My
Barry Hearn

About the Author

Barry Hearn OBE qualified as a Chartered Accountant in 1970 and spent several years with a major firm of international accountants. In 1974, he became chairman of Lucania Snooker Clubs and began to involve the snooker-hall chain in amateur tournaments.

In 1976 Steve Davis began playing at the Romford Lucania Club and the two struck up a partnership which transformed the world of snooker. With the formation of the Matchroom organisation in 1982, Hearn managed most of the world's top snooker players and promoted the sport around the world. He subsequently developed Matchroom Sport as global promoters and TV producers of boxing, darts, pool, netball, golf and a host of other sports.

In late 2021, Hearn was honoured with an OBE for services to sport. Married to Susan, a highly successful breeder of racehorses, Hearn has two children and four grandchildren. He lives in Essex.

My Life

Knockouts, Snookers, Bullseyes, Tight Lines and Sweet Deals

Barry Hearn

With Nick Pitt

HODDER

First published in Great Britain in 2022 by Hodder & Stoughton
An Hachette UK company

This paperback edition published in 2023

1

A CIP catalogue record for this title is available from the British Library

Paperback ISBN 9781529393347

Typeset in Sabon MT Std by Manipal Technologies Limited

Printed and bound in Great Britain by Clays Ltd, Elcograf S.p.A.

Hodder & Stoughton policy is to use papers that are natural, renewable and
recyclable products and made from wood grown in sustainable forests. The logging
and manufacturing processes are expected to conform to the environmental
regulations of the country of origin.

Hodder & Stoughton Ltd
Carmelite House
50 Victoria Embankment
London EC4Y 0DZ

www.hodder.co.uk

To my family,

You have always come first, with business a close second.

First Word

I kept telling myself, over and over again: don't do anything stupid. It was 20 April 1981, and I was sitting high up in the dark recesses of the Crucible Theatre, Sheffield, watching the final of the World Snooker Championship unfold below.

Steve Davis was playing in his first world final, against Doug Mountjoy. In truth, there wasn't much tension in that famous auditorium. Steve was in cruise control, leading seventeen frames to twelve, needing one more frame to win. He was in among the balls. Victory was inevitable.

Yet I was trembling. My heart was racing. I felt light-headed, woozy. That was because I knew, aged thirty-two, that my world was about to be turned crazy, that all I craved would soon be within my grasp.

Five years earlier, when I ran a chain of snooker halls around London, with a few other irons in the fire, Steve, aged eighteen, had walked into my Romford snooker hall, walked into my life.

It took a while for me to realise that the gawky youngster with long ginger hair and a dubious sweater might be a truly great player. It took longer for us to get to know and trust each other so much that we were not bound together as manager and player but as brothers-in-arms with a shared dream. We used to sit in my Romford office with mugs of tea, talking about what it would be like to win the World Championship. Sometimes, tears would be rolling down our cheeks at the thought of two boys from council houses conquering the world.

By 1981, Steve had established himself as the dominant force in the game. In fact, I remember one of his opponents checked out of his hotel on the morning of his match against Steve in that season's UK Championship, knowing he would lose. He was right: Steve went on to win the 1980 championship, his first major trophy.

When it came to the big one, the World Championship, Steve beat three of the game's finest – Jimmy White, Alex Higgins and Terry Griffiths – on his way to the semi-final, where he met Cliff Thorburn, the Grinder. After two sessions, Steve trailed eight frames to six. As we walked back to our hotel, we passed a fountain and I told Steve that if he could get ahead of Thorburn in the evening session, I would jump in that fountain. I was wearing expensive shoes, crocodile skin, and needless to say they got ruined.

Now, in the final, he was calmly potting his way to the title. I was anything but calm and it didn't help that I could only sit and watch and tell myself: don't do anything stupid.

The pink was frame ball, match ball and championship ball. Steve took a deep breath, wasted no time and stroked it home. He stood still, closed his eyes and seemed to say a silent prayer before turning to shake hands with Mountjoy. Typical Steve: understated.

I don't know how I got there, but within seconds I was down on the auditorium floor, racing across to give Steve a hug, more like a rugby tackle. Later on, Steve said he was just letting it all sink in when he saw me charging towards him, fists and teeth clenched, hitting him like a tank.

That scene still gets played on TV, part of my embarrassing past. But I'm not really embarrassed. If you don't feel passion, don't get emotional, then there is no point to sport.

It was the fulfilment of our dream, but just the beginning. I knew that the world title would change our lives, bring opportunities almost beyond imagination. But I didn't know the half of it. As a player, Steve would go on to dominate snooker in the 1980s, the boom years; as a businessman and impresario, I helped to create and shamelessly exploit that boom.

I moved on, promoting boxing, pool, ten-pin bowling, darts, fishing, netball, golf, poker, gymnastics, you name it. I bought the football club I supported as a boy and ever after, Leyton Orient. I built a global TV sporting company and guided many of the greats, from Chris Eubank and Anthony Joshua to Ronnie O'Sullivan and Phil Taylor.

In business terms, I grew up and became responsible; in sporting terms, I never lost the thrill, the adrenalin, the exhilaration I felt when Steve potted that pink and I just lost it. Now and again, I still do.

I'm Barry Hearn. This is my story.

My commandments might not have impressed Moses,
but they've helped me hugely and they might help you.
Credit: University of East London

1

My Ten Commandments

Three decades after Steve Davis won the World Snooker Championship and changed our lives, I was in New York on business when I had a phone call from a friend called Michael Davies, a young Englishman who had moved Stateside to make his mark in the world of television and entertainment. Michael was famous because he was smart enough to buy the US rights to *Who Wants to Be a Millionaire?* and had built a very successful business involving chat shows, quizzes and even, at one stage, darts, as my partner when we staged shows at the Mohegan Sun in Connecticut.

Michael, a soccer nut (Chelsea fan), had started a podcast called *Men in Blazers,* aimed at soccer fans in the US. Along with a friend, Roger Bennett (Everton fan), Michael had put together a podcast of irreverent chat, explaining the intricacies and culture of the beautiful game. It was timely because soccer, as they insist on calling it, was taking off at last in America, and the podcast was aimed at a young audience, college kids and the like.

So, I had this call from Michael in 2013 asking would I free up some time to be interviewed by Roger for their podcast. I didn't think it was much of a gig, but as a mate I would always say yes, so I got together with this likable rogue, Roger Bennett, and we spoke for about an hour about all things football. Now my bed of nails at that time was the chairmanship of Leyton Orient. I knew, therefore, all about the strange obsessions and masochistic tendencies of those of us whose burden is to support and love a Cinderella football club. I can't say I took the podcast too seriously, so I gave a very off-the-cuff interview, lots of expletives, lots of funny stories, as I tried to put across the passion that we Brits have for our national game.

A few weeks later, Roger phoned and said it had gone down amazingly well! They got it; they loved it. Roger made out I had become some sort of cult figure, which I took with a pinch of salt. He asked me if, next time I was in New York, as a favour, we could have an evening together, with Michael. I said of course, I'll let you have some dates the next time I'm due over.

About a month afterwards I sent a note saying it looks like I'm going to be there in February so pick a day. We agreed on 12 February. Shortly before I travelled, I rang Michael. 'All OK for the twelfth. Where are we going to meet?'

'At the theatre.'

'Theatre? I thought we were going to have a meal or something, the three of us.'

'Oh no. I've booked a theatre in Greenwich Village. *An Evening with Barry Hearn*. And it's sold out. I sold all 700 seats in a day and now I'm selling tickets for standing-room only.'

I felt a spasm of panic. In the past, I had always just winged it when giving a talk or a speech, no preparation, no notes, trusting that the gift of the gab would come to the rescue and – mostly – it had. But this was different. This was scary.

'What on earth am I going to do in a theatre in New York?'

'Well, why don't you just talk about life. Come up with a list of principles that have stood you in good stead in life and chat about some examples, stories and so on.'

So I have Michael Davies to thank and blame. As soon as I put the phone down I began to write down my ten principles. And during the New York rush hour on Wednesday, 12 February 2014, I was in a cab from the Hotel Plaza Athénée, where I always stay in New York, on my way to the Poisson Rouge theatre on Bleecker Street, Greenwich Village.

The place was packed and I had a good, stiff drink in the green room. Michael asked me how I wanted to be introduced and whether I wanted some walk-on music, like at a darts event.

'Yes,' I said. 'Carly Simon singing "Nobody Does it Better".' (All right, I know, some of you might reckon 'You're So Vain' would be more appropriate, but I really believe that at what I do, sports promotion, I am the best there is. That may be vain, but isn't vanity better than false modesty?)

Carly sang her heart out as I walked on at 7.30pm sharp, smart-suited. The punters – 700 seated and maybe 200 standing – were rocking. Michael Davies and Roger Bennett prompted me and I was away, giving them the Full Bazza.

Here, in a family-friendly version, F-words and other offences deleted, are my ten principles:

1. It is better to be born lucky than good-looking

Too many people seem to think they're entitled to success while others believe their success is all down to their own efforts. Absolute rubbish! Ask any honest successful person and he will tell you that we all need a bit of luck – and my life has been scattered with unbelievable bits of luck.

Back in my early days in business, I took a call from KPMG, my accountants, to ask if I was interested in acquiring a chain of snooker halls, just before the BBC went nationwide with snooker. Then one day in 1975 Steve Davis walked into the snooker club I was running in Romford. He became world champion, I built up the sport commercially and we both made our fortunes. Later on, when my business was crumbling, Sky TV was launched. They wanted wall-to-wall sport and I was saved. Then there was getting involved with Chris Eubank, who helped make me a force in boxing promotion; and best of all there was my greatest slice of luck, which was meeting my wife, Susan, on a railway platform. There's quite a story about that, which we'll come to.

Of course, there have been other times when my luck was such that only an idiot could have failed – and although I'm many things, I'm certainly not an idiot. What I have done is take advantage of the luck that has come my way. I believe in fate. Certain things are going to happen in your life and if you are good enough to take advantage of a lucky turn of the cards then you will be successful. But don't ever kid yourself that it's all down to you.

2. Tell the truth, it's easier than telling lies

I have to come clean here. When I was young, I used to lie all the time and I made a shedload of money by doing it. But I've learned the lesson: lying catches up with you. Telling the truth should come naturally. You don't have to remember what lies you told to whom. It is so much easier and makes you feel good about yourself, even to the extent of being blunt and direct. For example, 'I don't like you and I don't want to do business with you' is a phrase I have used many times during my life. Honesty should be your guiding light. While a lie can get you out of a short-term problem, the truth will come to your aid when you really need it, as people will appreciate that they may agree or disagree with you, but they will respect you for being honest.

3. Sheer work ethic can make you look like a genius

Academically, I was hardly a success, let alone a genius. I scraped into grammar school and somehow scrambled seven O levels, five of them at the bottom grade. I needed five passes to go on to A levels and to become an articled clerk on my way to becoming a qualified chartered accountant.

I studied geography, history and economics at A level, but after one year of messing about and playing too much sport I realised I was destined to fail all three unless I gave up geography. Somehow, I passed the other two and had the two A levels I needed to limit my accountancy course to four rather than five years.

Once I knuckled down – and my mother made sure of that – my work ethic was prodigious. That is probably what divides me from a lot of other people. I have been dedicated, organised and logical and I know that although I am not always the brightest candle in the room, I can burn longer than anyone else. Once I put my relentless hat on, there is no stopping me. I've also been blessed with another major asset: common sense.

In 1988, when things were really going tits-up, I owed the bank millions of pounds, having spent all the money I made from 1982. But I still kept going. I used to go into the office every day and I wouldn't leave until I had sent someone somewhere an invoice. Whether it was for £1,000 or £10,000 didn't matter. I had to be relentless. I would not allow a negative thought to enter my head throughout this two-year period, the worst two years of my life. It was the work ethic that got me through, the refusal to accept defeat, to be second best.

My advice to youngsters is not to expect favours from anyone; put the work in, put the graft in, put the hours in and you will emerge triumphant because your competitors will not match your effort.

4. Pressure is only felt by those that fail

The one word that really annoys me is 'pressure'. It is used as an excuse by those who fail. When a sportsman says he couldn't cope with the pressure, he is making the worst possible admission. When a businessman says he bailed out under pressure, he is just saying he gave in, as simple as that. Of course, there will be times when we encounter seemingly insurmountable problems and we just have to deal with them. But pressure is not the right word to use. I have yet to hear of a successful person in sport or business who doesn't actually enjoy the pressure and feed off it to show that they can cope where others fail.

5. You will run a better business and live a better life if you think poor

Never forget you want value for everything you do and never forget you expect to give value to others in everything you do. So think poor. We all tend to get complacent when things are going well. But complacency in business and sport is the worst sin of all. It destroys your aspirations, and you will hate yourself when you look back and say those terrible words, 'I should have . . .' Life is no rehearsal, and if you think poor you are making sure you never get complacent. Thinking poor does not mean you are a mean person. It means you want value and offer value. That is how you can guarantee you are getting 100 per cent out of the work you put in.

6. Unusual things happen every day of your life – it's how you deal with them that makes you unusual

The world is ever-changing, so be ready to adjust in midstream. It is too easy to stick to an approach that just ticks along, but life in business or sport doesn't work like that. There will be unexpected events for which no one can plan. What will separate you from the pack is how you deal with them. Optimism is essential and you must be as well prepared as you can possibly be. And you should be creative by trying to imagine what might happen. But you will never be completely right. How you adjust to the unforeseen will determine whether or not you are successful. (The Covid pandemic and how we dealt with it at Matchroom is a great example of how you can cope with the unforeseen.)

7. Life ends in tears, so smile for the rest of it

It sounds easy, but it is really important to be happy. All the time. It makes you feel good about yourself if you have a smile on your face every day and it means you appreciate what God has given you. I have been blessed never to have had to do a job that doesn't motivate me and make me feel good about myself. If I don't have a real passion for a sport, then I don't promote it. It's as easy as that.

Remember, it really pisses people off if they see you happy all the time, and my reply to anyone who asks, 'How are you?' is always 'Good as gold!' I never let anyone see me upset because it achieves nothing. We are fortunate people and others are much worse off, so we don't have the right to be upset. Just acknowledge your good fortune and keep that smile on your dial!

8. Your life doesn't change by sitting on the sofa

Few things annoy me more than people who tell me they don't have the time! By my reckoning, we have twenty-four hours in every day, sixty minutes in every hour and sixty seconds in every minute, so time is available if you put the effort in. I once asked a group of troubled kids at an East End police function how many of them got up on Saturday before midday and three out of twenty put their hands up. I knew we had a problem. There is always time if you take advantage of it. Whether it is going for a run or working through to the early hours to meet a deadline, time is something you create and something that can pass you by if you let it.

So get off the sofa, be active, make sure you use every hour of every day, because one day that hour will be your last and you would give anything in your possession to have a few hours more. Sleep when your body tells you to, but work as much as you can to achieve your goals.

9. Avoid being a secret – if you're good, admit it and shout it from the rooftops

I was always good at accountancy. In fact, modestly, I can tell you I was actually great! When I worked solely as an accountant, starting out, I was also exceptionally good at putting fees up and selling people the services we provided.

As a teenager, I realised that, with my background, recognition was hard to come by. I began working for an accountancy firm in the pin-stripe-suit era, but I occasionally wore a white suit, which as you can imagine didn't go down too well. I looked like John Travolta on a bad day, but it got me noticed and being noticed means you are no longer a secret. One of the partners, Alan McLintock, encountered me in the lift one day. 'Do you work for us?' he said. 'Yes,' I replied. 'Good lord.'

You need to have ability to get away with stunts like that, but the point is that if you remain a secret no one will know about you and no one will rate you, back you or even compete with you. If you're good, don't hesitate to tell people you're good. Shout it from the rooftops to make sure you get your chance, because without that chance it makes no difference how good you are.

10. When you need a hand, you are more likely to get a kick in the nuts

This is one of life's great mysteries. When you need no help there will be a queue of people offering to give you things. And when you do need help – well, Rule Ten says it all. Don't expect charity. Work hard and rely on your own efforts.

Well, my talk at the Poisson Rouge went down a storm. About a hundred of us went to a nearby bar and I soon learned that people had travelled from all over America for *An Evening with Barry Hearn*. That was gratifying and I felt like the hero of the hour. Even better, it has had some lasting effect. I regularly get messages and calls from people who were there and who say they follow my ten principles or that they have had them framed and displayed on their office walls.

Those principles go a long way to explaining who I am, why I've had success, and why I've had such a ball in this small adventure called life. The ten principles have served me well and if you adopt some of them yourself, they won't do you any harm and they will certainly bring rewards.

There's no fee.

Grammar-school boy: my mother enrolled me in the Verse
Appreciation Society and the Drama Society; I wanted to play
sport and make money

2

The Boy Barry

In 1982, when I had made a pile of money by selling the Lucania billiard-hall chain, I bought Mascalls, an eighteenth-century mansion comprising 12,514 square feet set in extensive grounds on a hill in Brentwood, looking out over London, to the City and beyond. It was my home for about twenty years and is now the head office of Matchroom. It was the kind of place where, generations ago, some member of the landed gentry might have said to his son and heir: 'One day, all this will be yours.'

Soon after I bought it, I was anxious to show my mum around, as a way of demonstrating that I had done well, so she might be proud of me. It was also a way of saying thank you. Mum had a good look round the house, drawing room, billiard room, butler's pantry, wine cellar and so on, and stepped onto the terrace to admire the view. Then she gave me a questioning look.

'You're not doing anything illegal are you?'

'No, Mum,' I replied. 'Chartered accountants make terrible gangsters.'

The truth is that without my mother's influence, I would never have been able to buy such a place, or to build a business as profitable as Matchroom. My debt to her will always be immense. In fact, many of my ten principles in business and life are actually the principles of Barbara Winifred Hearn.

My father, Maurice George Sidney Hearn, had a good war. He was a dispatch rider in the army and somehow managed to get the best gig going: teaching other soldiers to be motorbike riders. He was stationed in India and Ceylon (now Sri Lanka) and the pictures we still have in one of the family albums show him lying on beaches. I remember him telling me the war was the best time in his life. He never saw a German, never fired a gun, and had a very relaxing holiday that lasted three years. Maurice was rather a posh name, so in the army they called him Hank for some reason and years later my sister Christine went to Sri Lanka and, using old pictures in a family album for reference, managed to find the rock on which my father had engraved the word HANK in big block capitals.

After his 'holiday', my dad worked as a tram driver, bus driver and bus conductor in east London. I can remember sitting on his lap as a child while he drove a tram. Later on, he worked on a production line in a factory making televisions.

I was born on 19 June 1948 at 34 Gray Avenue, Dagenham, a small council house near the Ford motor works. That was my grandad and nan's house. My birth certificate, for Barry Maurice William Hearn, gives my father's occupation as 'Trolley Bus Conductor'.

We soon moved to 135 Chequers Road, a two-bedroomed terraced house in a new council-house development in Debden, Essex, which was built because so many East End houses had been destroyed by bombing. My sister Christine was born there and we shared a bedroom until I was eighteen.

Every Sunday afternoon, without fail, we would make the trip to Dagenham, as would the rest of the family – aunts and uncles, nephews, nieces – to the grandparents' house. That's my mother's parents, whose surname was Kippax. We looked forward to it every week and on Sunday we would all jump somehow or other onto and into Dad's motorbike and sidecar for the seven-mile trip from Debden to Dagenham. Later on we got a car, so it was made slightly easier, but when the car broke down, as it did quite often, we would walk three miles to the Old Maypole pub in Chigwell Row and then get a bus to Dagenham and vice versa on the way home.

We usually arrived about the time the drayman came round with the fish stall on the back from which you could buy prawns, cockles, shrimps and mussels. Cockles and winkles were always our favourite. We would boil them up in the kitchen and the kids would have to painstakingly pick out the winkles from their shells with a needle. Then it was a proper East End afternoon, food and lots of it, sandwiches, jellies and canned fruit, covered with Carnation evaporated milk.

Grandad Will was an oil-tanker driver for Texaco for well over thirty years; my nan, Gladys, had part-time jobs like collecting insurance money for penny-a-week policies that were intended to cover funeral costs for poor families. My grandad was a great big man with huge wrists. He was immensely powerful, probably because he had spent thirty years pulling those tankers' steering wheels round with no hydraulics. By the end of his working life, it left him with a visible shake. Every Sunday after tea he would regale us kids with tales of what he would do if he won £75,000 on Vernons football pools – which was the maximum win in those days. We sat at his feet and listened as he gave out money that he would never ever see in his whole life. 'I would give Mabel £500, I would give Barbara £1,000,' and so on and we would say, 'Grandad, what about us, what about us?' and he'd say to each of us in turn, 'I would give you £500,' and we would think, wow, £500, that's impossible to spend in your whole lifetime.

Of course, he never won the pools but that didn't stop his weekly dispensing of fortunes, occasionally changing the amount he was going to give us, depending on who had done well at school, or at sport, or if he felt any of us needed additional recognition. We were never going to see the money and we knew that, but then we also wondered if maybe, just maybe, we might. And there was another lesson: dreams should never die, and they do not have to be based on reality to inspire you.

When the time came to go home, it was always the same ritual. We had to queue up and shake hands with Grandad and say thank you for Sunday tea. He would shake our hands and squeeze our fingers so tight that tears would come to our eyes, but we knew that in that hand, that huge hand, there would be either two shillings or two-and-sixpence, and if we could just take the pain for a few seconds we were going to walk away with enough money to buy our sweets for the week.

I remember hearing a conversation Grandad had with my nan when he was approaching retirement, aged sixty-five.

'Gladys,' he said, 'I don't know what we are going to do when we retire. Our pension is going to be just a few pounds a week and we are not going to have any money to spend and I don't know how we are going to manage.'

To which my grandmother replied, 'Well, Will, we've always got our savings to fall back on.'

I'll never forget the astonishment on his face.

'Savings, what savings?' he said. He had no idea that my grandmother had always put away at least a pound a week throughout their marriage, for a rainy day. Like my father, my grandad never had a bank account. He just passed his sealed wage packet to his wife, my grandmother, all his working life.

'Will, throughout our life together I have always saved,' my grandmother said. 'I never bothered to tell you because it was for our retirement fund.'

'Well, how much have you got?' he said.

He nearly fell off his chair when she said, 'A little over six thousand pounds.'

Effectively, he *had* won the football pools, thanks to the conservative attitude and habits of his wife, Gladys.

It was a shame that although Grandad was wealthy in his world when he thought he was poor, he never enjoyed it because all he thought and talked about as time went on was retiring at sixty-five, reaching his target. Sunday afternoons stopped being so much fun. When he reached sixty-five and found out they had some money thanks to Gladys, they bought a lovely bungalow near Southend. He sat in his chair with Gladys servicing his every whim until he died a couple of years later, too early, from lung cancer. He had achieved something he never dreamed he would achieve but the drive in him had gone. He thought that retirement was reward enough. A great man, for sure, but not a great ending to his story.

Dad was about five feet nine inches, and Mum was smaller. But her father (my grandad Will) and brother were six-footers, so that's probably why I'm tall, six foot one, and well built.

The Hearns came originally from Maldon in Essex. There are quite a few laid to rest in the churchyard there, going back to the eighteenth century. After that, they migrated to the East End of London and were variously employed as building labourers, decorators and dockers. I never met my father's father, a decorator from Forest Gate. I was told he had a scar on his neck from ear to ear, courtesy of a German bayonet in the First World War. My paternal grandmother was christened Margaret Unwin. Her father, George Unwin, was a chief engineer in the fire brigade. The connection with Maldon probably explains why my parents chose to have their honeymoon there.

Although it sounds like a cliché, we really were poor but happy. Mum and Dad never argued. Mind you, no one argued with my mum. Christine and I could play in the nearby fields, go down to the river and explore Epping Forest. We felt free.

When I was about seven, I came home and found my father lying upstairs on my bed. He'd had his first heart attack, short of his thirtieth birthday. It was actually the day I brought home my first school report. It was a glowing report because I was quite smart, and I showed it to him. He started to cry, wondering whether he was going to live or die, whether he would get to see his kids grow up. He was very proud of both of us, my diamond sister and me.

Poor father was never quite the same again. He could still dig the garden, but not for too long. In those days, the doctor's advice following a heart attack was to sit in a chair for three months and not move. He was still allowed to smoke, though! He rolled his own but wasn't a heavy smoker. These days, as I know only too well, having had two heart attacks myself, they encourage you to get out of bed and keep your circulation going. They also have much better medication, and they make it clear that smoking has to stop.

At home, Dad used to make radiograms, building his own cabinets and selling them locally. Dad was good at making things and he used to make model airplanes, with engines. He set them off to fly in the surrounding fields and my job was to go and bring them back. Later on, he worked for Radio Rentals, repairing people's TVs. He found it easy and used to be back by lunchtime. Then he'd ring in to see if there were any more call-outs, but really he was doing a part-time job for full-time money.

Dad used to steal a valve a week from the TV factory and used them to build his own television set with a nine-inch screen. It was the only one in our street, so on Coronation Day, in 1953, just about the whole street was crammed into our tiny lounge. There was a fancy-dress competition for the Coronation. My mum dressed me up in a suit covered with the litter from the cinema, old tickets, popcorn boxes and so on. I won first prize: a model of the Coronation carriage, long since lost.

Ours was a traditional household. Dad's job was to earn the money and he would bring his wages back in cash every Friday evening. Mum and Dad would count it out and work out what would be spent on what. He used to bring home a bar of Cadbury's milk chocolate as well. Christine and I would get a square each and Mum and Dad shared the rest. Mum did all the cooking. We always had a roast dinner on Sundays with rhubarb crumble for pudding. Monday was cold meat and chips; Tuesday rissoles or spam fritters; fish on Fridays. One Christmas, when I was thirteen, we couldn't afford a turkey, so Dad said that the twelve pullets we kept in the backyard had to go. He strangled eight and I strangled four. We ate the lot.

Our mum was not one just to stay at home, though. She was a strong character and could get her way. Early on in their marriage, she made Dad give up motocross riding and she was always trying to improve herself. She took Italian classes at night-school but never advanced very much because she loved the first-year studies so much she kept taking them over and over again.

Mum was vivacious, glamorous and a bit of a snob, but needs must. She got a job as a cleaning lady five mornings a week for Mr and Mrs Locks, who lived in one of the big houses up on Tycehurst Hill. Mr Locks owned the local paper, the *Loughton, Chigwell, Buckhurst Hill and Woodford Gazette*.

As the boy in the family, I was expected to mow the lawn and wash the car, when we got one. Christine had to wash up and help Mum in the kitchen. I always looked after Christine. When I was nine and she was seven, I built a wooden go-kart. The wheels were held on with bent nails. We were out playing with it one day when a nail caught Christine's leg and caused a nasty cut, with blood running down her leg. We were quite a long way from home but near some shops, so I marched her into a chemist and told them to fix her up. They did that all right, but she has the scar to this day.

When I went to the local grammar school aged eleven, I didn't have long trousers, and I was almost six feet tall. If you want to be embarrassed, try going to an all-boys school wearing short trousers when everyone else is wearing long trousers. They took the piss, constantly. I dreaded going to school and I dreaded going home because a gang would be waiting for me underneath the railway arches. These were the kids off our East End council estate who were resentful of me because I had passed the eleven-plus exam and they hadn't. Every time I got off the bus they would kick and punch me, bullying me all the way home.

I took it for a few weeks and then I snapped. I chose the biggest one and gave him a proper good hiding. His pals ran away. I was foaming at the mouth. My mother came out and laid into me, giving me a beating for hitting that poor boy. That was unfair, but I didn't mind. I was proud of myself. I had stood up to be counted. I had learned a lesson in life. I could look after myself. And no one on that estate came near me again.

We were having Sunday lunch once when Christine was a bit older, and she came in crying because some boy had hit her.

Dad looked at me and said, 'What are you doing, sitting there?'

I was halfway through my dinner. 'Off you go,' he said. 'Sort it out and finish your dinner when you get back.'

I found the kid, sorted him out and went back to finish my dinner. Family first.

Christine, who was much closer to our dad than I was, always helped me as well. We both used to save up our pocket money, and when I wanted to buy a new cricket bat or whatever, she gave me her savings. I ordered her around, but I protected her as well. If we went out to a dance or whatever, she was allowed to stay out later so long as I was there to keep an eye on her. I also helped her with her schoolwork, teaching her algebra, geometry, arithmetic and French.

When Christine was given a bicycle for passing the eleven-plus, Mum and Dad tried to teach her to ride it, but she couldn't get the hang of it. I took her up to the top of a nearby hill on some waste ground, put her on the bike and pushed her down the hill. It worked. I used the same method when I taught her to swim: I just threw her into a swimming pool, the deep end.

My mum was a tough lady who believed in discipline. She used to lock me in the bedroom until my homework was done and when she identified certain working-class traits, such as the way I spoke, she sent me off to elocution lessons and later enrolled me in the Verse Appreciation Society and the Drama Society at Buckhurst Hill Grammar School. Of course, I cringed and resented it, but you didn't argue with my mother. And by that time I had learned to stick up for myself, which kept the teasing within limits. With a sick father and a strict mother, this may all sound harsh, but children adapt. I was very happy as a boy.

Our holidays were spent in the West Country. It would take us twelve hours to drive down, with at least one breakdown. Often it was the fanbelt, in which case Mum's old nylons would be brought into service. The first week would be spent working, harvesting peas, potatoes or strawberries. We'd get half a crown for filling a sack with peas. I struggled to fill two sacks in a day, which was eight hours. For the potatoes, we had to follow a trailer and bend over so that we could hardly walk by the end of the day. After a week, the holiday would start.

Mostly, it was camping, but we also used to stay at a bed and breakfast, Lower Zeals Farm. I loved the farmhouse and the country life. I'd get up at five in the morning to help milk the cows. I asked the farmer how much land he owned. 'As far as the eye can see, my boy,' he said. He didn't have any money, but I thought that was an amazing thing to be able to say. It stuck with me and that is why I've long been an investor in arable land. They don't make land any more, and I like to own it and look at it. It's also free from Inheritance Tax.

At Christmas in 1959, I was eleven years old and beginning to find my feet. I asked my mum and dad if I could start going to watch professional football, as some of the other kids in my school had been to some matches and I was jealous. My parents said I couldn't go to Arsenal, Tottenham, Chelsea or West Ham as they were big clubs, but I could go to Leyton Orient because they were a small, family club in the East End of London and had a reputation for being safe enough for kids.

On 30 January 1960 I made my first trip to Brisbane Road to watch the great Leyton Orient play a friendly match against Falkirk from the Scottish League. The match ended as a 2–2 draw. I still have the programme, with the late changes in the teams marked in biro as well as the scores from the half-time scoreboard. The attendance was 6,988, more than twice the number that turned up for my first league match as chairman of the club thirty-five years later. From day one, I was hooked on Leyton Orient as my club, and that has remained the case ever since, to my lasting pleasure, and cost.

I went to almost every game for the rest of that season and developed a great affinity with the club because it was a good place to be. Everybody seemed so kind and I never felt at any risk, even if we didn't win many matches.

My number-one hero at that time was a rough-and-tough centre-forward called Tommy Johnston; he was in his second spell at Orient and was a legend with the fans as he constantly scored goals. He had a withered arm, a legacy of an injury received when he was a miner, and always played with his arm bandaged, so he was easy to spot. I was never particularly good at football myself, but I was a centre-forward and modelled my style on his. Not pretty, but effective.

Tommy left the club in 1961 and so did I as I moved over to near neighbours Tottenham Hotspur. I was twelve years old and felt I was a proper geezer. I never forgot Tommy Johnston though, and when I later became owner of Leyton Orient, we renamed the South Stand the Tommy Johnston Stand, with a moving ceremony. His ashes were interred there – forever Orient.

Having experienced live football for the first time at Leyton Orient, I couldn't have picked a better time to go to Tottenham. The 1960/61 season at Spurs will always reside in the memories of their fans as they became the first team in the twentieth century to do the double of the First Division Championship and FA Cup. I found a new hero in Bobby Smith, the centre-forward who played in the same style as Tommy Johnston – a rough-and-tumble character who may not have been elegant but scored a hell of a lot of goals. Bobby Smith scored thirty-three goals in the season when Spurs won the double.

These were the days when 65,000 people went to White Hart Lane, and it wasn't the safest place in the world because of the huge crowd, but the atmosphere and the standard of football left me with deep, abiding memories. Great players such as Danny Blanchflower, John White and of course Bobby Smith were just three of a team that were almost unbeatable that season, and they were soon to be joined by the supreme goal-scorer, Jimmy Greaves.

When the players ran onto the pitch, youngsters like me would run on with autograph books and try to get them to sign before the match started. On one occasion, we were playing Blackpool, including the great Stanley Matthews. I ran onto the pitch trying to get the one autograph that had eluded me the entire season and that was the one and only Dave Mackay, a tough, no-nonsense man who tackled with proper tackles so that the other man was rarely left upright. He was a beast of a man and a great midfielder, but I didn't have his autograph and I was determined to get it. I ran straight towards him as he came out of the tunnel and, without looking up, he kicked the football he was holding and it hit me straight in the face and knocked me off my feet.

I can still remember lying there seeing stars and this huge face of Dave Mackay peering at me.

'Are you all right, lad?'

'Yes, Mr Mackay, I'm fine. Can I have your autograph please?'

'No, you can fuck off.'

At least forty years later, I was speaking at a function in the Midlands and there was a table of former Tottenham Hotspur players including, you guessed it, the one and only Dave Mackay. I walked over to him and said, 'Can I have your autograph now, Mr Mackay?' I recounted the story, and we had a good laugh, but I still ended up without his signature.

A week later a huge parcel arrived in my office. When I opened it, there was a picture of the great Spurs squad with Dave Mackay being held aloft by Jimmy Greaves, Alan Gilzean and Pat Jennings. Every player had signed it and there was an accompanying note from Dave Mackay: 'At last you have got my autograph.' That picture takes pride of place in my private office at home and will never be taken down.

I stayed with Tottenham for the 1960/61 and 61/62 seasons (when they won the FA Cup again but didn't do the double) and I had the odd visit to the Orient, but my mind was then set on other things, such as trying to earn some money.

But there was one experience at Brisbane Road that would stay with me for many years and had an emotional influence on my decision, many years later, to buy my boyhood club. In 1963, I was standing next to an old fellow who lived in Brisbane Road; he had a cloth cap on his head and was wearing an overcoat. It was freezing cold, half-time in the game, and we were having a chat. He asked me what I was doing that night and I said I was going to the pictures with my mum and dad. He asked me what we were going to see, and I said *Cleopatra* – it was one of those classic big-budget movies of the time, with Liz Taylor as the Queen of the Nile. The old man said to me, that's interesting – when the film is over and they play the National Anthem and everyone stands up (which is what we did in those days) just watch the credits at the end of the film and you will see that my daughter is in charge of costumes for that film. Her name is Edith Head.

I remembered the name and at the end of the film I did stand up during the National Anthem and I did watch the credits, and sure enough when it came to costume design there was the name Edith Head. Apparently, this old fellow's daughter had gone off to America and made herself a career in costume design for movies.

In fact, Edith Head was one of the most famous costume designers of all time in Hollywood and won a record eight Academy Awards and her dad, it seemed, was a normal bloke who lived in Brisbane Road and went to watch the Orient.

Now the strange thing is that I learned much later, after I bought the club, that the old fellow's story cannot have been true. Edith Head's father would have been 105 at the time and he had no connection with Leyton. But the yarn had a most powerful effect and there must have been some connection or there was no point in telling the story. A mystery.

My first effort at a properly structured business, with purchasing, marketing and so forth, came at grammar school. When I was sixteen, I found this girlie mag in Epping Forest and took it to school to show the lads. The centre pages were in colour and the rest were black-and-white. One lad wanted a colour picture, so I tore it out and sold it to him for sixpence. Others paid threepence for black-and-white pictures and I made ten shillings from the whole mag.

I was on to a good thing. I got one lad to go up to London and buy mags for me at a pound or less. I recruited a salesman for each school year, and I ran the financial side. I soon had a franchise going, making a few quid a week. The problem was storage: where to hide them? There was a big lad called Chunky Ryan. No one would go near him. I put him in charge of storage. He put them in his desk, knowing no one would dare look in there. At least, no boy would.

One day, we were being taught religious instruction by Mr Tomlinson.

'Where's Ryan? I want to mark his homework.'

'Not here, sir. He's gone to the dentist.'

'No problem. It'll be in his desk.'

He opened the desk.

Next morning, the deputy headmaster read out the names of six of us. 'Report to my office after assembly.' Chunky had grassed us up. We lined up outside his office. We could hear the cane. Wallop, wallop. Six of the best. I was last in the line.

'I don't think it's fair that I should be punished twice,' I lied when my turn came.

'What do you mean, twice?'

'Well, sir, my dad gave me a terrible beating when I told him what I'd done last night.'

'Oh, I see.'

He let me off, but that was a good business ruined.

It was my mother, as I have said, who decided my proper career. One day, when I was twelve, she came home from cleaning and announced that I was to become a chartered accountant. She had been speaking to Mr Locks, whose house she cleaned, and he had said that the thing about chartered accountants was that you never saw a poor one. I didn't know what a chartered accountant was, but I didn't argue. And that phrase, 'you'll never see a poor one', resonated with me. I had often been up the hill to look in awe at the big houses with their driveways and gardens, and all I could think was *I want one, and one way or another I'll get one, one day*. At school, whenever careers advice came up, I would tell the teacher to leave me out. I didn't need any advice because I was going to be a chartered accountant.

After working as a cleaner for years, my mother suddenly decided to get a full-time job. I was about sixteen and she was in her mid-forties when she applied for a job with the North Thames Gas Board as a showroom assistant. Dad tried to dissuade her, saying she should stay at home, not bother. She had no education to speak of and no track record apart from cleaning, and there were fifty applicants, but she got the job. At the interview, she was asked to just talk about anything, so she talked about her two children, and it worked.

Quite soon after she started her first career, we were able to buy our own house, 94 Buckhurst Way, Buckhurst Hill. Three bedrooms and a garage. I painted the whole house outside, front and back, over the school holidays. Moving out of council-house accommodation was a major breakthrough for us all. My mother never stopped trying to improve our lives. She had a driving force that I must have inherited. She ended up as area director of the North Thames Gas Board, a wonderful achievement.

Dad was one of those working-class men who accepted the way things were, knew his place. So long as he had his baccy and telly, he was happy. When his wages went up to twenty pounds a week, a thousand a year, we had a big celebration. My pocket money went up from two shillings to two-and-six a week.

I was different to Dad, and I didn't accept that the Conservatives should run the country as a kind of birthright. I joined the Young Socialists when I was sixteen and stuck a picture of Harold Wilson in my bedroom window, facing the street.

One thing I did inherit from my dad, apart from a dodgy heart, was a terrible temper. I could really lose it. The worst example came when I was sixteen and having a spitting row with him. 'And you can wipe that smile off your face,' he said, and hit me with his right hand. It split my left eyebrow. I got hold of him and held him up. I was going to kill him. Mum was screaming. Then I realised he really could die, and I put him down.

As it happened, I had the oral exam for my French O level the next day. I had a black eye and was wearing sunglasses. I rehearsed a phrase: *'Excusez-moi de porter les lunettes noirs, mais J'ai tombé dans les escaliers dimanche soir.'* I still failed.

My working life began when I became a teenager. My mum had seen in the paper that labour was needed at Waltham Abbey, where a group of Italians who had come over after the war were growing tomatoes in greenhouses. Waltham Abbey was a seven-mile bike ride. The bike had been my reward for passing the eleven-plus. I could only work three hours a day because I was under sixteen; the pay was two shillings and ten pence an hour (about 14p in today's money). The greenhouse was heated to a hundred degrees Fahrenheit and the work involved stripping leaves off the tomato plants so that the sun could shine directly on the tomatoes to ripen them.

The first day I went there, I asked if I was allowed to eat any tomatoes. 'Of course,' I was told. 'Eat as many as you like.' I must have eaten three or four pounds of them that first day and never let another tomato near my mouth for ten years.

Every day through the summer holidays I left the house around seven in the morning and cycled seven miles to work. At the end of each week, I got a pay packet of more than two pounds, a fortune. It was hard work, especially in that heat, so when I was fourteen or thereabouts, I got together with a friend, Phil Croxton, and we started washing cars. Phil had come up from Bristol, complete with a West Country accent, and our school headmaster asked me to look after him because he was a new kid and I was nicely useful by then. I could stand up for myself and people left me alone. When I was fourteen or fifteen, Phil and I started our first car-washing round for the big houses at the top of the hill.

From pocket money, with help from Christine no doubt, I saved up enough to buy a bucket, a sponge, a chamois leather (pricey but very important) and some washing-up liquid, and set off up to Alderton Hill, Tycehurst Hill and Sparleaze Hill, where the rich people lived. Unlike the folks down on Chequers Road, they all had cars. For the first few weekends, we knocked on every door and picked up the odd customer, charging five shillings a car.

One day we knocked on the door at 78 Tycehurst Hill. A man came to the door and I made my pitch, bucket in hand.

'How much do you charge?' the man said.

'Five shillings a car.'

'Do it properly and I'll pay you ten shillings.'

That man was Morris Blow, who was to have a huge influence on my life. He also had two big cars in the drive.

After a while, Phil Croxton went off the idea of car-washing, but I carried on and expanded into gardening, window-cleaning, house-cleaning, babysitting, anything to earn a few pounds. Morris was my main client. He paid me four or five pounds a weekend. I soon got to know his wife Pamela and daughter Deborah. Cindy and David were born subsequently, and I babysat for all the children. They were a Jewish family and treated me as one of their own. I even got to know Myra, Morris's mother-in-law. She hired me to clean the floors in her hairdressing salon in Loughton. They all called me Boy Barry and if I met any of them on the street today, I'm sure they would still call me Boy Barry, which I would take as a compliment, we were that close. I was part of the family.

With my dad in poor health, mostly staying at home, Morris became a kind of surrogate father to me. He was a Chelsea fan and took me to Stamford Bridge and all over the country for away games. He introduced me to golf and took me to my first black-tie evening. Just being around Morris was an education and a pleasure. He operated a family fruit business in Spitalfields Market but when the market closed he lost out badly. It was a terrible shock and loss when I was told that Morris had died in his sleep, at far too young an age.

Just before the Covid pandemic, I went to see Pamela, Morris's widow, unannounced. She opened the door and was clearly hard of hearing, with poor eyesight. She peered at me and eventually said, 'Is that Boy Barry?' We spent a treasured hour together, reminiscing.

In my late teenage years, as well as washing cars, babysitting and all the rest, I began to work on the doors, doing some security. It wasn't as dangerous then as it is now. I organised dances and formed a blues band; I played a bit of bass guitar, harmonica and occasionally second vocals. We were terrible but we did have one decent musician, Andy Hughes, lead guitar and vocalist. Jumbo Tyndall was bass guitarist and we had a drummer called Laurie Ashton, who styled himself Odd Bod Clarence the Third. There was so much Brylcreem on his hair that we got splattered whenever he shook his head.

We played a variety of blues music because that was quite fashionable at the time. Everything from John Lee Hooker to Muddy Waters came out of our lips with deep soulful overtones – not! In fact, we were probably the worst blues band in the world until the half-time break at our local gigs. At that point, one of us would grab whatever we were being paid, go to the nearest off-licence and spend the lot on bottles of gin, vodka and whisky. We were soon so drunk that in the second half we were a half-decent blues band.

There was another local band called Black Cat Bones. They were really good and got on *Ready Steady Go!* on ITV. We were sometimes their warm-up act. We went on first and no one minded how bad we were because Black Cat Bones were coming on next. It was a great period for music. The Beatles and the Rolling Stones came to our area and you could see them in a local hall or cinema for a few shillings, with everyone screaming and going nuts. Now and again I went up to London, to see Manfred Mann at the Marquee Club or Long John Baldry at the 100 Club.

But my forte was organisation. I managed to get the Dave Clark Five, on their way to stardom, to appear at my school.

I could handle myself, as I said, but one time when I put on a dance, it seemed I'd bitten off more than I could chew. I may have been too heavy-handed because a group of lads all waited for me when everyone was off home. They cornered me in the cloakroom, six or seven of them, terrible odds. Then the toughest kid in the neighbourhood, Bimbo Potts, turned up. No one went near Bimbo. He was a proper handful. I knew him, but not well. 'Hello, Barry,' he said when he walked in, as if choosing sides. My would-be attackers fled. Another example of Principle Number One: Better to be born lucky!

As a kid, I took street cricket very seriously. Sometimes there would be only two of us but we still managed to play England versus Australia, pretending to be Fred Trueman, Brian Statham, Richie Benaud or Denis Compton, mimicking their styles and writing down the scores. I often used to be Fred Titmus, the off-break bowler, and these days, over seventy and with a dodgy shoulder, I bowl off breaks, though I'm still keen to come off the long run and bowl seam-up.

I became good at making money, but my real love was sport. I played anything I could at grammar school and after my A levels I had a few months left at school to throw myself into sport. I was in the First XI cricket team and took over sixty wickets in ten matches in 1966. I had my first write-up in a national newspaper when the *Daily Mail* ran a back-page piece headlined 'Hearn set to break schools' wicket record'. The local paper even posed the dilemma about whether I would go into accountancy or county cricket. I was playing for Essex Young Amateurs at the time, but it was never going to be my career – nowhere near enough money in it at the time.

I had joined Buckhurst Hill Cricket Club as a thirteen-year-old, and was coached by Bob Greensmith, whose brother Bill played for Essex, but there wasn't much opportunity for juniors, who would be put down at tenth or eleventh in the batting line-up and rarely asked to bowl. One day, walking home from coaching at Buckhurst Hill, I came across South Loughton Cricket Club, a small club with a tiny pavilion next to the River Roding. As I was watching some boys playing, a guy called Norman Crowhurst, who ran a model airplane shop and had an enormous nose, came up and asked me if I played at all. I told him about Buckhurst Hill and he said I should join South Loughton because I would get coaching and plenty of chances to play and bat and bowl, so I joined the following season and played for them for many years, ending up as captain of the First XI. I was still a decent seam bowler and in 1969 I did the double of 100 wickets and 500 runs in a season, a lifetime achievement.

I've played the game for sixty years. After leaving South Loughton I played for Brookweald and then Brentwood and I've ended up as President of East Hanningfield Cricket Club, whose ground is very handy – it's on my estate. Every year, I still hope to be granted one more year with bat and ball, and I still look forward to the call from the captain every January to turn up for pre-season nets. I'm now playing for Essex over-seventies as well. It's not a bad standard, except for the fielding, as you can imagine, but I love the game as much as I did when I first started playing.

At Buckhurst Grammar School, I made the First XI in football as well. Instead of terrorising batsmen, I was a centre-forward who terrorised centre-halves and goalkeepers. In those days, football was very much a contact sport, so I never held back. When we played public schools, I had a chip on my shoulder about where they had come from and how nicely they spoke. If one of them said something like, 'Jolly good shot, old boy,' I would just whack him. Against those teams, I never heard the final whistle.

Academically, I was lazy until I realised that I must pass two A levels to reduce by a year the time I would have to spend as an articled clerk and qualify as an accountant. I knuckled down and managed to pass. In my final school report, the headmaster, J.H. Taylor (the son of the great golfer of the same name, who won five Open championships), wrote one sentence: 'There is more joy in heaven . . .'

Years later, Mr Taylor came up from Devon and made a speech to the old boys. I went along. 'Who would have thought that one of our most famous old boys would be a snooker manager?' he said. I sought him out afterwards and he remembered exactly what he had written as my send-off. I was gobsmacked.

After leaving school, I turned out at football for the old boys, the Old Buckwellians. I had two seasons with the Fighting Fourths, the Old Buckwellians Fourth XI. It was rough and the standard was not high, but I scored over thirty goals in one season and more the next. I broke my leg in the last game of the second season and my footballing days were effectively over.

At Buckhurst Hill Grammar, I was determined to win something in athletics. I tried everything, from pole vault to shot put and discus, as well as running every distance from 200m to 1500m. I always came second or third. In cross-country running, I had come eleventh in the Essex junior county championships, when you had to be in the top ten to qualify for the English national championships.

Then one day, looking at the noticeboard in the gym, I spotted that no one had entered for the one-mile sprint walk. At last, an opportunity. I trained flat out at this less than attractive discipline and found myself taking minutes off my best times. In the divisional championships, I won by over 400 yards. Then I went to the South East Essex championships and won by 200 yards. I went on to the Essex championships full of confidence. As we were warming up, I asked some of the other lads what their best times were. Eight minutes five seconds, eight minutes twenty seconds and so on. My best time was seven minutes forty seconds, and I thought this would be a doddle. But, as we know from Principle Number Five, complacency is a killer. I casually strolled round the first three laps to find some ginger-haired kid in front of me. I had to make a big final effort to catch him. As I went past him, I got disqualified for lifting. That meant I had broken into a run. I could easily have settled for coming second but I did all I could to win and ended up coming nowhere – the sporting story of my life.

One year, as we were going up in the world, we took a family coach trip to Italy. It was a great success and we decided to go again the following year, to a resort called Diano Marina. Mum, Dad and Christine went down in Dad's Vauxhall Viva for a couple of weeks. I had finished school and it was my time for independence. I went down on my brand-new, much-admired scooter, a Lambretta GT200 that had cost me £240, all saved for. I wasn't an out-and-out Mod but I was more Mod than Rocker, and wore a Parka. I took fifty quid and loads of cans of beans and chipolatas from Mum.

I went with a pal called Keith Thomas, who had a Vespa 150. Actually, he wasn't so much a pal, but I couldn't find anyone else to go with. He was an academic sort. Keith rode his scooter into the back of a lorry at Arras in northern France. It was mangled. He climbed onto my scooter, along with all our clothes and camping gear, and we rode down together like that. It took us four days and I walked bow-legged, like John Wayne, for a while.

We lived in a tent on the beach. I made some money playing table football against the Italians. There was a bar with a small television on the beach, which was where we watched the 1966 World Cup final. There were about sixty Brits watching and as many Germans. To begin with, we were all very friendly, but with the tension of the match, and extra time, it became raucous and then fighting broke out. No one got seriously hurt, but we won that game as well! A good many of us were arrested but just got a warning from the police. I thought England's victory would be the beginning of world football domination. Not quite.

St Mary's Church, Chigwell, 25 July 1970. Do you, Barry
Maurice William Hearn, take this woman, Susan Joan Clark,
to be your lawfully wedded wife? You bet.

3

A Vision of Perfection

When I left school with two undistinguished A levels – grade B in history, C in economics – my mother spoke to one of her uncles, who had a small tiling business in Southend. He managed to persuade his accountants, Bristow, Burrell & Co., a small City firm with an odd address, 68½ Upper Thames Street, to give me a job as an articled clerk. I started on Monday, 5 September 1966, suited and booted, on six pounds a week. I was eighteen years old and it was just about the first time I had been to the City.

My mother made my sandwiches every day, which meant I could cash in the luncheon vouchers we were given, and I took the tube into work. When I got home, I would have something to eat and then go to my bedroom to work on my accountancy correspondence course. I was virtually locked in by my mother, Monday to Friday. Mercifully, I had the weekends off. But I still kept up my car-washing, window-cleaning and gardening. I made more each weekend than I did during the week.

I also found my first and one-and-only serious girlfriend. I met her on the Thursday of my first week of work in the City, and since that girl is now my wonderful wife, Susan, that week must go down as the most important of my life. Getting Susan to go out with me was an episode that does not reflect well on me, except maybe it does. On Thursday, 8 September 1966, I had finished work and walked down to Bank station to get the tube back to Debden. As I arrived on the platform, I saw a young lady, a girl so beautiful it took my breath away. She had long hair down past her bum, the shortest of miniskirts and a white raincoat. We loved those raincoats because they reminded us of French girls, girls like Françoise Hardy, the singer we were all in love with because she looked so sexy in her white raincoat. There was this vision of loveliness on the platform at Bank station, and my luck was in because she was chatting to a lad I knew, the boyfriend.

On the tube, I got into conversation with him and this lovely young lady and when she got off at Woodford, the boyfriend and I were left on and I asked him what the score was with her. He said he had been going out with her for a couple of months and she was a lovely girl. The boyfriend knew me by reputation, that I could handle myself. Well, I asked him to do me a favour, to ring her up at eight o'clock that evening and tell her he didn't want to see her again, and to give me her phone number. We had a little discussion and the boyfriend saw the sense in it. At five past eight that evening I phoned Susan and asked her if she would go out with me on Saturday. She said she didn't have anything else to do, so why not? I knew the boyfriend had been as good as his word.

Susan Joan Clark was sixteen years old at the time and we have been together for more than fifty years. Funnily enough, about twenty years after we met, we bumped into the boyfriend at a party. Susan asked him why he had ditched her. 'Hasn't he told you?' he said. Then he told her I was so keen I wasn't going to take no for an answer. She was impressed, I think. It was another case of Principle Number One, being lucky, and taking advantage.

In fact, I had met Susan about a year earlier. We had a dance at my grammar school. She was a smart girl with shorter hair at the time and was not in the least impressed with my chat-up lines. She certainly didn't fancy me particularly and I can't blame her. She was especially keen on The Who at that time and when they played a concert at her school, she managed to get a lift home in the back of their van. But at least she agreed to go out with me a year later. I took her to see a film and from then on it was

34

official: we were going out together. We met every working day at lunchtime, underneath the Duke of Wellington statue at Bank station. We'd head for the Kardomah coffee house and have a cup of Bovril. Always Bovril. I was on six quid a week and she was on twenty. Every Friday, she would buy me twenty Benson & Hedges cigarettes and put a gallon of petrol in the car. We always went to a garage in Hainault, where it was four shillings and ninepence a gallon, the cheapest we could find.

From the very beginning, it seemed clear to everyone, not least me, that Susan and I were meant for each other. She was accepted straight away by my family and our parents all became friends as well. When we went to Italy again, Susan came with us. My Uncle John drove down as well with his family, towing his speedboat.

It would be wrong, though, to assume it was all sweetness and light. There has always been a tempestuous side to our relationship, with regular flare-ups along the way. I suppose you could call it dynamic. Once, we were almost having a fist-fight on Buckhurst Hill High Road. After five minutes of spitting fury, she suddenly turned round to me with arms outstretched and said, 'This is silly, let's stop arguing.' As I walked closer to her, believing we were friends again, she kneed me right in the testicles.

I had a great time at Bristow, Burrell & Co. and I learned fast. The audit manager, Charlie Lee, had spent three years on the Burma Road as a prisoner of the Japanese in the war. He was a tough old bastard who set very high standards. Out on an audit, we would listen to his stories for hours. I learned more from him than anyone in those early years. I got very good, very quick with figures. Sometimes in the office they would have a bet and set up a clean set of figures and it would be me against the comp operator in a speed trial. The comptometer was the machine they used to add figures and it was reckoned to be lightning fast. I was never beaten by any of the comp operators. The atmosphere in the office was great, but we weren't making much money.

Always keen to supplement my income, my ears pricked up one day in the office when one of the clerks, with connections, told me he was involved in organising a greyhound-racing betting coup. The plan was quite simple – he and his colleagues were going to go over to Dublin and steal a greyhound (in fact one of the favourites for the Greyhound Derby) from its kennels, bring it over to England and run it at a flapper track, i.e. a track where there is no real control from the greyhound authorities. This one was in Luton. The idea was that the dog would win comfortably to bring home a betting coup and would be taken back to Dublin the same night, no one any the wiser.

It sounded to me like the easiest way possible to make some quick money, so I was in. I invested fifty pounds. That may not sound like much, but back then it was to me. My work colleague and his dubious associates duly acquired the dog, took it to Luton and entered it under a false name. I was still concerned that I might lose my money, so I asked my colleague if the dog was definitely going to win.

'Look, on the times, we are so many seconds faster than anything else in this race, it really is impossible for it to lose,' he said. That was it. I was in, fifty pounds laid.

Just before the race, I was still very nervous, and I asked him the same question: 'Is this dog really going to win?' Once again, he reassured me that it was a certainty. However, he also said that the only possible problem was that the dog had been drawn in lane six, while he preferred to run in the inside lanes, one or two. But not to worry; he was so fast he could not be caught.

Well, the dog came out of trap six like a rocket, but because he liked to run in trap one he cut across immediately to the inside, hit another dog, flew up in the air, fell awkwardly and damaged his paws. He did get up after a while and was so much faster than the other dogs he almost won, beaten in a photo-finish. Maybe that was just as well. Had he not been injured, our ringer dog would have won by so far that we would have definitely been disqualified and not paid anyway.

Once again, I had learned a lesson in life. There is no such thing as a certainty. That lesson cost me fifty pounds.

I was working by day, studying by night, an early example of Principle Number Three, that the work ethic can make you look like a genius. Fortunately, Susan was equally dedicated and ambitious. She didn't pester me to go out and we usually got together just on Saturdays. Actually, I still made money when I was courting Susan. I would be babysitting for Morris Blow, earning three pounds as well as a pack of Senior Service cigarettes, a chocolate cake, maybe some gelfilte fish or lokshen soup, with the house to myself and my girlfriend.

Susan enrolled at East Ham Technical College. After leaving Loughton County High Grammar School, she went through O levels, A levels and a business degree, just collecting them as she went along because she was super-smart.

It was at this time, in the late 1960s, when I was always short of money, that I began playing the stock market by 'stagging' new share issues. It was a wheeze I was put on to by some of the lads in the office. The idea was to apply for shares in companies that were about to be quoted on the Stock Exchange for the first time. An attractive price was offered to attract investors and, if an application for the shares was successful, the shares could be sold immediately at a profit.

On a Monday morning, an issuing house, usually a bank, would release a prospectus and application forms and I would go along to the bank to pick up as many application forms as I could and spend the next couple of nights tearing out the forms and filling them in, each for the minimum number of shares permitted. I went for the minimum number because I knew that if the offer was oversubscribed, successful applications would be chosen by ballot. Making multiple applications at the minimum number maximised my chances in the ballot but kept the risk of receiving too many shares within limits. It was still a dangerous game because successful share applications had to be paid for.

I formed a small company called Clernark Securities, after Clark, Susan's surname, with 'ern' in the middle – not a particularly inspirational name. I asked friends and family for funds. My dad lent me £300, Susan's father put in £200 and an old friend, Mick Dunning, put in £112. I was off and running, but this was when matters started to get out of hand. Susan and I used to sit up all night, writing out applications for ourselves, for my mum, her father and various mates, each for the minimum number and each application with a cheque attached in case of success.

At first, all went well. I managed to get 200 shares in a company called Bardolin and sold them immediately for a profit of £47. That was handy, for I had just decided after a couple of years of courtship, with world wars regularly erupting between us, that Susan was the only girl I could spend the rest of my life with. I went round to her house in December 1968 and quietly asked her if she would do me the honour of becoming my wife.

'If you like,' she said.

It wasn't exactly the reaction I had been hoping for, but apparently she just didn't see any reason why not. I used my £47 profit to buy the engagement ring. Mission accomplished. Having been thrown at me so many times over the years, that ring has now been lost.

In the summer of 1969, Susan and I, along with Christine and Phil Croxton, went on a camping holiday to Mimizan, on the French coast, south of Bordeaux. We squeezed into my old Hillman Imp. The engine was at the rear and one time there was smoke pouring out of the engine and into the back seat. We made a hasty exit, waited for the car to cool down and carried on through France. We had two tiny tents in the campsite near the beach – one for me and Phil and the other for Susan and Christine. All very proper, as we weren't married. The Hillman didn't manage to complete the trip and was returned by a breakdown service a couple of weeks later.

That was also the summer of my greatest cricketing achievement, the 100 wickets and 500 runs double for South Loughton Cricket Club. For most of my cricketing life, I was a fast, or not-so-fast, bowler. I used to bowl off and leg cutters, with one finger down the seam, shifting it either way to get movement off the pitch. I ran in off sixteen paces and at my best was quite quick. I still remember the hundredth wicket, in the late summer of 1969. I bowled a leg cutter that lifted. The batsman fended it off, and it went 'down the throat' of Alan Petit Pierre, fielding at forward short leg.

I used to rope in Susan to do the scoring, just as I had roped in my sister Christine. They were both meticulous scorers, using different-coloured pens. Susan could have been a fine player, too. She bowled a really good leg break and could throw a cricket ball further than most of the team. She could whistle it in from the boundary. In those days, of course, women didn't play matches, not for a club like ours anyway. Scoring and making teas were their tasks. Susan managed to get off the tea rota by serving the best we'd ever had, beautiful sandwiches and cakes, laid out with serviettes. It was so lavish she was excused from doing it again. We would all have put on weight and the teas would have bankrupted the club.

That September, one Thursday, my dad spent an afternoon working on the Hillman Imp. Over dinner, unusually, he explained to my mum in detail what he had been doing with the engine. After the meal and a cup of tea, Mum was ironing while Dad was tickling Christine and chasing her around the kitchen and conservatory when he just collapsed and died. When I came back from a game of cricket, Fred, Susan's father, met me at the station and told me. Dad had got to know Susan but didn't see us married. He was forty-five when he died. His father had been forty-seven when he died, and his grandfather had also died young.

In many ways, my father's illness prepared me for my own health problems later in life. I expected them and it didn't scare me because it was largely out of my hands. I did, however, try to give myself every chance of survival by keeping fit, and now, in my seventy-fourth year, despite two heart attacks, it seems to have paid off. My father taught me one important lesson – never waste a second of your life, Son, and I never have.

Back at Bristow, Burrell and Co., once I got a taste for it, I was staging for every issue every week and it got so out of hand that I would often send in several hundred application forms with cheques totalling up to one or two million pounds, despite hardly having a thousand pounds in my Clernark Securities bank account. Very dangerous, very stupid, and totally illegal today.

In the first year, I made around £2,000, a fortune in those days. I paid out a dividend to my investors and spent the rest on a Lotus Europa Twin Cam car kit, price about £1,600. You had to build the car yourself and I am useless at anything mechanical, so I got a local mechanic to build it for me. The car was magnificent, especially after the Hillman Imp, and especially since it had come from somewhat ill-gotten gains.

After a couple of years, the market became more difficult as more people were jumping onto the bandwagon and guaranteed profits slowly began to become unavoidable losses. I applied for shares in a company called Myson and read in a newspaper to my horror that the issue was only just subscribed, which meant that every application was going to be successful and would have to be paid for. For me, this was a disaster, and brought the worst weekend of my life as I could see my career as a chartered accountant ending in disgrace when my bank manager saw piles of cheques arriving, signed by me but with no funds in my account.

When I went to see the bank manager on the Friday and was totally open with him, he wasn't very pleased. We agreed to leave it until Monday to see the scale of the disaster and I endured a sleepless weekend. On the Monday morning, my various nominees were receiving their mail. I was petrified that my credibility would be ruined, so I spoke to my stockbroker, Cyril Rebak, a young Jewish guy, and told him the truth, which, as I have explained in my principles, is the best policy. I told him I was going to be in big trouble and I needed to sell a lot of shares first thing so that I could get a cheque from him the same day to placate my bank manager.

A Vision of Perfection

Cyril reluctantly agreed to back me and warned me against such behaviour in future. That warning was unnecessary because I had already decided I couldn't go through another weekend like that. I sold around 40,000 shares before I even knew how many I had. That was to cover my liabilities. But when the post was delivered, I noticed that a lot of my applications had been thrown out as multiple entries. The same had happened with my nominees, so now my problem was that I had already sold 40,000 shares without knowing how many I owned. Furthermore, I had sold those shares at a discount, i.e. a loss, so I was already 5 per cent a share down. That added up to more money than I had in my bank account.

When I tallied up, I had been allocated 20,000 shares but had sold 40,000, so I contacted Cyril, my disgruntled stockbroker, again and explained the situation. He was furious that I had presold stock without knowing how much I held. But the blow was softened when he told me the price had collapsed and I now had the chance to buy back the 20,000 shares I had sold without owning them. Instead of a 5 per cent discount, there was now a 20 per cent discount per share.

Remember Principle Number One: it is better to be born lucky than good-looking. I had fortuitously turned a disaster into a substantial profit. I had upset my bank manager and stockbroker and I don't think they ever forgave me, but my feeling of relief was compensation. For those of you who struggled working out the maths, I effectively sold 20,000 shares at a 5 per cent loss, which cost me £1,000, but I bought back the remaining 20,000 shares at a 20 per cent discount, giving me a 15 per cent profit per share, a £3,000 gain, so I made a profit of £2,000. What a touch!

I never forgot how close I had been to disaster, and I never bought a single share in a public company again. When it came to investment, land and property would always be my thing.

With all the studying I was doing – and my mother made sure I was doing – it was impossible for me to fail my accountancy exams. Every time an exam result came through the post, my mother knew that if it was a thin envelope, it meant I had passed. If you passed, it was just congratulations; if you failed, it was a fat envelope containing details about resitting the exam. For my Intermediate results and Final Part One, I was sent a thin letter and she was ecstatic.

But after my Final Part Two, the last exam of all, I was sent a fat envelope. When I got home, I found Mum in tears at the bottom of the stairs. I opened it and explained that for the final exam, a thin envelope meant you had failed and a fat envelope, which had details about arranging your membership of the association, meant you had passed. The tears dried and she was the proudest mother in the world. I had qualified as an accountant in March 1970, a few months before my twenty-second birthday.

Having qualified, I went to see my boss at Bristow, Burrell and Co., Frederic Pledge, and asked for a salary increase from the twelve pounds a week I was getting by then. I told him I was planning to get married. 'Well,' said Mr Pledge, 'when your articles are completed in September, are you going to stay here or leave?' I said I would be leaving. 'Then I don't see the point in putting up your money,' he said. That was another life lesson: there are times when you need to keep that big mouth shut.

Susan and I were married on 25 July 1970. The ceremony was at St Mary's Church, Chigwell, and the reception at Victory Hall, Chigwell, a parish hall suitable for very small weddings, and this was a small wedding. On the morning, I drove round to the local off-licence and spent fifty pounds on booze. The relations, mostly on Susan's side, made sandwiches and there was a dodgy caterer who served a very dodgy meal. Susan looked gorgeous and Phil Croxton, my old mate from washing cars, cleaning windows and so on, was best man. We had a great party, a proper knees-up, East End style.

Phil Croxton had been a great mate. In our wild days we used to gate-crash parties and get into fights. Well, I did. He was a terrible fighter. After school, he went to work in a tailor's shop and went out for a while with Christine. We even thought they might get married. Then he opted out of society and became a beach bum in Cornwall. Years later, I looked him up. He had bought an acre of land, a pig and a greenhouse and somehow or other he made a living. Much later, we tracked him down and he came to my sixtieth birthday party. Phil went on to own and operate the Fowey Aquarium. I had a tour of the place, and it didn't appear to have much more than some cod and whiting, but Phil seemed content.

Susan and I started our married life living with my grandparents in 34 Gray Avenue, the house where I was born. We had put down our deposit of £300 on a £6,000 semi-detached house on the Cambridge Road, Sawbridgeworth, right on the A11, and moved in after spending ten days with my grandparents. I carried Susan over the threshold and our adventure began.

Susan has been the boss from day one. In fact, of all the people I have met around the world, and some of them have not been friendly, she is the only one who has ever frightened me. She also has her lovely old-school way of looking after her husband and children and is the most loyal human being you could ever find. One example from a few years later: when our son, Eddie, was at nursery school and misbehaving as usual, one of the other mothers took matters into her own hands and slapped him around the legs. Susan floored her with a right-hand punch and they both got banned from the school. Proper girl. When we first moved into 50 Cambridge Road, there was lino on the floor, no furniture to speak of and no curtains. And by the way, as well as everything else, I was still cleaning cars and all the rest. We were blissfully happy.

Once my articles had been completed, I joined a big accountancy firm, Thomson McLintock, and also established my own practice, Hearn & Co., with small builders, publicans, garage owners and the like as clients. I would do their accounts and tax returns.

When we got home from work, Susan would cook some supper and then I would go up to one bedroom to do tax work and draft letters and Susan would go to another bedroom to do the typing. We soon had the house kitted out and life was sweet.

Before long, I was an audit manager at Thomson McLintock. The partner who promoted me called me into his office. 'Congratulations,' he said. 'You are the youngest audit manager in the two-hundred-year history of this firm. But you do realise that this is as far as you go?'

What he meant was that I could forget the idea of becoming a partner. I didn't have the family connections, the university education, and I hadn't been to the right school. That's how it was in those days. I knew that to fulfil my dreams I would have to move on.

Early in 1973, I was doing the annual audit of a fashion company called Deryck Healey International. The company was making about £200,000 a year, which was a lot of money in those days, but the books were in a terrible state and I had to 'qualify' my report, which meant I was not satisfied with the accuracy of their records.

I went to see Tom Blyth, their legal director, and explained that their bookkeeping was awful. It wasn't surprising, because their accounts team was run by a former shoe salesman. Tom was not happy with my criticisms, but I refused to budge. I told him they should get themselves a finance director to sort things out.

'What about you?' Tom asked.

'No,' I explained. 'I have my career mapped out. I am the youngest ever audit manager at Thomson McLintock and I've built a private practice and an investment company as well. I have a young wife and a small mortgage on a cheap house. Eventually, I want to leave the company and set up on my own.' In other words, I was looking to become a rather boring provincial accountant based in a small office above a butcher's shop in some high street.

'What if we pay you £5,000 a year?'

I was on £3,500 at the time, but I said: 'Money can't buy Barry Hearn.'

That was a whopping lie. The director went to see the chairman, Deryck Healey himself, then came back and offered me £7,500 plus bonuses.

'I'll start on Monday,' I said.

I phoned Susan to tell her I'd been offered and accepted a job. 'You've already got a job,' she said. I explained the deal. She could hardly believe it. It was life-changing. She booked a table at the Straw Hat Chinese restaurant in Sawbridgeworth, very fancy: we were going to celebrate.

Now I was finance director of Deryck Healey International, fashion design consultants specialising in fabric design and colour forecasting. They employed about a hundred fashion consultants working from Kensal House, a beautiful Georgian mansion in Kensal Green. Clients included ICI for the UK and Europe as well as major firms in America, Japan, South Africa and Australia. From the moment I walked into the place, I felt like a duck out of water. I was among people of fashion, in the 1970s. There were men in the office wearing make-up and a distinct aroma of marijuana in the library. These were things I had never come across. Homosexuality as well. It was unnerving to begin with. There was I, the accounts man, in suit and tie, so they saw me as the square guy, a freak.

Deryck Healey himself was born in South Africa. He was a lovely man whose wife had died of cancer and he had ended up living with another really nice guy called Graham Roberts. Deryck wasn't really a businessman; he was creative, passionate about his work rather than profits. He taught me a great lesson, one that has stood me in good stead: follow your passions and instincts and the money should take care of itself. For that reason, he was one of the most important people in my life.

We once had some customers from a company called Texfi Industries over from the States. They wanted to buy a simple range of designs for double-knit production and Deryck asked me how much we should charge them. I worked out the hours it would take to produce what they wanted and told Deryck it was a very small deal, probably in the region of $20,000.

'Fine,' Deryck said. 'Why don't you join us for the meeting?'

We sat down with these loud-mouth Americans. Deryck clearly didn't like them and when they asked him how much this small design job was going to cost them, he said, 'Gentlemen, it is a three-year deal at $200,000 a year.'

I thought he must have misheard me, but the Americans agreed, signed a contract and we were off and running with another very profitable arrangement.

'I said $20,000,' I told Deryck after they had left. 'And you charged them $200,000.'

'Yes, Barry. But you have just met them. If we are going to work with people like that, we add a nought to our price!'

It was another good lesson for me. We are in business to make money and to build good working relationships, but if there is going to be aggravation or problems, make sure you get well paid for your trouble.

Our business with Texfi Industries almost brought me an introduction to Elvis Presley and certainly got me into deep trouble with Susan. As financial director for Deryck Healey International, I was in charge of all contract negotiations and on a visit to America I arranged a meeting with the Texfi financial team to run through a few points. Our children had not yet been born and Susan was travelling with me. When we arrived at our hotel in Greensboro, North Carolina, the place, usually quiet, was rocking. I asked the receptionist what was going on. Elvis was in town, performing that very evening. Susan had long been a huge fan of the King but had never even dreamed of seeing him live. She was desperate to go and was not best pleased when I refused to cancel my business meeting over dinner. Very reluctantly, Susan joined us for dinner. It was ultra-boring, not much got done and all night she was thinking she could have been watching Elvis Presley live. When we went to our room at about one in the morning, we thought the ceiling was going to cave in, there was so much noise. Susan rang reception, who told her that Mr Presley and his entourage were having a party in their suite, directly above our room.

In an instant, Susan went from an Elvis Presley fan to an angry hotel customer and told the woman to make sure the noise stopped immediately. If not, 'I will send my husband upstairs to sort it out.' I was much relieved when the noise died down and we went back to sleep.

Next morning, I went to play golf at Pinehurst and Susan stayed in the hotel. She went down to the hairdressers and was complaining to the stylist that her husband had been a bastard by insisting on going to a business meeting and that she had missed a once-in-a-lifetime chance to see Elvis.

'But you have seen him,' the stylist said. 'He just walked past you in the corridor as you came in here.' Susan hadn't noticed. It was still my fault. Elvis died a few months later so I never had the chance to put matters right. Forty-odd years on, Susan still mentions the episode every other week, as one of the many errors for which she will never forgive me.

She had a happier time when we went to Paris for a weekend break, staying with Christine and her husband Frank Dawkins, who worked in computers. They had a small apartment. We started a card game when we got there and just kept playing until, on the Sunday, someone said we were in Paris and hadn't seen or done anything except play cards. So, we took the Metro and went to Sacré-Coeur. We wandered around there for a bit then decided we'd go back to the card game. We were playing for money and just about all the ready money we had in the world was on the table. We were young and crazy back then. In the end just one person cleaned up the lot, and, no surprise, that was Susan.

Missing out on Elvis was not forgotten but years later Susan did manage to catch Luciano Pavarotti, live and very exclusively. We were staying at the Sandy Lane Hotel in Barbados, which had been recommended to me by Sir Charles Forte. He had told me years earlier to stay in his hotels whenever I could, and I did. Sandy Lane was in the Trust House Forte Group. Susan found it pretentious but was happy to discover that Pavarotti was staying there and that he used to sing arias while floating on his back like a whale in the sea. You could swim round him and get a private performance.

When I went to check out, I was presented with a bill for $700. I knew it should have been much, much bigger, so I asked what it was for. Phone calls. When I asked where the rest of my bill was, the receptionist just said, 'Mr Hearn, it has been a pleasure to have you staying here.' It was another act of generous hospitality from Sir Charles, one of my most valued benefactors.

Deryck Healey International was doing well and the directors wanted to diversify. I was put in charge of the operation. I took them into property, but the business we bought went bust. I took them into garment production, which made sense because they were designers, but we ran into problems. I could sell the garments, and I went to fashion shows all over the world, living the life, and we had two factories in south London, employing around five hundred people, but we just couldn't make the garments well enough or on time. That company also went into liquidation.

I was down and depressed and I needed that all-important stroke of luck. It came in 1974 when my old accountancy firm, Thomson McLintock, called and asked if I was still looking to diversify for Deryck Healey International. 'We have a chain of snooker halls that one of our clients is keen to sell,' they said. 'Interested?'

I had never been in a snooker hall in my life, but I looked at the numbers and they were making a small profit. More significant were the freehold properties they owned in high streets. I started negotiations but they failed because I wouldn't pay what the owner wanted for them. He decided to give the company away to charity rather than sell it for less than he thought it was worth. But then I had another piece of good fortune. An amendment to Capital Gains Tax had been introduced, which meant that even if you gave away an asset you still had to pay tax on it as a disposal. I left it for a while and then phoned the man again, suggested we talk, and booked a table at Quaglino's, which I knew was his favourite restaurant. Now he realised that if he gave away the business he'd still be stung with a tax bill. We did the deal on the back of a napkin in ten minutes. I paid £632,000, or I should say Deryck Healey International paid, but by then the company was struggling in the 1970s recession, so we had to get a bank loan and the bank took 15 per cent of the equity. Still, job done, and that was how I became chairman of Lucania Temperance Billiard Halls (London) Ltd.

The timing could not have been better and once again it wasn't down to my foresight but to luck. Principle Number One. The BBC had begun limited coverage of the World Snooker Championship when I bought Lucania. It became a huge success and I was hailed as a genius for making a big investment in a sport no one had rated but which became one of the biggest sports in the country, thanks to the BBC.

All good, but little did I know that another huge slice of outrageous good fortune was just around the corner.

Two brothers-in-arms who enriched my life: Steve Davis (top) and the one and only Freddie King. Credit (top): David Muscroft

4

Two Godfathers, chalk and cheese

The decade from the mid-1970s to the mid-1980s was the most hectic, crazy and momentous of my life. Katie and Eddie, our two brilliant children, were born; I rode the snooker boom; and I formed Matchroom as I progressed from being something of a chancer to a serious businessman. Working sixteen-hour days, seven days a week, I ran three businesses and made my first fortune. I still had time to play cricket and enjoy a wild sporting and social life. In those ten years, we moved from our first marital home to a purpose-built modern house in Ongar, and then to Mascalls, a mansion.

At the beginning of that decade, I also met two extraordinary people who shared those years with me and who were instrumental in my success. I owe them more than I can say. Both of them became godparents to my children.

You've probably guessed the identity of the first: Steve Davis, the snooker genius who became a friend, really a brother. But before we meet Steve as a gawky teenager in 1975, let me introduce you to my other comrade-in-arms, someone who could not have been a more different character. Steve was shy and quiet, awkward everywhere except on a snooker table. The other fellow, Freddie King, well, he was just Freddie King.

The first time I met Freddie was on the golf course. I looked at his face, on which his battle scars were clearly visible, especially with regards to his nose.

'You must have done a bit,' I said.

'What do you mean, done a bit?' he said, aggressively.

'Well, looking at your face, you have obviously been a boxer.'

'Are you talking about my nose?'

'Yes.'

'You should keep quiet, or *you'll* get one like this.'

Freddie was not a big man, but he was lively to say the least and had a short fuse. For some reason, he tended to get the hump on golf courses. Another time, when I knew him much better, we were playing at Hainault, a municipal course in Essex, and a four-ball group ahead of us was taking an age to putt out on the first green. Freddie made some sort of gesture and shouted for them to get a move on. One of them took exception to this and called Freddie to come up, clearly wanting to sort him out. Freddie left his bag of clubs, marched up to the green and knocked the fellow out with his first shot. The second ran over to join in and Freddie sparked him as well. Number three tried to run away but Freddie caught him and whacked him too, so we ended up with three bodies on the green. The fourth fellow disappeared. What impressed me most was that Freddie returned to his bag, selected an eight iron and calmly played his approach shot to the middle of the green. I was fond of Freddie and I enjoyed our games of golf, but I never took him to Sunningdale.

If you have formed the impression that Freddie could be spontaneously violent, you are not wrong. But I want to stress that there was much more to him than that. He was loyal to a fault, completely trustworthy once you had his confidence, and a true friend. He had to wrestle with contradictions in his nature because he relied on his reputation as a hard nut yet craved respectability. He wanted to be legitimate, a good citizen.

My dealings with Freddie came about because he worked for one of my clients in my accountancy business. I did the accounts and tax returns for three brothers operating in East Ham. They had a small operation involving jukeboxes, slot machines and coin-operated pool tables. Freddie was their site finder, which was the key role for that kind of business, persuading pubs and clubs to install their machines. He worked in Smithfield meat market during the day and in the evenings did his site-finding as well as coaching at the Waltham Forest Amateur Boxing Club. Freddie had been a notable amateur boxer himself at lightweight and had once beaten Dick McTaggart, an Olympic gold medallist and one of the most celebrated of all British amateurs. They said Freddie put the nut in to beat him. Maybe he did. Freddie's professional record was respectable, but he never fulfilled his championship dreams.

The eldest of the three brothers, the one with the brains, wasn't partial to hard work, but he was partial to nicking. According to Freddie, he orchestrated the great silver scam of that period, and Freddie was involved. The eldest brother found out that pre-1947 half-crowns and florins (two shillings) were worth more for their silver content than their face value. To begin with, he got a local bank manager in Upminster to get all his tellers to look out for those coins and keep them to one side. He had another fellow who would give him twice the face value and everyone had a slice. Then he found out that a villain from Manchester was doing it wholesale, getting coins from all over the country and taking vanloads of them to Antwerp for melting down. It turned out the driver was someone Freddie knew and the eldest brother told Freddie he should tell the driver he was going to be robbed and he had to be bashed up to make it look right. Freddie just made it look like the fellow had been bashed up, taking some sandpaper and scraping the fellow's face. Anyway, on the way back from Antwerp they stopped the van and nicked all the money.

A nice bung all round and everyone reckoned the fellow behind it in Manchester wouldn't go to the police, as moving cash around was illegal. But he did and they all got nicked. Freddie spent fourteen days in Wandsworth Prison and then got his sentence suspended on appeal. But those fourteen days made him really ashamed. He cried in the dock during the appeal, said he would never do it again, that he had a young boy to look after. And it was true: he really wanted to be loved and respected and he didn't want to let down his mum.

The brothers from East Ham were actually a nice bunch and I went to see the eldest a few times in Ford Open Prison down at Arundel in Sussex and met loads of old faces, including Charlie Kray. I helped the eldest brother legitimise all his properties. He had them all over east London and I set up companies for him. I used to sneak in papers and get him to sign them.

But as far as their jukebox and one-armed-bandit business went, I couldn't afford to be involved. I had monitored the business and it was clear that sooner or later they would get their collars felt by the police because they were operating without a licence under the Gaming Act. I told Freddie and said I was up for buying the business if the brothers were up for selling it. Freddie was in awe of me because I was a director of a company and he wanted to be straight. I said we could go halves and Freddie said he would back me. I put in five grand and Freddie put in thirty grand. He had it under the bed. Literally.

We called a meeting with the brothers at my house in Ongar. Susan was in hospital having Katie. This was a tricky meeting. I explained to the brothers that the business had to go legitimate and get a licence but that because of their criminal records they couldn't be involved, and I should buy the business from them. This did not go down too well, but when they realised that Freddie was now on my side, they settled down and eventually a deal was struck. If Susan had known what was going on in her house while she was away, she would have been apoplectic.

First up, we had to get licences under the Gaming Act. We had to go up before a judge. I told him I was a chartered accountant, with my own small firm and so on, and the judge was happy with that. Then he read Freddie's application and credentials – meat porter, suspended prison sentence – and the judge said to me, 'What sort of person are you here with today?'

'Someone who made a mistake, a genuine person who wants a second chance,' I said.

Freddie repeated his speech about having a young boy, wanting to be legitimate, make his mum proud. The judge said it was against his better judgement, but he would grant the licences.

'Just make sure everything is legal,' he concluded.

Freddie was reinvented. He got out of the meat market, became a director of our company, with a visiting card pronouncing it, and was as proud as anything.

I sold my accountancy firm because I was just too busy. I was finance director of Deryck Healey International, chairman of Lucania Billiard Halls and now joint-owner, fifty-fifty with Freddie, of Stelka Automatics.

We dovetailed well. Freddie carried on with the site-finding and I did the books and explored deals with other operators. We identified half a dozen small businesses in east London and bought them all. Then we went for Stannite Automatics, an old family firm that had a number of quality sites, working men's clubs, Conservative clubs, all with the best machines. They also had three amusement arcades, in Dymchurch, Eastbourne and Lancing. We paid £100,000, which was a good deal because it included the freehold of the arcades and a factory in Tottenham. Freddie and I had been running everything from under some railway arches in Leytonstone, rent seven pounds a week, and everything shook when a train went past. Now we had the factory in Tottenham, with nice offices. Freddie was like a pig in muck.

The brothers had about fifty machines when we bought their business. One after another, we bought out our rivals and ended up with 2,000 machines in the East End, with our headquarters in the factory in Tottenham and thirty employees. We were the biggest operator in the East End and stayed on our patch. There was an unwritten rule that one family or firm had east London, another had north, another west and another south London. Straying into another firm's territory was not a good idea.

During that period of acquiring smaller businesses, I came across a young fresh-faced kid from north London called Frank Warren. I had heard that he had a small pool table and jukebox operation in a few pubs, but I think most of his income came from stocking cigarette machines. He was of interest as we were mopping up as many operations as we could. Freddie arranged a meeting between us in an East End pub with two items on the agenda. First, I was interested in buying his small business. I believe he had around twenty sites, so it was no great size. However, he put a value on them that was far in excess of market value (a habit of his with which I was to become familiar), so there was no way we could do a deal. Too expensive, let's move on. The second item on the agenda was boxing.

Warren had started promoting unlicensed boxing and was gaining a reputation for putting together some great contests. Some of these fights have become part of boxing's folklore. Warren's star turn was Lenny McLean, alias the Guv'nor. McLean was a beast of a man who roared when he jumped in the ring, putting the fear of God in his opponents. He was a real handful and when I went to a few of his fights the atmosphere was electric, but it was rather barbaric. Now, Freddie King had told me he had an experienced fighter he was sure would beat McLean, if properly trained. This fighter had had a successful amateur career. He was an ex-policeman who had ended up working in the meat market. We put it to Warren to see if he was interested in staging this fight. He was. I asked him what the deal was, and he said each fighter would get a grand but we would have to have a side-bet to make it more interesting. The bet would be £20,000. That didn't worry me. I thought £20,000 was a reasonable bet and in those days I used to gamble quite a lot anyway. But before committing myself, I asked Freddie King two questions.

Question one: 'Can our guy really beat Lenny McLean?'
Answer: 'Yes.'
Question two: 'If our man wins, will we get the £20,000?'
Answer: 'I cannot guarantee that.'
The fight never happened.

Making money was easy to begin with. We would buy a machine for £1,000 on ninety days' credit, and we had that back in three months. We did fruit machines, jukeboxes, pool tables, and when Space Invaders came in, we made a small fortune. Freddie had a nice Mercedes but he went round in a bashed-up Volkswagen so that it didn't seem we were doing that well. But after six months or so, the pub landlords wanted a bigger share. Business tailed off, so we had to keep finding new venues.

It was a cash business and there were a lot of funny and not-so-funny faces around at the time, but we never really had any aggravation. None that I saw, anyway. On the rare occasion that something went wrong, Freddie would just wink at me and say, 'Barry, I'll get it sorted,' and sure enough he did, every time. On one occasion, a team of naughty people stole our master key, which meant they could open any machine of ours. I was horrified because it meant we would have to change the locks on 2,000 machines. Then Freddie said he knew who had done it, it was a firm down by the docks. He said he would get it sorted but it was probably better if I didn't know about it. The next day, the master key was back on my desk.

'Leave it to me,' was Freddie's watchword and I'm sure he used to protect me, knowing that I had to be above reproach. Once, when I went socialising with Susan at the Epping Forest Country Club (proprietors included Sean Connery and Bobby Moore), I had an altercation with one of the bouncers – my fault, really – and I ended up with some facial damage. Someone had put his hand on Susan, and I whacked him. I got dragged out and beaten up by the bouncers, who had all been brought down from Blackpool. I went back in again, which was a mistake. The next day, when Freddie saw what had happened to me, he went berserk.

I hadn't seen him in a rage like that for ages. A few days later, a team of lively fellows went to the country club and sorted out all the bouncers. No one died, but it was carnage. I read about it in the paper and asked Freddie if it had anything to do with him. He just smiled.

If I wasn't in the Stelka offices, I was usually to be found in my office underneath the Lucania Billiard Hall in South Street, Romford. I was there one afternoon in 1975 when Les Coates, the manager of the place, phoned down.

'You might want to come upstairs, Barry. There's a kid playing up here and he looks a bit special.'

I had nothing much to do so I wandered upstairs and there was a crowd around Table Thirteen where Vic Harris, our top player and the Essex champion, was playing this tall, skinny kid with ginger hair down to his shoulders and a jumper of dubious quality and taste. Steve Davis.

Now the odd thing is that once I got to know him, I always called him 'Davis'. Forty-five years on, I still do. But writing about him, 'Davis' somehow doesn't sound right for someone so important to me. So here I'll call him Steve.

According to Steve, on that very first occasion I saw him, he was sizing up a complicated four-cushion escape from a snooker. I don't remember that, and I certainly didn't watch him and instantly conclude that one of the best players ever to hold a cue had come among us. But I could see that he had tremendous focus and it wasn't long before I knew that he also had unwavering determination to be the best he could possibly be.

The arrival of Steve Davis could not have come at a better time for me. I was hooked on the game. From the moment I walked into my first billiard hall, after buying the Lucania chain, I felt at home. I looked around at the customers and saw myself. During the day, there were the unemployed, a few villains, some sick and disabled people, and in the evening the office workers came in. I was more at home with the layabouts; after all, I had very little to do during the day and for those of us like that it was either going to the billiard hall or the betting shop.

I had to try snooker, so I picked up a cue and in time became proficient. My highest break in a match was fifty-four and in practice eighty-seven. But I was tough to beat, especially when there was money involved.

Once the snooker boom was under way, if you didn't have a table by ten o'clock in the morning you had no chance of getting one until six o'clock at night. The places were buzzing and the queues by the fruit machines and Space Invaders were often seven people deep. Everyone was doing something for money, whether they were selling stolen goods in the corner of the billiard hall or playing money matches.

The first time I walked into our Lewisham hall, I saw a shotgun underneath Table One.

'That's not right,' I said to the manager. 'You'll have to have a word with those four geezers.'

'I'm not talking to them,' he said. 'I'll leave that one to you.'

We decided to ignore it and carried on having a cup of tea until they left, with the shotgun.

Money matches were everywhere – you could walk into any billiard hall and get a game for a decent sum, at any time, any place, although of course the cleverer players were the ones who went home with the money and that wasn't always me.

We used to have plenty of players in the winter in the Lucania halls but fewer in the summer months, so I came up with the idea of staging a one-day national Lucania tournament in September, exclusively open to players who played at least twice a week in our clubs. The idea was to spread and boost our turnover. We put up £1,000 in prize money, a good sum in those days. After Steve Davis had been to our club a couple of times, he asked me if he could play in our next Lucania tournament. It was just about the first time he spoke to me. In fact, he hardly spoke to anyone for two years after he arrived. I told him the rules: he had to play in a Lucania at least twice a week. He lived with his parents in a council flat in Plumstead and it took him two hours door-to-door to get to Romford, with three buses and a walk through the foot tunnel next to the Woolwich Ferry. But he came every week, several times a week in fact, usually playing Vic Harris, never for money.

To start with, Steve was on standby for the 1975 Lucania tournament. Then someone pulled out and I phoned Steve to give him the news that he was in. The family didn't have a phone at home, but I tracked him down at the Plumstead Common Working Men's Club, where he practised with his father and coach, Bill. You wouldn't know he was thrilled from his response, but I know he was.

The tournament attracted top amateur players from all over the Southeast. It was played at Romford, with eight tables, starting at 10.30 in the morning and finishing around midnight. Steve beat Vic Harris, the number-two seed, in the quarter-final, Wally West of Hounslow Lucania in the semis and met Geoff Foulds, one of the best players in London and the defending champion, in the final. Foulds won by three frames to one.

I organised a tour around the country for Foulds and Steve, who took on some of the best players around, including Mike Hallett, Tony Knowles and Terry Griffiths. They went in Foulds's car, which had engine trouble. When Foulds got fed up and went back to get on with his work, I took over and drove Steve down to Wales. He had very little personality, zero charisma really, but I began to get to know him a bit. We gradually became closer until I was like an elder brother to him.

It dawned on me that in Steve I had an ace in the hole. He may have been socially inept, but he had an almost eerie self-assurance on the snooker table. I wanted to organise more events, so I dreamed up a Romford tournament involving four top professionals and four amateurs, who would be given a fourteen-point start in each frame. The pros were Ray Reardon, Dennis Taylor, Patsy Fagan and Doug Mountjoy; Geoff Foulds, Vic Harris, Russell Jarmak and Steve Davis were the amateurs.

As well as the main snooker room with thirteen tables, there was another with six. For matches like this we would shift five of the tables, put in seating for spectators and make it a match room, hence Matchroom. It was a knockout event, and the amateurs slaughtered the pros. They won all four quarter-finals and Steve went on to beat Foulds in the final around two in the morning. The place was heaving and the atmosphere fantastic. Steve won a trophy and £200. I did rather better because I had backed all four amateurs to win their quarter-finals and Steve to win the whole thing at six to one.

After that I adopted a policy of backing Steve whenever he played, and I encouraged the Romford Mob to do the same. Pretty soon he became known as the Golden Nugget, our banker. He rarely failed to deliver. Some months before, Steve had rung me in a rare state of excitement after he had made his first 147 break – fifteen reds, fifteen blacks and all the colours – in practice at the Plumstead Common Working Men's Club, so I knew he could build breaks. But his great gift was controlling opponents. His safety was so good he would tie them in knots and as soon as they left him an opening, he would ruthlessly clear up. Steve has said that he liked to 'deny oxygen' to his opponents. I likened his approach to taking an opponent's brain and putting it in a jam-jar on the mantelpiece.

All he lacked was experience, so I arranged a series of matches, pitching Steve against the best players in the world, all held in what was becoming the famous Romford Matchroom. Over the years, Steve took on John Spencer, Alex Higgins, Ray Reardon, Cliff Thorburn, Jimmy White and others. In 1977, he beat Spencer, the reigning world champion, five frames to one; he beat Higgins 5–3 and Reardon 14–11 in a two-day match. I had to lure the top players with handsome fees, only marginally offset by selling tickets. One marathon match against Higgins over the best of sixty-five frames went on for four days, with Steve winning 33–23. These were some of the greatest nights of my life.

Naturally, I bet on Steve on these occasions, and naturally I almost always won. Steve never bet on matches. He was happy to get £25 for an evening plus a bonus out of the winnings, and to share a Chinese or Indian meal when a match was over. He knew that the experience he was gaining was invaluable. In some ways, Steve was innocent – he still shared a bedroom with his brother, seven years his junior – but on the table he was assured, with a killer instinct.

While Steve was an amateur, he had ten or seven points a frame start, not that he needed it. When he turned professional, it was on level terms, but he knew the table and he had the Romford Roar behind him, so he was just about invincible. We also went around the country for money games. He played Jimmy White in Manchester once and the Romford boys were buzzing, putting on money with all the locals. (I always made a point of looking for a handy exit to make sure we could get out in one piece, but we rarely needed it.) I had already placed several thousand pounds with local punters when Steve walked in, with a brutal cold. He could hardly breathe. Shit! Jimmy destroyed Steve that night, but that was a very rare losing evening.

I was keen for Steve to turn professional. It took some persuasion because his dad, Bill Davis, wanted Steve to win all the amateur events, including the World Amateur Championship, before turning pro. Steve just wanted to play snooker. We went up to Blackpool for the 1978 UK Pairs Championship. Steve and Tony Meo won so easily it wasn't true, winning 6–0 in the semi-final and final. We were as happy as sandboys, which may have helped, because Steve signed the management contract with me against a lamp-post on the Blackpool front. It was our first and only contract because our trust in each other grew stronger and stronger and a handshake was always enough. We saw ourselves as a team, two council-house kids going out to conquer the world, Steve with his ability, me with my mouth. I gave Steve a car, his first one, from the Lucania pool: an old Maxi worth about £200.

Professional snooker was pretty much a closed shop at that time, so I phoned Ray Reardon, a major influence in the World Professional Billiards and Snooker Association, and explained that Steve really wanted to turn pro but only if his membership was proposed by Ray Reardon, as he admired him so much. That did the trick. Ray took it as a compliment and proposed Steve with his blessing. We were off and running.

I had fallen in love with snooker, so when I bought a plot of land in Ongar, Essex, and built a five-bedroom house, I thought it would be a great idea to build an underground snooker room beneath the patio, with a lovely view over farmland. We left 50 Cambridge Road, Sawbridgeworth, and moved in to 77 Fyfield Road, Ongar. Susan started playing snooker and we had some great games. I gave her a 21-point start in each frame and the bets were quite big – none bigger than best-of-three frames and the loser had to get up in the night if the children woke up. That was real pressure.

The trouble was that my dream snooker room leaked, and we never solved the problem. Steve and I had marathon matches there, best-of-101 frames over months. Sometimes we had to play in wellington boots, wading through two inches of water. I had a seventy-point start in every frame. Quite often, I'd be fifty points ahead with one red left on the table and Steve wouldn't give up. He'd snooker me time after time until my brain was addled. That was when I realised how ruthless he could be. The bet was that the loser had to wash the winner's car. That meant washing the Maxi. Steve used to walk round, inspecting it as I grovelled with the bucket and sponge. 'There's a bit of dirt on the exhaust pipe,' he'd say.

I was playing snooker every day, all afternoon usually, in Romford, sometimes for amounts of money that make me shudder. This was probably the most exciting and enjoyable period of my life. Unlike today, and for most of my time in business, I did not put in the hours. I was too busy having fun. Among the characters in the Romford hall were such legends as Blind Les, Newcastle John, Crunchy Warne, Frank Mizzlebrook, Putts, Fat Sid, Patsy Hutchinson, Ronnie Cutmore and his dad and the one and only Robbo Brazier, of whom much more anon.

I fondly remember Mark Lazarus, his son Nicky, his brother Bobby and dear old Jo Lazarus. Mark scored the winning goal for Queens Park Rangers in the 1967 League Cup final and played for Leyton Orient for some time, but I think he was most at home in a billiard hall or a boxing gym. Mark was useful, to say the least. I sparred with him a few times and I was always on my toes just in case. Bobby Lazarus was the one I used to play snooker against for too much money in the late 1970s and the one person who was more frightened of his wife than I am of mine.

We were playing a money match up in Romford one Sunday when his wife walked in with his dinner on a plate, steaming hot.

'You spend all your life in here, you can eat your fucking dinner here as well,' she screamed as she threw his food all over Table Thirteen, our best table, before storming out. The place went silent; Bobby looked bashful. We cleaned the table up and carried on with our game.

One day I had seen a picture in the *Daily Mail* colour supplement: a group of our Romford guys in front of the Chicken Ranch, a well-known brothel just outside Las Vegas, having the time of their lives in the desert. One of them was Bobby Lazarus and when I saw him in the billiard hall, I told him I had seen his face on the front cover of that day's magazine. He went white.

'Are you OK?' I said.

'No,' he said. 'We have the *Daily Mail* delivered at home.' He ran out and returned an hour later looking terrible, because when he got home all his clothes had been thrown out of the bedroom window and were on the lawn.

'Bobby,' I said, 'I think your wife has gone too far this time. You just had your picture taken. No one said you was up to anything naughty.'

'It's not really like that, Barry,' he said. 'I told her I was in Brighton buying a car.'

My record, bet-wise, was a match against Bobby for £6,000 a side. I put up my £6,000 and Bobby raised his stake with help from his many mates. We were about as bad as each other. We started at ten o'clock at night and played until four in the morning. Neither of us would take a risk with so much money at stake. After all, you could buy a house for £6,000 in those days so it was serious stuff.

If I won a big-money match like that (and I did beat Bobby), I would get into our house at Ongar in the early hours, turn the lights on in the bedroom and throw the money up in the air. If I lost, I used to get undressed downstairs, put my clothes in the cupboard underneath the stairs and then sneak upstairs and hope Susan didn't wake up. She did once and asked me what I was doing getting in at that time of night. I said to her firmly, 'I've just been to the toilet. What are you talking about?'

'Oh, sorry, I thought you'd been out late.' It wasn't often I pulled the wool over Susan's eyes.

Another great game I remember was against the legendary Ron Gross at his Neasden Snooker Centre. Ron was a noted amateur player but he had one weakness, which I decided to exploit when I played him for £3,000 a side in his Neasden club. There were big-money matches there all the time and Ron loved to be involved. He was such a lovely character that win or lose, you really didn't mind, because it was a grand occasion. I believe we played the best of fifteen frames and agreed to have a break after every five frames. After the first five, Ron was 4–1 up despite giving me fourteen points a frame start. After the next five frames, Ron led 7–3 and the money looked safe for him. That was when Ron's problem came in. He did love a drink. Super-confident after the second session, he suddenly appeared with a bottle of whisky, which he polished off over the next couple of frames. He didn't win another frame, but he was still great company and took his loss like a man. Perfectly sober, I left with his three grand in my pocket and a warm memory of a man who was fun company every time he picked up a cue. I think he would have been a lot wealthier if he hadn't been so partial to a drink.

One match, though, got me into serious trouble. Susan was expecting our second child, Eddie, and once her waters had broken I took her to Epping Forest Hospital and then went to work. When she had Katie, our eldest, she had been in labour for ages, so I wasn't worried about leaving for a while. At lunchtime, I was playing Crunchy Warne for £50, best-of-three frames, when I had a call to say Susan's labour had started. It was one frame all and I had never beaten Crunchy, so I carried on and finished the game. I won, too.

I drove at speed to the hospital and as I arrived I saw Susan being pushed somewhere on a trolley.

'Best of luck. Hope it all goes well,' I said.

'Where have you been, you bastard? I had him twenty minutes ago.'

I've never lived that down.

I was smoking and drinking too much and not getting much exercise so, with Freddie King's encouragement, I joined Waltham Forest Amateur Boxing Club. I was in my late twenties and loved every minute of it. I always liked fighting. Even when I was younger, I knew I could look after myself and, being on the big side, I didn't really have much to worry about with the company I kept.

From the moment I walked into the club in Hoe Street, Walthamstow, I loved it. Freddie had an amazing atmosphere in the gym. Initially, he told me I didn't have to fight anybody, he just wanted to get me fit. But after a few weeks he threw me a pair of gloves as he walked past and told me I was in next.

Now, with my ego it is quite impossible to swallow or bottle it, so I did as I was told and soon found out I had the heart for it but not the technique. Week in, week out, I got battered by just about everybody. There was an East End family, the Furlong brothers, who could all fight. The best of them was Tony Furlong, who had boxed for England and was a league above me. When my turn came and Freddie shouted out, 'Barry, you are in with Tony,' my heart used to sink but I took my medicine like a man and learned a few lessons.

I would spar two or three times a week. On the drive home, my eyes were usually swelling and the road would disappear in front of me.

'Why are you doing this?' Susan used to ask. 'Are you mad?'

My reply was simple: 'I love it.'

Most of the lads in the gym could look after me quite well, but my spirits used to rise when Freddie told me I was sparring with one fighter in particular. His name was Alfie Cole and he was about as bad as me. They say two donkeys make a great race and we had some terrific sparring sessions. Truthfully, I ended up well in front. Alfie was as game as they come. He didn't stop coming forward and I didn't stop bashing him up.

Twenty-five years later, I was in Kent looking at a fishing lake to see if it would be capable of staging the final of *Fish'O'Mania* or even one of the qualifying heats. I walked round the lake and as I was leaving I saw someone on the clubhouse roof doing some repairs. I took no notice. As I got to my car, a voice shouted out, 'Are you going to make me a cup of tea, then?'

I looked around and couldn't see anyone other than this bloke on the roof.

'Are you talking to me?' I shouted back.

'Too right, I am. Make me a cup of tea.'

He came down the ladder, looking belligerent. I didn't have a clue what was going on. When he came close, he was snarling but I half-recognised the face. Alfie? Yes, he'd had a few more wars, but it was Alfie. Alfie Cole! We greeted each other pleasantly and had a good chat about the old days. But when I told him I used to love to spar with him, that he was so useless I could bash him up whenever I felt like it, he took umbrage and said he used to handle me with ease. It seems ridiculous but we nearly ended up in the car park trying to find out who really was the better man. We parted as friends, honour intact, proving that the camaraderie established in the confines of a boxing gym is everlasting.

Freddie King got banned from the Waltham Forest club for some altercation, no surprise, and went to the Garden City ABC in Debden, my old patch. I moved across with him and he trained me one-to-one, which was great. When I was twenty-eight, I was getting ready to make my competitive debut on an amateur dinner-show, as a light-heavyweight. One evening there weren't any other light-heavies to spar with, so Freddie put me in with a heavyweight. 'Don't worry,' Freddie said. 'He couldn't beat up his wife. Enjoy yourself.' I did, for two rounds, moving nicely. At the end of the second round, Freddie said, 'Why not knock him out?' He knew I wasn't usually a big puncher and that I longed for a knockout. In the third and last round, my opponent was battered. There were fifteen seconds to go, and I knew it was now or never. I threw a big right hand and missed. At that moment, when I was off-balance, he hit me with a left hook, catching me on the right shoulder. The shoulder was broken as I lay on the canvas. I looked up and I could see the happiness on my opponent's face.

In the hospital, I heard Freddie phoning Susan to say, don't worry but Barry's in hospital, and I could hear Susan laughing at the other end. She thought I was mad to be boxing but I enjoyed it so much. The damaged shoulder was the end of my formal participation in the noble art. It also affected my cricket. With limited mobility in the shoulder, I was never the same as a bowler.

In the late 1970s I could not have been happier. Now that my son and heir, Eddie, had been born, our perfect family was complete. Steve had turned professional and we were ready to conquer the world, the slot-machine business was going well with Freddie King having a ball, and we had plenty of money. Unfortunately, Deryck Healey International was in trouble. In fact, the snooker-hall business was just about keeping it afloat. The legal director, Tom Blyth, committed suicide and the managing director was having trouble coping. Deryck Healey himself could not come to terms with the fact that changes had to be made. I went to see him and said that if he did not cut his workforce, he was going bust. He said he couldn't do it, that he had recruited his people out of universities and art colleges and he did not have the heart to sack any of them.

Deryck disappeared for a few months and I did the dirty work for him. I have to admit, I was ruthless back then. If something had to be done, I'd do it. These days, I understand Deryck's point of view. I now know how important staff are and that they must always be treated with respect. People matter, and we should never forget that.

I did learn that lesson from Deryck and I am proud that so many of our staff at Matchroom have been with us for decades. Loyalty has worked both ways. Two who must be introduced straight away are Steve Dawson and Michelle Wassell. Steve was recommended to me by KPMG, who asked me if I was looking for a good accountant. I was, and Steve has become my right-hand man, absolutely irreplaceable. He makes sure everything is done correctly. I might have the ideas and do the deals, but Steve makes them happen. He does the slog of contracts and paperwork. Best of all, his integrity is beyond question. He's the straightest man I know. Michelle joined in 1986, the year after Steve, as my personal assistant. When she came for interview, she reminded me of my diamond sister, Christine, and I thought it would be a safe appointment. It was better than that, for Michelle is also a diamond. Totally reliable and honest, she organises my business life.

Anyway, I reorganised Deryck Healey's textile company in 1978, making half the staff redundant, and carried on expanding the snooker-hall business. My price for saving the company and doing the dirty business was that Deryck should sell me a third of the company for £30,000 and that when the time came to sell, the decision to do so would be mine alone.

The 1980s, which were to be Steve's decade as the king of snooker, really got going when he played Alex Higgins in the final of the 1980 UK Championship, Steve's first major final. We had long had a private agreement that when he came to within a frame of victory at any tournament, he would take a quick toilet break and we would meet in the toilets to discuss his winner's speech. So when he was leading fifteen frames to six, a frame away from beating Higgins, I went down to the toilets and waited for him. After a while, he came in. 'This could be very unlucky, you know,' he said, as if we were tempting fate. We weren't. Steve made a cool century break to take the title. He won £6,000, which he thought was pretty good, until I told him I had bet £650 on him to win the championship, at odds of ten to one, making £6,500, plus, of course, 20 per cent of his prize money. Steve never knew or even asked what the prize money was. He just wanted victories and trophies, knowing that the money would come.

The celebrations following Steve's first major title went on long into the night. But the only title that really counts, and the one we had set our hearts on, was the world title. That came the following year, 1981, the year that Steve established himself as the dominant force in the game, the man they all feared. Steve won five major championships that year, including the big one. The 1980s was a golden era for the game, with some big personalities who became household names, but none of them was truly dedicated and professional until Steve came along. He was the first, and others, notably Stephen Hendry, Ronnie O'Sullivan, John Higgins and Mark Williams had to copy his professionalism to match him.

The great breakthrough for Steve, and me, came in the 1981 World Championship. To reach the final, Steve beat four great players – Jimmy White, Alex Higgins, Terry Griffiths and Cliff Thorburn, the Grinder. The final, against Doug Mountjoy, was comparatively plain sailing.

At the opening of this book, I described how I felt as Steve closed out the match, how I kept telling myself not to do anything stupid, which is exactly what I did, rushing down to the auditorium floor and almost taking him out with a rugby tackle. That just showed how much it meant to me.

Here is Steve's published description from the receiving end:

> I closed my eyes for a moment to take it all in. Then I saw Barry Hearn charging towards me with his fists and teeth clenched. He hit me like a tank. We had dreamt of this moment for so long. Everybody could see what it meant to us. The scene was unreal. I don't think the World Championship knew what had hit it.

For seven years, I could do no wrong. The fruit-machine business was booming, with a small army of people going round collecting money for me every day. The acquisition of a load of amusement arcades scattered across the Southeast added to the fun, and the profits. The snooker business, with Steve firmly established as the best in the world, was even more lucrative. Then in 1982 I had the phone call I always knew would come. It came from a company called Riley Leisure and they asked if Lucania Temperance Billiard Halls (London) Ltd was available for purchase. I told them, 'Everything is for sale if the price is right.'

After some haggling, I went to see Deryck Healey to tell him we were selling the snooker business. He asked me what he would get, and I told him it would be two-thirds of £3.1m and I would get the rest. Deryck was true to his word and said it was a great price – go get the money. When I sat down to close the deal with Riley Leisure, I realised that I would essentially be out of a job and I needed compensation for that. I asked for the Romford property in its entirety, including, of course, the snooker centre and the now-famous Matchroom. They agreed.

I had more money than I had ever dreamed of, and for the first time I wasn't overdrawn at the bank. I was thirty-four and seriously contemplated retirement, to devote myself to cricket, golf and fishing. Not for long. I knew myself well enough to realise that I needed to do deals as much as I needed oxygen to live. I decided to spend the surplus, which would drive me back to business.

In partnership with Steve, I bought a Mayfair property, 3 Grosvenor Street, on the corner of Bond Street, which comprised a basement, a street-floor shop, two floors of offices and a flat. As part of a tax-saving scheme, we bought 500 acres of forest in Scotland, next door to Billy Connolly's holding. We planted a couple of million fir trees, and I used to go up there every year, plane to Glasgow then helicopter, to see how they were growing. Our 500 acres was opposite the Mull of Kintyre. I'd look across the water and sing Beatles songs. There was nothing to do up there, so I mostly just had a little look – they were growing a bit every year, surprise, surprise – and flew back. We put in a reservoir and stocked it with trout, but I never fished it. One year, the land agent asked me if I wanted to do any shooting. I'd had a pop at clay pigeons but never anything alive. This bloke was there with a huge gun. He looked through the sights and said, 'This one's for you, Mr Hearn,' handing me the gun.

I looked through the sights and I could see this magnificent stag about 500 yards away. It was on the top of a crag, surveying the valley.

'It's yours,' he said again.

'No,' I said. 'I can't do this.' He was quite upset.

I also used my cash from selling the Lucania business to buy Mascalls, an eighteenth-century mansion with views over Docklands and the City of London. As soon as I saw the place, in the company of estate agents working for the Ford Motor Company, I fell in love with it. At that time Ford had a number of large country houses for its senior executives and Mascalls was their President of Europe's residence. Ford decided that such extravagance had to stop and put Mascalls and other properties on the market.

'No way are we buying that,' Susan said. It was massive – over 12,000 square feet – and needed extensive repairs and renovation.

For once, I won the argument. The price originally was £260,000. I struck a deal at £240,000. It took two years to renovate Mascalls, then in 1984 we sold our lovely house in Ongar and moved in. We now had this magnificent house with staff, two lovely children, and I was walking around with a smile on my face every day. That was when I showed my mother round and she asked if I was doing anything illegal.

Top of the Pots: Chas & Dave, the pop duo, at the table; Steve Davis, Dennis Taylor, Tony Meo, Terry Griffiths and Willie Thorne mildly amused.

5

Snooker Loopy

The morning after Steve won the World Championship, he was front-page news; every journalist wanted to speak to him and the phone never stopped ringing with offers of endorsements, sponsorships, exhibition matches and so forth. One call came from someone with a strange accent, asking if I would bring Steve Davis for an exhibition tournament – in Thailand. I didn't even know where Thailand was and I didn't know what to say when the man, who said he was from Channel 7 in Bangkok, asked me what it would cost to have Steve Davis visit his country. I said $20,000 but when the man immediately agreed, I realised I had said it too quickly and gone too low.

'Is there anything else you want?' he said.

I quickly corrected. 'Yes. First-class airline tickets.'

'Of course.'

'The best suite in the best hotel in Bangkok.'

'Naturally.'

'A police escort front and back when we go anywhere.'

'Our pleasure. Anything else?'

'We'll need to bring someone for him to play. I can arrange for Tony Meo to come.'

'No problem, of course. Anything else?'

'I can't think of anything right now.'

Within a day, the contract was signed and the Cathay Pacific tickets were on my desk. The boys loved first class. We were asked if we could please look like film stars, with white suits and sunglasses, when we landed in Bangkok. Naturally, we obliged and when we walked into the terminal there were two or three hundred young women screaming as if we were The Beatles, holding placards: 'Kiss me Steve', 'We love you Barry', 'Welcome to Thailand'. Just outside the airport, there was a thirty-foot poster of Steve. A reception was held for us on the first night, and everyone was there, from the British Ambassador to the Governor of Bangkok. TV cameras were everywhere, and people started screaming when Steve walked into the room. We had the time of our lives, laughing all the way, and Steve had the chance to show the Thais how to really play snooker.

There was just one fly in the ointment, shortly before we left. I was in bed when the phone rang at seven am. Bangkok police. We want to talk about your visit to Thailand. OK, I said, let's fix a time. No, we're downstairs.

Steve and Tony Meo were already in the back of a police van. We were taken to a police station and led down into the basement. Tony was in bits but Steve seemed amused. I told them to leave the talking to me. The officers kept asking me how much money we had made in Thailand and I kept saying we were just over to publicise the game. In fact, we had been paid in cash on arrival. I had it in a suitcase in my hotel room. This questioning went on for an hour or two and then I lost patience.

'This man here makes eight million baht a year,' I said, pointing to Steve. 'And this man makes four million baht a year,' pointing to Tony. 'And I make two million baht a year. We came here to spread the game of snooker to Thailand. Do what you like with us, but we will not be coming back.'

It worked. Apologies were forthcoming and we were free to go. Fortunately, they never searched my hotel room. I managed to get the cash out of the country and over the years we often returned to Bangkok. We had all fallen in love with Thailand, the Land of Smiles.

Thai culture included Muay Thai, an ancient martial art to which I was introduced by Somphop Srisomwongse. As well as being head of Channel 7 over there, he was a Muay Thai and boxing promoter. He had a Muay Thai training camp at his house and when I stayed with him on one visit I did a few training sessions. It was incredibly tough. I was offered a chance to spar with some of their fighters. No way. They were no more than eight stone, but eight-stone killers. They lived and trained in the most basic conditions and were grateful to win a bicycle or a T-shirt after some brutal competition.

No wonder so many of them went on to become world champions as boxers. One I knew well was Sot Chitalada, the flyweight world champion who came over to London to fight Charlie Magri in 1984. Magri had been a world champion himself, but Sot knew he had his measure.

'Do you like to bet?' Sot asked me a few days before the fight.

'Yes.'

'OK, I'll do you a favour. What round would you like me to knock out Magri? I can take him out whenever you like.'

I just smiled.

'OK,' Sot said. 'Let's say round five. I take him out in round five.'

Actually, I didn't put a penny on it. It didn't seem right to bet against the British fighter and I liked Magri. He was an East Ender.

On the night, I was close to Sot's corner. He saw me and called out, 'Round five.'

Sot carried Magri for three rounds. In the fourth, he decided to set up Magri for the finish and knocked him all over the place. It was all going to plan, until Magri's trainer, Terry Lawless, decided Magri had had enough and pulled him out at the end of the fourth round. Sot had won by stoppage after four rounds. He was mortified because he thought he had cost me a lot of money. Fortunately, my patriotism had rescued me.

My first trip to Thailand with Steve and Tony Meo was the start of the Matchroom love affair with the Far East and the start of the snooker boom in Asia. We went to Kuala Lumpur, Singapore, Hong Kong and China, where we put on our first show in the Great Hall of the People for the Chinese Government's top brass. We'd had a request from Deng Xiaoping, the Paramount Leader of the People's Republic, no less, to watch some billiards. Apparently, it reminded him of his youth in Shanghai, where the game was played extensively. Billiards and snooker had become illegal under Chairman Mao, but it had survived underground. I took Steve over to play with Rex Williams, one of the veterans who still played billiards as well as snooker. To be honest, it wasn't the most exciting event I've seen, but Deng seemed happy.

Most of those trips were sponsored by a French brandy house, Camus Cognac, who were making a big pitch for the Asian market. I can just about remember being in a Bangkok nightclub when we were drinking several bottles of the stuff. I had to stop because I couldn't feel my legs. We were young, we were crazy, we were having a great time and, best of all, someone else was picking up the bill.

One time, I was on a round-the-world trip with Steve Davis. We were flying home in first class when this fellow who was in business class came up to see me.

'My name is Michael Cohen and we're going to do some business together,' he said. He was short and balding, full of chutzpah and an absolute bundle of energy. As I quickly learned, Michael, agent extraordinaire to the stars, is never quiet and could do a deal when locked in a toilet. Not long after meeting him, we were on our way to his house in The Bishops Avenue, Hampstead–very fancy. It was me and Susan, plus Steve because Michael had a snooker table and wanted to play. As we went down The Bishops Avenue, Susan asked what number his house was, and I realised I didn't have it. Then I saw a place that was even swankier than the rest, with fountains, all lit up like a casino hotel on Las Vegas Strip. That must be it, I said. It was. Michael does everything to excess: he had fifty different desserts for his son's bar mitzvah.

Michael had a black stretch limo, a Cadillac. 'If you ever need to borrow it, let me know,' he said. There weren't many such limos around back then and they really stood out. I did borrow it and Robbo, my driver, drove it. Pretty soon, I thought we should get one.

My first one was black and I bought it 'off the shelf'. The second was custom-made for me by Dillinger-Gaines Coachworks in New York. I asked them to create something special, a super-stretch white Cadillac, with office facilities, a quadrophonic sound system, TV, fridge, bar area, and the Matchroom logo on the exterior paintwork as well as the upholstery, plus darkened windows. It cost $64,000, delivered. When it arrived, the engine had a speed governor, limiting it to 55mph, which was the speed limit then in the States. We took that off straight away. The licence number was THE 147S. It was what we called our 'lucky motor' and it became the most famous limo of all time in the UK. You could park Ferraris around it and people would just stare at our limo. On one occasion, we were cruising up the M1 when some young fellows in a Ford started chasing us, blaring their horn, lights flashing. They drew alongside the driver's seat, occupied by Robbo.

'Who's in the back?' they yelled.

Robbo lowered the electric window.

'Michael Jackson,' he shouted, before closing the window and accelerating away.

The 1980s belonged to Steve. He was in the world final eight times and won six of them in that decade. It was also the decade of the Romford Roar, the Romford Mafia, call us what you like. Travelling up to Sheffield in our stretch Cadillac limo was our annual pilgrimage.

Invariably, we stayed at the Grosvenor House Hotel and when Steve had a match, we would walk down to the Crucible Theatre, always using the same route, always walking on the lucky cellar doors outside the Brown Bear pub on Norfolk Street, walking tall as if we owned the place, which we did. It's fair to say we were flash bastards, not universally popular. But we didn't care.

I used the limo as a family car when we went racing, and during my marathon-running phase, I'd run behind it every morning from home to the office, Robbo driving the Cadillac, with a clean suit for me in the back and the *Rocky* theme blaring out. Susan hated it, said it was pretentious. I eventually sold it when we had done 200,000 miles and it was falling to bits. A fellow I know bought it for £8,000 and restored it. He sold it for five times that to an escort agency in Southend. They used it for sex on the M25. Pick you up anywhere; one lap of the M25; as many girls as you like.

In the Crucible, Bill Davis and Robbo, real name Robert Brazier, would watch Steve's matches on the monitors in the media room. They rarely betrayed emotion. Bill Davis still served as Steve's coach. He had been a mechanic for London Transport buses but his main occupation once Steve made it to the top seemed to be watching his son and smoking cigars.

Robbo had been a lorry driver. He was one of the Romford crew, a regular in the Lucania, and became our driver and Steve's minder. He was completely unreliable except when it came to Steve's cue case. You'd have to kill him to get that off him. Robbo was addicted to gambling. When he first worked for me, he had been made redundant by Texaco, who used him as a security guard. He got twenty grand severance money and did the lot. Overnight, he went from a £5-a-bet man to a £500-a-bet man. He usually lost, of course, but he made a good bit when he had a lump on a young boxer we had, Herbie Hide, at 200–1 to win the world heavyweight title one day. Well, Herbie got his world-title shot and I told Robbie to lay the bet off, cover himself and put £10,000 on the other fellow so he was certain to win. Robbie wouldn't do it, but Herbie won anyway, a sensational stoppage to give me and Freddie King a world heavyweight champion.

Ladbrokes didn't want to pay up; they said Herbie had only won the WBO version of the title. I called the Ladbrokes boss and told him to cough up, that it didn't specify which version of the title on the betting slip. The cheque came in, made out to me, and I grabbed Robbo by the scruff of the neck, took him down to the council offices and spent £20,000 paying off the mortgage on his house. For the first time in his life, he had an asset. Robbo was the best gambler I ever saw with ten quid. He would turn it into £300 by being smart. But give him a grand and he'd lose it like a lunatic.

In our heyday, Robbo became style-conscious. Gordon Burn, a fine writer and one of the scruffiest journalists I ever met, was merciless when Robbo displayed a new hairdo: 'an elaborate, lacquered, burnt-sienna production that looks like two onion bhajis sitting side by side on a plate'.

Early in 1982, I was able to tell the press: 'This year Steve Davis will earn £350,000 before he takes his cue out of its case . . . if he is fully rested, I don't think he can be beaten.'

Now that *was* tempting fate. At the World Championship that year, as defending champion, number-one seed and overwhelming favourite, Steve was drawn to play Tony Knowles in the first round.

It never crossed Steve's mind, or mine, that he could be beaten, but when we left the Crucible after the first session, on a Friday night, Knowles was leading by eight frames to one. And it was first to ten frames. At the Grosvenor House, Steve ordered a huge steak and I ordered champagne.

'This is not a good time to have a party,' Steve said.

'We usually drink this stuff when we win a tournament,' I said. 'I'm not waiting. Let's have it now.'

Instead of getting morose, we had a celebration. Next morning, Steve went in-off from the first break-off shot and soon lost 10–1. Actually, it got worse. Tony Meo and Terry Griffiths, both part of our fledgling Matchroom team, and the only two players capable of seriously challenging Steve at that time, were also beaten in the first round. We went home with our tails between our legs. No doubt our detractors were thrilled. That was the year that Alex Higgins famously won his second and last world title.

And that familiar lesson from Principle Number Five had been administered again: complacency is a killer.

What should you do when you're down? Get back up; fight back; be positive; don't let your enemies see that you've been hurt. Back in Romford, we had a party, a losers' party. It also happened to be my thirty-fourth birthday.

Now, if there was one activity at which we excelled in Romford, apart from snooker, it was throwing parties. Usually, we would have an evening in the Matchroom snooker room upstairs and then peel down to my office on the ground floor and party until the early hours. People used to wake up in the middle of the roundabout in Romford with a bottle of something in their pocket having passed out trying to walk home. Once, someone stole a horse on his walk home and was arrested by the police at the top of nearby Hog Hill for riding a horse in the middle of the night on the main road.

Mostly, those were celebrations after some notable victory and, as they say about the 1960s, if you can remember much about them, you weren't there. But without doubt the greatest party of all was our losers' party.

The Romford crowd was in full attendance as well as Steve Davis's parents, my wife Susan, Terry Griffiths and his wife Annette, along with Willie Thorne and Tony Meo. Joe Coral, the bookmaker and devoted snooker fan, sat and enjoyed his usual glass of scotch. Joe was one of life's most notable characters. He claimed to be a communist but was always welcome in the Queen Mother's box at Cheltenham. He said his hobbies were 'billiards, bridge and booze – there was another one, but I've forgotten what it was'. He died in 1996, aged ninety-two.

There was some decorum at first. The losers' party coincided with a change in use for our famous Matchroom, where so many great matches had been played. It was to become the Matchroom Club, an upmarket snooker club that would be a source of great fun for many years. The final match to mark the close of the old Matchroom was, naturally, a match between Steve and myself. I had my customary seventy-point start and was holding my own, at least with the banter, when the table-fitters arrived and stripped down the table.

Honours even, we all proceeded downstairs for jellied eels, oceans of alcohol, dancing and crazy games, Romford style. The Phantom Flan Flinger put in an appearance, I remember, and the manager of the Harlow Lucania broke his nose pushing a peanut in the peanut race across the carpet.

During those mad times, and at that mad party in particular, I was as happy as I have ever been. The fact that we could celebrate losing was also a demonstration of how best to recover from a loss. You only look forward, you never lose your positivity, you accept that losses happen, take them on the chin, brush yourself down, try to be better next time. It is called character, and when you throw a big party, win or lose, you throw a blinding party.

There is a written record of that night. At that time, two sisters, Jean and Mary Rafferty, were working on a book about the snooker scene, *The Cruel Game*. Jean produced the words; Mary took the photographs. The book gives a good idea of what was going on in those days, of the way Steve and I put snooker on the map, put Romford and the working-class people of Romford on the map. It was appropriate that our company became Matchroom Sport in that year, 1982, the year I suppose when we had to start to grow up.

But first let us conclude that losers' party. The final chapter of *The Cruel Game*, correctly titled 'The Party to End Them All', captured the essence. Here is Jean Rafferty's final paragraph:

> There are pale streaks in the sky but not the twitter of a bird as dawn comes to Romford High Street. Two policemen look up from their inspection of the empty street and locked shops as the partygoers straggle down the High Street. They laugh at the crazy hats and general air of gaiety and want to know where everybody's been. Barry Hearn's party, says a girl in a pink ra-ra skirt and gold boots, her striped boater clinging at a rakish angle to her head. One of the policemen shrugs. 'Never heard of him,' he says. The other looks appalled. 'You can tell how long *he's* been in Romford,' he says.

The losers' party has become a part of snooker's folklore, but it was also just the beginning of a succession of parties, for any excuse, for Matchroom as well as me and my children.

The highlight for me was my sixtieth birthday party at Mascalls, followed up ten years later by an extravaganza beyond compare. Our big bashes, with hundreds of people flying in from all over the world to attend, have produced wonderful memories, but my favourite party was a lot lower key, with far fewer people.

I was invited by Eddie to play golf with him on my seventieth birthday and I thought that was really cool, a round of golf on your birthday with your son and heir. The destination was secret but when he turned left just before Stansted Airport into the private jet area, I knew something was up. It wasn't just that Eddie had hired a top-end private jet to fly us to France to play at the fabulous Les Bordes golf club in the Loire Valley, but as I got into the plane I was greeted by some of my best pals. There was Steve Davis, of course, my son-in-law Dan, Adrian Powell, Bob Scott, Ian Payne, Steve Dawson. We had a fabulous and alcoholic round of golf and jetted back because I had booked a small family dinner at a local restaurant. When I got home, however, I smelled that something wasn't quite right as there was a car in my drive I wasn't used to seeing. I arrived thinking I had five minutes to shower before I went out to the restaurant with just me and the kids, and I found a reception planned in my back garden. My golf mates, who hadn't said a word about it all day, were there as well with wives and partners.

Music began to come from a small marquee next to where we were to dine alfresco. Not just music, but a song from my favourite artist of all time, Tom Paxton, who was standing there, guitar in hand, playing live one of my favourite songs "Forest Lawn". This was one of the greatest and best surprises of my life and the fact that the kids had taken the trouble to fly Tom in from Canada at his advanced age, eighty-one, was surreal. I was starstruck and insisted Tom sit next to me at dinner. The food was sublime, the wine excellent and Eddie gave a terrific speech, after which we had two 45-minute spots from Tom, just for me and my pals. That was my best birthday party ever. And by the way, "Forest Lawn" will be sung at my funeral. Instructions have been given!

Back in 1982, as well as Steve, I already had Tony Meo and Terry Griffiths under contract and part of our Matchroom team. Griffiths, who won the world title in 1979, was a marvellous player and marvellous man, with a very dry sense of humour and a deep pride in his Welsh roots.

Steve was the best player in the world by a country mile, but his most memorable matches, as far as the public was concerned, tended to be the ones he lost. That's life, I guess. There was the Tony Knowles shock and then, most famously of all, the 1985 World Championship final against Dennis Taylor.

On the first day, Steve took an 8–0 lead in a canter. Taylor never looked like winning a frame. In the second frame of the evening session, Steve had a difficult green to pot. He would not usually have taken it on, but what the heck, he was 8–0 up. Was it complacency? I don't know. He missed, Taylor cleared the table and had a glimmer of hope. By the end of the first day Steve was only 9–7 ahead.

The following day, it was nip and tuck with Steve edging ahead and Taylor continuing to pull him back until they reached seventeen frames each and that memorable final-frame decider. It started after 11pm and went on for an hour and ten minutes until only the black was left: one ball for the world title. Eighteen and a half million people were watching on TV, one of the biggest audiences for a sporting event in British television history. Standing next to Susan and Robbo, I experienced the closing drama from behind the backstage curtain because I could not bear to watch. Steve had a cut on the black to win, a shot I expected him to make nine times out of ten. I turned away and heard the click of the balls and then the mass groan that told me he had missed. Taylor had an easy pot and made no mistake.

Snooker, an obscure pastime ten years earlier, had become a major sport. Back in 1978, when the BBC started day-by-day coverage, they screened thirty-five hours of action. In 1985 that had increased to 130 hours. Prize money for the Championship had gone up from £24,000 to £300,000. Today, it has gone up to £2.5m, with £500,000 to the winner.

There was another strange aspect to the Taylor match: it made Steve more popular, perhaps because he took defeat with such good grace. Instead of being seen as a machine, he was human, a good guy. In any case, he made it to the next four Crucible finals and won three of them. Business as usual.

Dennis Taylor, with his big glasses and sunny personality, was the housewife's choice, so as soon as he had won the title, I decided to sign him up. The original Matchroom team was a trio, Steve Davis, Tony Meo and Terry Griffiths, none of whom were best pleased by Taylor's arrival, especially Griffiths. He was a great person and player, but he never stopped moaning. We were making loads of money, going first class, staying in hotel suites, and he never stopped moaning, except to comb his hair. But it made sense to me to have the reigning world champion and Taylor was soon joining us on our overseas trips. Cliff Thorburn, Neal Foulds (son of Geoff), Willie Thorne and Jimmy White all joined as well over the following couple of years, so we had an eight-man Matchroom team, with most of the world's top players. This was the era when we went endorsement crazy. There was Matchroom aftershave, Matchroom slippers, Matchroom duvet covers, Matchroom pillowcases and even Matchroom timeshare apartments on the Costa del Sol. Hardly a day went by when we didn't send out an invoice – heaven!

For four or five years we went on an annual Far East tour, away for a month or so, to Shanghai, Beijing, Kuala Lumpur, Singapore and Thailand. Every player made a minimum of fifty or sixty grand from each trip. We had a deal with Riley snooker tables. We endorsed them and made £200 for every table we helped to sell. We sold a thousand in Hong Kong alone. We would go to a club, play a frame of snooker, do some trick shots and move on. We'd do six clubs a day. The players were knackered, but they all made a nice few quid out of it.

One evening in Hong Kong, we had 4,000 people watching as Jimmy White was playing in the Hong Kong Masters. They all loved Jimmy. At the end, we had a trick-shot competition. Steve did his trick shots, then Dennis Taylor did his. We held the best back to last. That was Terry Griffiths, who was marvellous with trick shots. I was master of ceremonies on the microphone.

I gave it the big build-up: 'Now, the 1979 world champion and a great trick-shot artist, the one and only TERRRRRY GRIFFITHSSS.'

The spotlight shone on the entrance. No Terry. Oh, bollocks, I'll say it all again. He must be there by now. I did the big build-up once more. Nothing. Now I'm in trouble. Then I saw his head appear and he makes his entrance, walking like a drunkard, which was odd for a teetotaller like Terry. He came right up to me. I put my hand over the microphone.

'Are you all right, Terry?'

'Fine. I've just had one of Jimmy's fags. Those big roll-your-own ones. They're great, aren't they?'

Needless to say, Terry messed up every trick shot.

The problem for most of the players was not making money but hanging on to it. Jimmy White tried every toxic substance known to man, most of them very expensive; Willie Thorne went gambling; Tony Meo spent his money on cars and clothes. And however many times I told them, they didn't appreciate that they would have to pay tax.

Steve Davis was the opposite. He never spent the money he earned. I used to keep his cheque book in my drawer, but we never wrote a cheque. He never earned much more than £1m a year but he earned at that level for many years. He now owns several houses including two massive ones, some rental properties, an interest in a few businesses plus a few million in the bank. He's not extravagant, he doesn't gamble or use cocaine. In fact, he makes Jack Benny look like a philanthropist.

When we went out, Steve never had any money on him. He assumed I would pay and it really pissed off Susan. Once we were in the Méridien Beach Plaza in Monte Carlo, having a drink with a group of footballers and personalities. Steve came in, went to the bar, bought a small beer and came over to join us.

'Davis, get yourself to that bar and buy everyone in this place a drink,' Susan said. 'NOW.'

He did as he was told.

What was I like during this crazy period? Gordon Burn, the dishevelled writer I had a soft spot for, put it like this:

> Hearn's Matchroom headquarters in Romford was bullshit central, with Barry giving GBH of the earhole to anybody who cared to push his button and get him started on aspirational this, and socially hygienic that, and how everybody associated with the Matchroom set-up stood to make fortunes.

Ouch, but not far off.

It was at this juncture, the mid-1980s, that I had a strange phone call from a snooker fan who wanted to give me a present. He said he was so pleased with being able to watch Steve Davis winning World Championships that he wondered whether I would accept a gift, a free racehorse.

Now I have always believed there is no such thing as a free lunch but, liking a bet, on greyhounds or horses, it was a very tempting proposal. I agreed to watch the horse run before deciding whether or not to accept his gift.

I went to Doncaster to watch Charming Charles, a gelding, in a two-mile hurdle race, and learned that the horse had apparently been a wedding present for Lady Diana and Prince Charles but he had been rather naughty in the stables and they got rid of him. He did seem to have some ability since he led throughout the race until falling at the final hurdle. He got up and trotted home with a smile on his face. By now I was hooked on the idea of becoming a racehorse owner. When you are born in Dagenham and your dad's a bus driver, the idea of owning a racehorse is quite an aspirational target. I didn't know anything about about being a racehorse owner, but nothing new there: another leap into the beyond.

My friendly snooker fan repeated that the horse was a gift, but it had to be trained by Dave Morrell, who had looked after the horse for him and did not charge too much. At the time, this made perfect sense to me and I arranged to visit Morrell's stables just outside Market Rasen. I took Steve Davis and Tony Meo with me because I sensed a useful photo opportunity. We met Dave the trainer and were not massively impressed with the facilities. Still, we sat on the horse, some publicity photos were taken, and the deal was done. Charming Charles became the first racehorse I owned.

As I said, I liked a bet in those days; in fact, I liked a big bet, so when Dave the trainer decided to run the horse at Kempton Park, I asked him what his chances were. 'We will win this easy,' he said.

I may not have known much about racehorse ownership, but I did know that when there are twenty-four runners in a race, as there were that day at Kempton, it is impossible with any certainty to predict a winner. Nevertheless, Dave was insistent and, because I am a very gullible type of person, I backed it to win £100,000 – £3,000 at 33–1.

The horse came twenty-second out of twenty-four and to put it mildly I was not best pleased. In fact, strong words were exchanged with Dave the trainer. He had a pile of excuses, then he said: 'Don't worry, I'll enter it again at Market Rasen in a week's time. It's my local course and he will definitely, definitely win there.' I decided to let him live a little longer on the basis of a promise that a betting coup was now a mere formality.

The following week, we duly drove up to Market Rasen. Our party comprised Robbo, me, Susan and Tony Meo, who also liked to bet. Our trainer, Dave, was as optimistic as ever. I took him to one side. 'Dave, I do not need to have a bet,' I said. 'I am happy to be here just to watch the racing. However, I will have a substantial bet if you tell me with some certainty that this horse is going to win or be close to winning. But please do not give me any bullshit because I do not need it, and if you claim this horse is going to win and I believe you and it runs like it ran last week, then I am going to be extremely unhappy with you.' (Or words to that effect.)

Dave's reply was to the point: 'Barry, we are going to win today. I know this track like the back of my hand. Charming Charles will be third or fourth on the first circuit, then on the second circuit, on the far side of the track where the ground is better, he will go ten lengths clear. Nothing will get close to him and he will trot in comfortably.'

This sounded so credible that I could not wait to organise my own mini-version of a betting coup. I had three bookmakers' accounts at the time, each with a limit of £500. Charming Charles was an 8–1 shot and I placed £500 on him at those odds on each of those accounts.

There were about ten on-course bookmakers in the ring, none of whom would take a bet of more than fifty pounds. I had quite a bit of cash on me and I distributed several thousand pounds between myself, Susan, Robbo and Tony Meo. I gave everyone instructions to wait until two minutes before the off and then to put fifty pounds to win on Charming Charles and to keep putting on fifty pounds until either I said enough is enough or the bookmakers stopped taking the bets.

We lined up and hit the bookmakers over and over again with fifty-pound bets, starting at 8–1 and finishing at 2–1. Charming Charles had become the clear favourite purely on the weight of money. We staked over £2,000.

As the horses came under starter's orders, I experienced a surging adrenalin rush. My eyes never left Charming Charles, who looked every inch a winner. Off they went and after the first circuit Charming Charles was in exactly the position Dave had predicted, third or fourth. Perhaps Dave the trainer actually knew what he was talking about.

On the second circuit on the far side, just as Dave had foreseen, Charming Charles reached the better ground and went ten lengths clear. Dave is a genius. And Charming Charles never got caught, never got close to being caught, and flew home a clear winner. I have never felt more excited in my life and Susan, Robbo and Tony Meo were equally overcome.

Then a Tannoy announcement: 'Stewards' enquiry, betting enquiry – will connections of the winning horse please report to the stewards' room?'

I went to the stewards' room with Dave the trainer and asked what the problem was. The stewards said they were not happy, that I'd had significant sums on the horse. I agreed. Then they said that last week at Kempton it came twenty-second and today it won by ten lengths. It does not look right.

I looked at those fellows in their country tweeds. 'Let me get this right,' I said. 'Last week I backed the horse to win £100,000 and it lost. Today I have backed it to win less money and it won. Are you telling me I am not going to get paid?'

'No, we are going to let the result stand, but we are warning you as to your future conduct.'

I thought that was a pretty good result. I wasn't worried about the warning and I was still overjoyed at the horse's performance and even happier to think that I was going to get paid out because I had probably won somewhere around £30,000.

I knew my bookmakers' accounts were solid, but we had a whole pile of winning betting tickets that we had to redeem from ten very disgruntled Market Rasen bookmakers. They were in a circle muttering about 'these Cockney bastards coming down and taking all our money', and I gave the pile of tickets to Robbo, to collect the winnings. As a working-class man, Robbo hated bookmakers with a vengeance, and he was happy to go into their midst with a wad of winning tickets. He just walked in there with a broad grin on his face and came out with the perfect line:

'Gentlemen, get your fares ready please.' Every one of them paid in full. Only one did not have enough cash and he sent on a cheque three days later. Hats off to the bookmakers of Market Rasen.

You should have seen us in the white Mercedes on the way home. I was the only one who wasn't pissed, so I was driving. The other three were all asleep. I pulled into a Little Chef café, ordered teas and Eccles cakes and told them all to put the money on the table. There was a lot of cash. It was in used notes, so it looked like millions. When the waitress served the tea and cakes, she almost passed out. She must have wondered if we had just robbed a bank. It wasn't a generous thought, but I reckoned that a good bit of that cash was going to disappear if I didn't get hold of it straight away. Robbo, in particular, had no principles, so he would have nicked the lot. I scooped it up and left them each enough for a drink. A good drink.

The local newspapers up near Market Rasen the next day did not read well. It was as if a mob of East End gangsters had come up to their little track and robbed everyone blind. Of course, the truth was simply that Dave the trainer got lucky. Charming Charles never won again. But my love of owning racehorses and going to the races for a day out had been firmly established.

Even more bizarre than the Charming Charles caper was the time I went for a jolly at Lingfield races with Michael Cohen and one of his clients, Jeremy Beadle, who became a great friend of mine. I know Jeremy was not universally admired. In fact, he played so many pranks on the British public that he got booed pretty much everywhere he went. Let me assure you, he was much more than a prankster. He was ultra-smart, very knowledgeable and generous to a fault. In fact, a great man. Always available for a good cause, it was reckoned when he died much too young in 2008 that he had raised £100m for charity.

Jeremy's weakness, of course, was that he loved practical jokes, which brings me back to that day at Lingfield. Our party included Michael, his wife and mother, as well as Jeremy and his wife, Sue. At the end of the day's racing, we all headed back to Michael's black limo. Now Jeremy had got it into his head that it would be hilarious if he picked up Michael, all five feet of him, deposited him in the boot of the limo and locked him in. So he casually asked Michael to open the boot.

I appreciate that this may not sound all that funny, but we'd had a great day at the races and a few drinks, and when we saw Jeremy pick up Michael, put him in the boot and slam it shut we all thought it was the funniest thing we'd ever seen.

Except for Michael's mother, the Jewish matriarch. 'My son is in there and he's going to run out of oxygen,' she screamed. 'Now get him out. Immediately!'

After thirty seconds, we realised the joke was past its sell-by date and it was time to release Michael. But where was the key? We looked everywhere, inside and outside the car, while Michael's mother went from crazy to apoplectic, sure that her darling son was going to die. We shouted at Michael in the boot. 'Where's the key? Where's the key?'

We heard a faint voice from within: 'It's in my pocket.'

We tried to lever open the boot. No luck. Eventually, we went into the back of the limo, took out the back-rests and managed to pull the diminutive agent through the gap to safety and sweet fresh air.

Another surreal episode involved a pop song, 'Snooker Loopy'. This time, I have to admit, it was my idea. I phoned Chas Hodges, one half of Chas and Dave, and suggested we do a Matchroom song with them, just as they had with the Tottenham Hotspur team. The singers were the eight Matchroom players and me. It had a somewhat catchy melody and a few disc jockeys started playing it. It climbed the charts until it made the top thirty and the video was played on *Top of the Pops*. That gave us another boost and in May 1986 it reached number six.

> *Snooker loopy nuts are we*
> *Me and him and them and me*
> *We'll show you what we can do*
> *With a load of balls and a snooker cue*

Pot the reds, then screw back
For the yellow, green, brown, blue, pink and black,
Snooker loopy nuts are we
We're all snooker loopy

No threat to Leonard Cohen, nor was the follow-up single, 'The Romford Rap'. For that one, we recorded a video at the Hippodrome with the Matchroom Mob dressed in coloured suits: Neal Foulds in yellow, Dennis Taylor green, Tony Meo brown, Terry Griffiths blue, Willie Thorne pink and Steve black. I'll leave you to guess what Jimmy White was. It was, well, embarrassing.

Those happy sing-song days didn't end happily for all our players. Tony Meo, who had been with us almost from the start, couldn't win often enough. His form deteriorated and he ended up disillusioned. In the early days, the names that kept coming up on the circuit were the boys from Tooting, Jimmy White and Tony Meo, from a club called Zan's. Actually, Tony was a much better player than Jimmy back then, but he was a bit older, about fifteen when Jimmy was thirteen.

The first time I met Jimmy he had a broken leg but was still potting balls off the lampshade. He couldn't read or write until he was twenty-two, but at fourteen he could work out a four-horse accumulator faster than anyone else I knew.

Tony was unbeatable in pairs events with Steve Davis but he didn't have the temperament for singles match play, especially in pressure situations. He was great for exhibitions, not for tournaments. The only 'ranking' title he won was the 1989 British Open, which wasn't enough for a world-class player. He complained I only cared about Steve Davis and I told him I only cared about winners.

'Used and abused' was the phrase he repeated, but there were lots of people who would have liked to have been used and abused like him. He earned a lot of money but never kept it. On those Far East tours, the players were making fifteen or twenty grand a week. I always said to them: 'Less tax.' But Tony never seemed to understand he had to pay tax. In the end he fell out of love with the game and dropped off the tour.

Willie Thorne was another who never fulfilled his potential. Technically, he was as good as anyone and was known for making maximum breaks for fun, but somehow it didn't really matter to him. His parents had their own snooker hall in Leicester, so perhaps he was rather spoilt. Despite his obvious attributes, Willie only won one ranking title – the 1985 Classic – but he made the final of the 1985 UK Championship and led Steve Davis 13–8, only to lose 16–14. Willie missed an unbelievable blue off the spot when well ahead and Steve, smelling blood, steamrollered Willie to win.

Willie just wasn't hungry for success. And, as all those who knew him and lent him money were well aware, he was a gambling addict.

He came to see me in the Romford office one day. 'Bazza,' he said, 'I've got a problem. I owe a lot of money to a lot of people.'

'I've told you before, Willie, you don't have the money to gamble.'

'Please help me out.'

'OK. Let's do a list.'

It was one bookmaker after another: Corals, Ladbrokes, William Hill, Gus Demmy in Manchester, Stan James, Fred Done and others. It added up to debts of £240,000. I knew the bosses of all the bookmakers, so I hit the phone, first to Corals.

'You've let Willie Thorne have credit, haven't you? Why did you do that? He owes you £24,000 and you've done your bollocks. He's not going to pay. He can't pay.'

It was the same when I phoned the other bookies. A lot of them said, 'We'll ban him, you know.'

And I said: 'Please do.'

Poor Willie was such a lovely man, but like all addicts he never told even himself the truth and he piled up debts with just about everybody. It wasn't as if he was any good at gambling. He always seemed to lose and, as he once said, 'You know, in a one-horse race I would finish runner-up.'

Through most of our relationship, I kept a watch to make sure he didn't pile up too many debts, but after a while I just couldn't be bothered to constantly look after all the problems he created, and we parted company. Not that Willie changed. He was the same until the day he died in Spain in June 2020.

The last time he came to see me about helping him out was at Sheffield in 2017 when he explained that he had serious problems with some heavy-handed people that wanted paying. He begged me for a £25,000 loan and promised he would pay it back at the end of the World Championship from his BBC commentator's fees.

I wrote him a cheque for old times' sake, and as I handed it over to him I said, 'Willie, we both know I am never going to see this again, which is fine, but this is the last time you will ever get a penny from me.'

Of course, Willie professed that it was only a short-term loan and gave me a cheque dated to the final day of the World Championship. That cheque is still bouncing around somewhere and that was the last I saw of the twenty-five grand.

Actually, it was a good move in the long run as Willie came on time and time again for further loans and I was able to say I told you, I'm never going to lend you another penny. A great player and much missed, but a very weak person.

Firefighting when players had problems was a big part of my role, especially with Jimmy White. I spent years keeping him out of the papers. But it didn't always work. There was a tabloid reporter called Brian Radford. I had known him for a while and liked him. In fact, when we decided to do Steve Davis's first book, we offered Radford the job. He got well paid and it was a big breakthrough for him, a young reporter. He came to play cricket with me a few times and brought his son, so I knew him socially as well.

Radford phoned me one day. 'What's this story on Jimmy White?' he said.

I knew the story. The *News of the World* had found him in some nightclub, snorting cocaine with a ten-pound note.

'Does Jimmy want to give his side of the story?' Radford asked. That was the usual line. Anything to extend the story. But I wasn't buying it.

'No, he doesn't.'

'Well, can I come to see you?'

He came to Matchroom's Romford headquarters and brought this other bloke with him. They sat opposite me in my office.

'What do you want to talk about?' I said.

'Jimmy. We've got pictures. What do you think about players taking cocaine?'

I saw a different person in front of me. Not a friend.

'Who's he?' I said, pointing to the other fellow, who hadn't said a word.

'A colleague.'

I went round the desk and told the fellow to stand up. 'Are you wired up?'

I took his jacket off him and he *was* wired up.

I turned to Radford. 'Brian, all the years I've known you and you've brought this prick into my office all wired up. This is how you treat me. You can fuck off. I don't want to see you again, ever.' I slung them out.

It wasn't the last I heard of Radford. Someone put some stuff through his letterbox to burn his house down. There was limited damage. Radford thought I had done it, but I hadn't. I've never done anything like that. He hated me and went round trying to get muck on me. He may have gained a reputation as a tabloid hack, but he lost all respect.

At the time, you want to lash out, but there's a bigger picture, I know. In sports management, we use the press for our own benefit all the time and there's a price to pay when you sell your soul to the devil, Faust-like.

Still, that was a rare fly in the ointment. The Matchroom snooker business was going well, and it all came so easily. Taking the game around the world, from China to Brazil, and supporting Steve Davis as world number one was all marvellous.

Every player in the Matchroom team knew that, while I always did my best to represent their interests, Steve held a special place in my affections. We were like brothers. But I also had a high regard for Terry Griffiths, who had been with me from almost the beginning and was a loyal team member. Terry won the English Amateur Championship in our Romford club in 1977 and afterwards I suggested he play Steve in an exhibition. Terry won, and went on to win the 1979 World Championship, but he rarely got the better of Steve. As he says himself, Steve's supremacy cost him millions of pounds.

Terry had long held two big ambitions: to have his own substantial house built and to open his own snooker club in Llanelli, his home town. He achieved both, and the official opening of his club just before Christmas 1987 was a memorable occasion. Terry was approached by Jimmy White, who offered to do the honours by playing a match against Terry in front of the good and the great, and not so good and great, of Llanelli. Steve also wanted to officially open the club, but Terry had already accepted Jimmy's offer. We knew what was going on and we knew that Terry felt embarrassed about it all.

We got together with Jimmy and planned a surprise. Jimmy went to Llanelli and told Terry he had a few mates coming from London for the evening and he needed three seats reserved. No problem. Jimmy and Terry started their match and when they came to an interval, we made our way up the stairs – Steve, with his cue, me and Robbo.

Terry seemed confused. 'How did you get here?' he said. I was just laughing.

'Don't worry,' I said. 'Steve will play a frame against Jimmy at the end and perform a few trick shots.' Terry was thrilled. His club was opened by the two best players in the world. It was a great evening and at the end Terry went into his office by himself and cried his eyes out. He was always an emotional, terrific man.

As if I didn't have enough to do at the height of the snooker boom, I bought myself a small present for Christmas, 1985: a manual on how to train for and run marathons. It was a crazy idea because I had no distance-running experience. I still gave it everything. Starting on page one, I followed it to the letter. First day: walk for twenty minutes; second day: twenty-five minutes. Gradually, start running, then build up the distances. I managed to wangle a place in the 1986 London Marathon, which gave me four months to prepare. That's not really long enough, but I was diligent. On the day, it was windy, but I got round in three hours, fifty-two minutes, which is very respectable.

Straight after the London Marathon I was in São Paulo, Brazil, with Steve Davis and Tony Meo. They were taking on the local snooker champions, Rui Chapéu and Roberto Carlos, under Brazilian rules. Their tables were smaller and only one red was used. It was re-spotted each time it was potted. Chapéu was a celebrity who always won and had his own TV show. He wore a flat white cap, which he said he would take off if he was ever beaten. He went three frames up on Steve and I could see that Steve's neck was flushed red. That always meant he had the hump. He knuckled down and beat Chapéu, who didn't remove his hat and forever lost his street credibility.

In Brazil, I was going for a short run every day just to keep myself in shape. After one morning jog, an old man came up to me and asked if I would run with him on Sunday, to which I agreed. I gave him my room number and the name of our hotel and left it at that. What I didn't know, as I went out on the Saturday night for a few drinks with Steve and Tony, was that the old man had entered me in the São Paulo Marathon.

The old man knocked on my door at six in the morning and said let's go. I'd only just got in after a good night out, but I thought it was quite amusing, why not give it a go, and we went down to the start. It got hot, very hot. I subsequently discovered the race was called Death Race 2000 because there were 2,000 entrants and the organisers expected fatalities. It got hotter, and someone forgot to put out any water over the final five miles. As I crossed the line after four and a half hours, I was out of it. If you had asked me my name, I couldn't have told you.

I am not easily put off. I had found another passion and, like my other passions, it consumed me. I gave it my all, and soon I had help. I bumped into an old friend, Annie Briggs of Ceefax, the BBC text service. She was a decent runner herself and advised me to get in touch with her trainer, Sandy Risley. He turned out to be an aggressive little bastard, as well as a great trainer and great friend. He could run forever, despite having only one lung, and had already notched up over a hundred marathons.

Nothing was too much trouble for Sandy. Most days he would arrive at Mascalls at six in the morning and we would have a session. Once a week, we would do a tough eighteen-mile run at Snodland in Kent, where Sandy lived in the hills. Running up gradients of one in four is great training. It gives you massive stamina and answers any doubts that might be lurking in your head. Sandy got me super-fit for a man of my age, thirty-eight, and bearing in mind I was somewhat overweight. I ran the New York Marathon together with Annie Briggs in 1986. I ran three hours, forty-six minutes and she beat me. Next up, I ran the London Marathon again in 1987 and ran a personal best of three hours, twenty-two minutes. Let me tell you, that is a bloody good time! I was well over an hour behind the winner but in the top third of the runners that year. My son Eddie thought it would be quite easy when he ran his only marathon in 2014. He trained like a madman, but he was still north of four hours, so for once I have bragging rights in the family.

I had the running addiction. I would run from Mascalls to the Matchroom Romford office most mornings. Robbie, my driver, used to follow me in the white stretch Cadillac, with my shirt, socks, clean pants, suit and shoes. That was five and a half miles and I would run home after work as well. I entered half-marathons, ten-mile and five-mile races virtually every week and with Sandy's help managed some respectable times. At my peak, I was running seventy-five miles a week. I ran two New York marathons, four Londons and the one in Brazil, plus one in Hong Kong and a local one, so I completed nine in all.

Sandy Risley accompanied me to the New York Marathon in 1987. He was a lot older and a bit slower than me but I had terrible trouble with blisters after sixteen miles. I stopped and Sandy came across me after the medics had taped me up. I was waiting for an ambulance to take me back to the start.

'We haven't come all this way not to finish, have we?' Sandy said. 'Now come on, get up.' So I did and Sandy managed to get me to the finish, running backwards all the way to encourage me. What a man. Later on, he helped out at Leyton Orient as fitness trainer and then as kit manager, and he was an important part of the Matchroom Boxing team, as the 'whip', the person responsible for the gloves and making sure the fighters are ready when their time comes to go to the ring.

Sandy was always available to help and I once asked him to see what he could do with Jimmy White, fitness-wise. He took Jimmy into the gym at Mascalls and asked him to hold his arms straight out and do some breathing exercises. Jimmy passed out halfway through and Sandy said, 'I think he has some way to go before we can call him fit.'

In his extraordinary lifetime, Sandy completed over 150 marathons. He contracted cancer around 2005 but trained almost every day, throughout his illness and treatment, until he died in 2020, aged eighty-six. A year before he died, I went round to his home with my kit on. 'Get out of bed,' I told him, 'we're going to do five miles and then have breakfast.'

'I can't run, I've got cancer,' he said, so I reminded him of the New York race when I wanted to give up and he wouldn't let me. The run was painful for him and slow, but it was a bloody good breakfast. That was the last time I saw him. His funeral was packed with all the people he had helped, from boxing, football and athletics. As I say, a great man.

In the Hong Kong Marathon in 1988 I injured my Achilles tendon and had terrible pain in my lower back. I wanted to pull out with just a mile to go. Marlene Lee, head of Prism, the media agency we used, came to my rescue and ran that last mile with me. I would never have made it without her. I had another crack at the London Marathon that year and trained really hard, mostly because I found myself up against Rocco Forte, Lord Forte's son and successor at the head of the Forte empire.

I had bumped into Rocco on many occasions and always noted how elegantly he was turned out. Clearly, he was as fit as a butcher's dog. Like me, he had developed a love of long-distance running. We used to chat about the pain, the pleasure and exhilaration in finishing a marathon and the dedication that went into trying to be as good as you can be. I knew that Rocco's times were a lot better than mine but I was still ambitious and we engaged in a little banter about which of us would be faster in the 1988 London Marathon, for which we had both entered. We had a bet. Rocco suggested the loser should pay £2,000 to charity. I wasn't going to tell him, but I knew I didn't have much chance. In any case, I didn't mind losing because I'd had such value and consideration from Forte hotels over the years, thanks to his father. I agreed.

I knew that Rocco was trying to get inside three hours, which was beyond me, but training went reasonably well and I ran the race in three hours, thirty-two minutes, twenty-nine seconds. Not bad, but I realised I must have lost the bet and I phoned Rocco's secretary the day after the race to find out where my cheque should be sent. She asked me how I knew I had lost. I said I had only run three hours, thirty-two minutes, and I knew Rocco was trying to beat three hours.

'Well, Rocco had a nightmare,' she said. 'I need to know your exact time. Three hours, thirty-two minutes and how many seconds?'

'Wait a moment. Twenty-nine seconds.'

'Rocco was three hours, thirty-two minutes, seventeen seconds.'

Twelve seconds! If I had just put in a little more effort I would have saved myself two grand. Still, the best man won on the day and in sport you can never argue with that.

For marathon running, the writing was on the wall, but not for fitness. I remained dedicated to regular exercise, usually in the gym, and it remains a fundamental part of my life. It helps me think more clearly and maintains my determination to succeed. I am also convinced that without my training regime, which started in earnest with long-distance running, I would not have survived two heart attacks and been an active sportsman into my seventies.

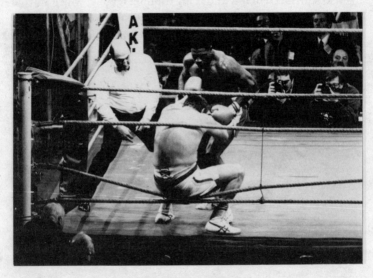

October 1987, my entry into big-time boxing. Frank Bruno batters
Joe Bugner to defeat in eight rounds at White Hart Lane.
Credit: Michael Fresco/Evening Standard/eyevine

6

No Tinned Tomatoes

Number Six of my ten principles says that unusual things happen every day of your life and it is how you deal with them that makes you unusual.

And so it was, one day in the mid-1980s, that I took a phone call in my Romford office. The fellow at the other end sounded posh, very posh, and that put me off straight away.

'It's Edward Asprey here, and I wonder whether Steve Davis can give some snooker coaching, some lessons, for one of my clients.'

I figured he must be from Asprey's, the top New Bond Street jewellers, but I wasn't in the mood to tug the forelock.

'Excuse me,' I said. 'Steve Davis is the world snooker champion, a world-renowned sportsman. He makes a lot of money and he does not waste his time teaching people who can't play how to play.'

'Fair enough. But I think you might be interested when you hear who my client is.'

'And who might that be?'

'The Sultan of Brunei.'

I did not know much about international royalty, but I did know that the Sultan of Brunei was one of the wealthiest men in the world. Now Mr Asprey had my full attention.

'Oh, I see.'

'Now how much would Steve Davis expect to be paid for coaching the Sultan's son, Prince Billah?'

This was where Rule Six kicked in.

'Twenty thousand pounds an hour,' I said.

'That sounds fine. Can we book ten hours, then, and could you arrange for a snooker table to be set up in the Dorchester Hotel for the coaching sessions to take place?'

No problem. We did everything Edward Asprey requested. Steve started coaching Prince Billah, a teenager who, it turned out, didn't particularly want to be coached in any case. At one point, Steve suggested a technical improvement: the prince should try getting his chin closer to the cue before taking his shot. That was ignored. I think he was just bored and wanted someone to play. During one session, Prince Billah asked Steve if he would mind refereeing the next frame so that he could play his bodyguard. *That's a bit cheeky,* Steve thought. *I'm world champion and I'm about to referee a match between two people who can't play. That's not on.* Then he thought, *Well, it is twenty thousand an hour, so perhaps I'll do as I'm told.* That was the perfect reaction, and he spun a coin to see who would break.

This all went on for ten days. Prince Billah wanted more players, so Tony Meo, Terry Griffiths, Jimmy White and the whole Matchroom camp were roped in at rather less than twenty grand an hour, but still significant money. Our bill for the first ten sessions was around £400,000.

Our splendid involvement with the Sultan went on for four years, with wonderful visits to the Dorchester and their palatial home in north London. At the end of the final session, we all queued up for boxes of goodies from Asprey: key rings, picture frames, all solid gold and engraved with the compliments of Prince Billah. Alas, the prince developed a love of nine-ball pool rather than snooker and the party came to an end, as all good parties do. But it provided me with another invaluable lesson: never turn down anyone until you know who they are and what they are prepared to pay.

It was also during the snooker boom years that I became acquainted with Rocco Forte's father, Charles Forte, or Baron Forte as he was by then. He was a huge snooker fan and follower of Steve Davis. He also wanted some lessons from Steve and I set them up. Steve was well paid, but I was the real beneficiary because thanks to Lord Forte I have hardly had a problem with hotel accommodation ever since.

Charles Forte was small and dapper, beautifully turned out, with an air of elegance. I think he liked me because he saw someone, like himself, from a relatively humble background who was making something of himself. He had started out with a milk bar in the Strand in 1935, and built one of the biggest hotel chains in the world.

When we first met, he told me I really should only stay at his hotels around the world. I took note because they were some of the finest. The Plaza Athénée in New York instantly became my home in that great city, and I haven't stayed anywhere else in New York for the past thirty-five years. In Paris, it's also the Plaza Athénée; in Barbados, Sandy Lane; and in London the Waldorf on the Aldwych.

The Waldorf was Lord Forte's favourite. In those days, it was a really upmarket gentlemen's hotel and Lord Forte used to boast that it had the finest dining room in London. Today, no longer part of the Forte group, it is still an excellent hotel but less grand, more corporate. Nevertheless, I still hold all my meetings in London at the Waldorf, as I have for thirty years. I have my own seat, I know everyone in the place and I spend a fortune on cups of tea. I have also closed millions upon millions of pounds' worth of deals in that hotel.

When it comes to the necessities of life – sleeping, eating, doing deals – I am a creature of habit. The accountant's mistrust of risk, I suppose. When I was working for Deryck Healey, he once took me to Mr Chow in Knightsbridge, one of the earliest fine-dining Chinese restaurants, very trendy in the 1970s. I have been going back there ever since and almost invariably I have the same meal

I ate with Deryck all those years ago: seaweed, honey prawns, crispy duck, lobster and filet mignon.

For breakfast (until they stopped serving it, most regrettably), it was always Simpson's in the Strand. I first went there for an early meeting with my friend, Paul Ridley, when he was sports editor of the *Sun*. We asked for tinned tomatoes. The waiter looked down his nose at us ruffians. 'This is Simpson's. We don't serve tinned tomatoes.'

To which we both replied, 'Young man, learn a lesson in life. Think about your customer, listen to your customer and always give the customer what he wants. We won't be back here again unless you have tinned tomatoes.'

For the next couple of decades, Simpson's had a special stock of tinned tomatoes in their larder, and I breakfasted there on countless occasions.

Matchroom snooker, for many years, was a cash cow. But we hardly had to try. I needed a fresh challenge; I needed to break down doors again. My chance to do just that came with an unexpected phone call from Terry Lawless, the boxing trainer and manager whose stable included Frank Bruno, the European heavyweight champion.

Lawless was a member of a group of four men, sometimes called the Syndicate, sometimes the Cartel, who had ruled British boxing for years. The other three were Mickey Duff, the matchmaker and manager, Mike Barrett, a promoter, and Jarvis Astaire, who you might call the Godfather, or Chairman of the Board. They had controlled all the major London venues and the television revenues, all from the BBC, for years. But young Frank Warren was challenging their monopoly and had managed to get ITV interested in boxing. I'm not sure whether Lawless was acting on behalf of the Cartel or beginning to fly solo, but he got in touch and suggested I should get involved with boxing promotion.

My first show with Lawless featured an up-and-coming heavyweight, Gary Mason, against Andre van den Oetelaar at the Cliffs Pavilion, Southend, in 1987. I loved it, a new buzz. I had always been a fight fan and although God had not given me the ability to be the heavyweight champion of the world, I knew I had the ability to be the best promoter in the world.

Within a month of my first step into the waters of professional boxing, I was in at the deep end. I was having lunch with Susan in a Chinese restaurant in Southend, discussing my ambitious plans for boxing. Susan has always been very critical of me, in the nicest way, and she listened for a while and then said, 'Don't just talk about it, do it.'

I had been nurturing the idea of a fight between Bruno, Britain's best contemporary heavyweight, and much loved, and Joe Bugner, formerly Britain's best heavyweight, and much derided. It was a fight I really wanted to see, as a fan, which is not a bad rule of thumb. When Susan said just do it, I asked to use the restaurant's phone and called Bugner, who was at home in Melbourne, Australia.

'Joe, it's Barry Hearn here. How would you like to come over and fight Frank Bruno?'

'That's going to cost you a lot of money.'

'I'll give you two hundred and fifty thousand pounds.'

'What plane do you want me on?'

I had Bugner, but Bruno was under contract to the Cartel. He was all set to fight Trevor Berbick in London, but Berbick injured his back and had to fly home to Canada. Seizing the moment, I went round to Lawless's house in Hornchurch and asked to see Bruno. I offered Bruno £300,000 to fight Bugner. With no alternative fight on the table, and desperate to earn some money, Bruno and Lawless signed. It also helped that Mickey Duff was out of the country, so he couldn't put pressure on Lawless. Deal done. But where to stage it? I fancied an open-air event at White Hart Lane, the Spurs ground, so went to see Irving Scholar, the Spurs chairman. Scholar was brilliant to deal with because, like me, he did not know what he was talking about when it came to staging big-time boxing, but he knew he wanted the profile for Tottenham, as well as four ringside seats for himself and his friend Martin Edwards, the chairman of Manchester United.

Basically, I took his trousers down. Tottenham were to get 10 per cent of the gate money but in return they were paying for everything: the ground, the ring covering, stewards, security, police, the lot. Tottenham lost money on the event but at least Scholar had a great time.

Next up: sponsorship. I phoned my friend Mike Foster, the marketing director of Courage Brewery, who had just acquired Foster's lager in Australia. I thought it was a marketing brainwave, pitching England's favourite son, Frank Bruno, against an adopted Australian, Joe Bugner. I told Mike I wanted £100,000 for sponsorship and he said, 'This is a no-brainer, I will come back to you on Monday.' But no-brainer turned into no deal because Foster's decided to get involved with Formula One. There are times when people make decisions that are fundamentally wrong. Can you imagine Lewis Hamilton getting out of a car with a pint of lager in his hand? It made no sense. Never mind. I managed to get Makita, an engineering and toolmaking company, to come on board, for the same £100,000.

I thought my next task, TV rights, would be an easy sell. Wrong. I went to see Jonathan Martin, the BBC head of sport, and told him I had Bruno and Bugner under contract to fight in October. I thought it was perfect for the BBC, who had screened all Bruno's professional fights as he rose to prominence. But it seemed that Martin did not welcome upstarts like me, preferring to deal exclusively with the Cartel, as he had for many years.

Martin looked down his nose and said, 'I do not believe this is a fight for the British boxing public.' To say that I was astonished is an understatement. Bruno had been fed punch fodder for too long and the BBC had been roundly criticised for screening mismatches. Martin was surely not acting in the best interests of his employers.

Now I had a big problem because I did not have a broadcaster. I knew tickets were going well and I knew what I was in for in terms of the costs of the show, but the cream on the cake was a good domestic TV deal. I had heard about a fellow called Greg Dyke who was at the time running London Weekend Television, which was part of ITV. (He later became director-general of the BBC and chairman of the Football Association.) I knew ITV had done some boxing with Frank Warren, with Bugner as their big draw, and that the Cartel's monopoly was effectively broken.

I went along to the LWT offices on the South Bank unannounced, walked into reception and asked for Greg Dyke. The receptionist put me through.

'Dyke here.'

'Mr Dyke, you do not know me. My name is Barry Hearn and I am involved in snooker.'

'Yes, I've heard of you.'

'Well, I have an idea for you that involves boxing and I think you will like it.'

'Fine. Next time you are in London let me know and we will meet up and discuss.'

'Well actually, Mr Dyke, I am in your reception area.'

'Oh, OK, come on up.'

It was a meeting that remains fresh in my mind. Dyke was an enthusiastic man, very creative, and wanted to cover sport for LWT in a different way. After some discussion, Dyke got down to the business at hand.

'I like this,' he said. 'I want to do this fight, so how much do you want for it?'

Such was my ignorance of boxing promotion at the time that I had to guess, off the cuff.

'I need £200,000,' I said.

'I do not believe you can deliver this fight. Boxing is a tough business and you are a newcomer. But if the fight does happen, I will give you £250,000.'

To this day, that is the only time a TV operator has paid me more money than I asked for.

Sure enough, the newcomer, me, had further hurdles to overcome. Jarvis Astaire, the Cartel's main man, rang me up and asked me to come and see him in his office overlooking Cavendish Square in the West End.

'You have stolen something that belongs to me,' he said.

'What's that?'

'Bruno.'

'How does that work?' I said.

'He's my man. I own Bruno. Get that straight.'

'If your partner sold me your car, that's not illegal, is it? Lawless is your partner and I've signed Bruno from him, for one fight.'

To prevent any legal trouble, I cut Astaire and Mickey Duff into the deal. I didn't care. I wasn't doing it for the money. I was doing it for the thrill. As it happened, I also made money.

It was always risky to put on an open-air show in October, but I was convinced we could justify using a stadium. On the first day tickets went on sale, we took £1m. In the end we sold 33,000 tickets. Bearing in mind that I had no idea what I was doing and that within a month I was going from a small-hall show in Southend to a mega-promotion at White Hart Lane, staging Bruno versus Bugner was an enormous amount of work, with an enormous amount to learn. I recollect seeing tickets scattered all over the floor in my office underneath the Romford billiard hall, hundreds of thousands of pounds' worth of tickets with no control at all. I have no idea whether we ever 'reconciled' the gate, but if we did, we must have been miles out because people were flying in and out, grabbing piles of tickets, settling up, bringing back tickets. It was chaos, but that was how we began to understand how to run a proper promotional business.

On the night of the fight, all went well with the undercard. Gary Mason and other Lawless fighters won nicely, but I knew the moment of truth, the main event, lay ahead. Actually, I was shitting bricks. I was hit by the realisation that we were going live to the nation on ITV, that the sponsors were there, along with 33,000 fans who were waiting to be entertained. We had to deliver.

I was wondering what boxing promoters do just prior to the main event and I remembered an old Mickey Rooney black-and-white film where he went in to see the fighters to wish them luck. Good enough for Mickey Rooney, good enough for me. I knocked on the door of Bruno's dressing-room. No answer, so I went in. It was like a morgue. Bruno was sitting with his head down, just concentrating, and everyone else was too frightened to say a word. I wished Bruno the best of luck and he mumbled 'thanks'.

When I approached Bugner's dressing-room, all I could hear was loud music. Bugner was an old pro. He had fought Muhammad Ali in Kuala Lumpur; he had fought at Madison Square Garden; nothing was going to faze him. He knew what he was doing, and he knew he was there for the money. When I entered, Bugner was showing Marlene, his wife, two dressing-gowns. (Incidentally, I would rather fight Mr Bugner than Mrs Bugner any day of the week.)

'Marlene, which of these do you prefer me in?' he said in his high-pitched, best Australian voice.

It was all relaxed, a fun place to be, but I felt I should make a little motivational speech.

'Joe, I just want to say thank you. You have helped sell this fight every day you have been in the UK. You have turned up at press conferences with plastic crocodiles over your shoulder; you have worn an Aussie hat with corks hanging from it and you have sold 33,000 tickets. If you can win this fight, there is a young man in America called Mike Tyson who looks useful. Beat Bruno and I will pay you a fortune to fight Tyson in London.'

Bugner's response filled me with dread. 'Barry, you are paying me a lot of money to be here, for which I am grateful, and I am going to do my best. But if he hurts me, I am going down.'

Hardly fighting talk. I was convinced he was not going to try an inch, that Bruno was going to tap him with a jab, he would fall over, take his money and fly back to Australia. The end of my promotional career in boxing before it had even started. Fortunately, I had underestimated Bugner. He was a good pro who knew how to survive and look aggressive. Bruno did not go for the kill early on, but he won just about every round. In the eighth round, he clipped Bugner with a half-decent punch and it was all over. Everyone had value for money and my career as a boxing promoter was saved.

Two days later, Bugner rang me up. He'd been having trouble with his first wife, Melody, who was suing him for maintenance arrears. Joe thanked me, said he did his best for me and told me I would read a story in the papers the next day saying he was on his way to Scotland for some personal appearance. Actually, he explained, he was just buying time because he would be on a plane back to Australia. In fact, he was already on his way to the airport.

Despite the aggravation, I was feeling pretty pleased with myself. The show had comfortably made seven figures in profit and ITV were delighted with record figures, 18.5m viewers. I decided to get into boxing, big-time. The idea was that I would promote shows but also build up a stable of boxers managed by me and trained by Freddie King. After more than a decade in the fruit-machine business, I reckoned it was time to get out. The breweries, pubs and clubs were getting savvy and wanted new machines regularly, while we liked to just install and service them. By 1988, we had 2,000 machines out on hire but were only making £100,000 a year, in other words one pound per week per machine. There was always the problem of other firms trying to muscle in as well. I sold the business to Bell Fruit Leisure Ltd for £1m, split between Freddie and me, and we kept the arcades.

Six months later, a bloke flew into Romford by helicopter to see me. He came with two minders in dark glasses.

'Who are those two with the shades?' I asked.

'They're just with me.'

I didn't like the fellow one little bit, but he wanted to buy the arcades and I wanted to sell.

'I want two hundred grand,' I said.

'I'll give you one-fifty.'

'Do you like to gamble?' I said.

'Yes, I have racehorses.'

'Well, if you're a proper player, I'll toss you for the fifty grand.'

I flipped the coin. He called. I won. After ten years, I was finally out of the amusement-machine business. Job done.

Now it was all about boxing and I was addicted, promoting a show nearly every week, but I still had to wait until September 1989, nearly two years, before I could claim I had my first champion, Mark Reefer, on one of my greatest nights at the legendary York Hall, Bethnal Green.

Learning the boxing business was a long and very expensive process. I made a lot of mistakes and trusted a lot of people who did not deserve my trust, but I also met some real boxing people, such as Tommy Gilmour from Scotland, Tommy Conroy from Sunderland, Jack Trickett from Manchester and Ron Gray from Birmingham. I would trust all of them, and some others, with a handshake rather than a contract. There were others where I would count my fingers after a handshake.

Looking back, I can see that this period marked the beginning of the breakdown of my relationship with Freddie King. Freddie was a great boxing trainer who developed a succession of world champions. He was also happy to get his share from the sale of the fruit-machine business, which we had sold at exactly the right time, commercially, because Bell Fruit went bust a few years later. But Freddie was not content. He had lost the credibility of being the managing director. As he got older, he suffered from early-onset dementia and could be a pain.

A rift started when Freddie wanted a higher profile, public acclamation, as a boxing trainer. We almost came to blows one time out at a boxing show in Germany. We both had the red mist and went outside to fight. I was fifty and he was ten years older. I was much bigger, too. But there's no doubt who would have been hurt. Me. Fortunately, one of the other trainers, Alex Gower, came out and told us we were mates and that if we tore into each other, we'd both regret it for the rest of our lives.

Our relationship was disintegrating. Freddie was getting more aggressive, and he wasn't the same person he'd been when we first met. I had also moved on.

Freddie was godfather to our two children, but I didn't see much of him during the last ten years of his life. It ended so sadly and no doubt we were both to blame, but I still count him as one of the best friends I ever had. Freddie passed in April 2018 at the age of seventy-nine, and just about every fighter he had ever been involved with attended his funeral, such was the depth of feeling for the man. I was proud to be among them.

It was time for a bigger, better office. With some much-needed funds from the sale of Stelka Stannite, we paid £300,000 for a house on Western Road, Romford. It would be the Matchroom HQ for sixteen years.

With Mascalls as the family home, and an excellent office in a prime position on Romford's main street, perhaps I fancied myself a man of property. But the late 1980s were difficult times. The UK was in recession and we were losing money on every show. We were burdened by overdrafts at the banks and paying 13 per cent interest. Then I recalled the story of a little pub in New York that was wedged between two skyscrapers and went for a fortune because it was such a strategic site. Our building was one of two houses squeezed in between office blocks and I wondered if the same might apply. So when we had a letter from the council saying they were going to auction the house next door it seemed a perfect opportunity to make some serious money. If we owned both houses, we could knock them down one day and either sell the site or build a huge office block ourselves.

The house next door had a lot more land behind it so I thought it must be worth much more than the £300,000 I had paid for ours. As always when doing deals, I get the views of experts but the final decision is mine. With the development potential, and taking into account the additional space, a valuer put an estimate of £2.2m on it. Trying to be clever (invariably a mistake), I instructed Steve Dawson to bid £1.1m at the auction. I reckoned that if we got it for £1.1m we could sell it quickly for £2.2m and pay off £1m from our overdraft. Easy.

We were top bidder with £1.1m and I instructed our property agents to put the house on the market with all speed and please get me £2.2m or more. This needed to come off because I didn't actually have the £1.1m we had bid. I had to go to the bank cap in hand. On the basis of my reputation and the fact that I was a good customer and that I already owed them a couple of million pounds, they advanced me £1.1m at an exorbitant rate of interest.

After six months in a declining property market, we had no offers from anyone. I had it valued again. £600,000. Instead of solving my indebtedness, I had added to it. What made it worse was that Susan took the piss out of me all the time, explaining to anyone who would listen that I was supposed to be smart but had managed to acquire an asset that no one wanted and that was costing 13 per cent interest per annum. It was embarrassing.

This was a mistake that took fifteen years to correct. Meanwhile, we used the house next door as accommodation for sparring partners. The interest was still killing us, but our business began to pick up and eventually we were able to repay the bank loan.

Remember Principle Number One: It is better to be born lucky than good-looking. It kicked in again because the light at the end of the tunnel that we had been in for fifteen years turned out not to be a train coming towards us but the land of milk and honey.

After the Millennium there was a lot of development and activity going on in Romford town centre and I decided we should try to get planning permission on our two properties. I knew the head of planning on the council and put it to him that we should have permission for residential as well as office use. That was unusual in town centres but somehow planning permission was granted and we managed to do a deal with a local builder in which we sold him the extra house and the land behind it and also gave him a contract to build a seven-storey office block on our old house, which we still own to this day. It was one of the best deals I've ever done.

During this difficult time, there was always a ray of sunshine in the form of a fellow called John, whose smile and charm I will never forget. It started with a letter I received soon after we moved into our new office in 1989. The letter came from a kid in Uganda who just signed himself 'John'. He explained that he had won a bronze medal for boxing in the Olympics and he wanted me to be his promoter and manager. Now I get a lot of letters like this and there is no way I would consider taking someone out of Uganda who does not sell tickets. I regret to say the letter was never answered. Three months later, Michelle came up to my office and said, 'There is a young man named John downstairs, from Uganda.'

Immediately I recalled his letter and felt guilty. Suddenly this smiling Ugandan was sitting in my office.

'I can fight, Mr Hearn,' he said. 'I won a bronze medal in the Olympics and I want you to be my promoter and manager.' I explained that our business model in boxing was all about local kids, not overseas fighters.

'I have flown here on a single ticket and I have nowhere else to go,' he said, with a smile I cannot get out of my head, even today.

'Let's see if you can fight,' I said. 'Let's go to the gym right now. Bring your gear.'

I took him down to the gym and grabbed a couple of the boys. Find out how good this kid is, I told them. Apparently, he won a bronze medal in the Olympics. Well, he wasn't bad; he was terrible. He was target practice for anyone who could fight, and he had the shit kicked out of him. Poor John went down more times than a whore's knickers. Every time he got up and was still smiling. I found out later that in the Olympics he had two byes in the early rounds and his first fight was in the semi-finals, which he lost.

At the end of the session, I walked him back to the office. 'Let me be honest,' I said. 'You are not very good.'

The smile remained. 'Well, it has been a long trip and I will get better, and I promise you one day I will be a champion.'

I did not believe him, but I could not escape that smile. Feeling sorry for him, I put him up in the house next door where the sparring partners lived and told him to train for another week to see how he got on. It was the same story every day and every evening. He would turn up on time, smile and get battered. At first, he was great sparring because fighters could practise shots on him without worrying about return fire. But after a while even the toughest fighters did not want to hit him because they liked him so much.

I tried to get John off my hands. I kept telling him he was not going to make a champion; he was only going to get hurt and he should consider an alternative career. When he said he had nothing else in mind I asked him whether he had ever tried gardening. He said that whatever that was he could do it and I employed him for about six months, gardening at Mascalls. He was quite a decent gardener, so enthusiastic he would run up hills with wheelbarrows. John became part of the furniture, everybody liked him and we really did not have the heart to sling him out on the street. Then one day he came to see me and said, 'I have to leave. I think you are right. I am not going to make it here in boxing, so I am going to go to Canada where the standard of boxing may not be so high, and I will have a new start in that country.' John left and I was relieved to be rid of him.

A dozen years or more later, I was queuing at a first-class check-in at Heathrow Airport on my way to New York when I felt a tap on my shoulder. I turned round to see an extremely well-dressed man with the most enormous smile.

'Mr Barry, it is me, it is John,' he said.

He had put on quite a bit of weight, had a big rosy face and looked immaculate.

'John, John, what has happened to you?'

'You were right. I went to Canada, I tried to carry on fighting but even over there I was not good enough, so I got a job in a travel agency and worked very hard. After a few years I started my own travel agency and now I have several agencies all over Canada, the States and even a couple in Europe.'

He had transformed his life, but what had never left him was that smile, that unforgettable smile.

Lots of people want to fight and think they can. Their problems start when they climb those steps and get into the ring. I had a call one day from Michael Flatley, the world-famous and immensely wealthy Irish-American dancer. Never mind dancing; he wanted to be a boxer. He said his father thought nothing of his dancing and would never really respect him unless he could turn professional as a boxer and win a title. Could I help?

Actually, Michael had done some amateur boxing and had fought in the Chicago Golden Gloves tournament in his youth. Michael came along to the Romford gym. It was supposed to be a private session, no publicity, but he brought along his own film crew.

I chose two young journeymen professionals to give Michael a try-out. They had both lost more than they had won but were decent fighters. I gave them each a couple of hundred quid and told them to go easy, not to hit Michael in the face.

Michael climbed into the ring and set to with one of the professionals. I could see that Michael had limited ability, but he was game, holding his own. Then, as I later found out, he got into a clinch with his opponent and told him he should go down the next time he hit him. It would look good for the film they were recording. Now every professional boxer, good or bad, is proud.

The idea of going down to order, of being decked by a dancer, was too much to bear. The kid waded into Michael, trying to take his head off. I jumped in and stopped it before Michael was seriously damaged. That was the end of Michael's excursion into the noble art, but full respect to him for giving it a go.

'Mr Hearn, I am an athlete and I know what I am worth.' The first words spoken to me by Christopher Livingstone Eubank, and how right he was. Credit: Sam Teare/Bskyb/Shutterstock

7

Simply the Best

Complacency, remember, is the great enemy, especially in commercial life. I was soon to learn that perhaps I wasn't quite as clever as I thought I was, that making money was not always just a matter of hard work and enthusiasm, that good times, inevitably, are followed by bad. When we hit the recession of the late 1980s, I was plunged into the toughest period of my business life. Event after event lost money. Companies that might have been sponsors were all losing money and cutting back. I borrowed more and more money just to keep the business afloat. Asset after asset had to go. The forest in Scotland and the Mayfair property were both sold and I still owed the banks millions of pounds.

Finding sponsors and getting TV income was as tough as it could be. But we did find a major sponsor, StormSeal, a double-glazing company run by some Manchester brothers who had ideas, perhaps delusions, of greatness. They had success early doors, acquiring businesses like I had done at Stelka Stannite to give them a broader customer base, with benefits of scale and size. They wanted a marketing plan where their name could be seen on TV, especially by working-class people who were buying double-glazed windows. It was the fashion; everybody wanted to be double-glazed to keep the heat in and the noise out, a double whammy. So StormSeal contacted me, wanting to sponsor some of our events. It was one of the most welcome phone calls I ever took, and sure enough they spent a lot of money with us, sponsoring snooker and boxing.

But all good plans have to be built on solid foundations or the house falls down. The StormSeal guys were so aggressively acquisitive they were probably guilty of stretching their resources beyond their borrowing capacities. Nevertheless, they continued to sponsor, continued to acquire and grew bigger and bigger. In 1990 they agreed to sponsor the UK Snooker Championship, one of the game's blue-ribbon events. The price was £600,000 and they had no problem signing the contract. We looked forward to yet another successful tournament. However, a few weeks before the championship, I had a phone call from StormSeal to say they were just going through another acquisition of a major company and rather than pay the sponsorship money two weeks before the event, which was the basic contract rule, would I mind if they paid two weeks after it? Looking back, I wonder how I could have been so stupid, but the relationship was strong, they had a good track record with us, and I agreed that they could have the deferment. That meant the event was taking place with the sponsor's name all over the venue but no sponsor's money in the bank. Well, one day the piper has to be paid and StormSeal had made one acquisition too many, so the whole house came tumbling down. Two days after the Championship, it was clear we were not going to see our £600,000. That was not just a loss, but a massive problem: we had to shell out the same amount, £600,000, in prize money and we did not have the money to do it. Throughout December, we tried everything we knew to get our money from StormSeal. I even drove up to Manchester and hid in the managing director's office, grabbed hold of him when he arrived and managed to get £50,000 out of him. It wasn't £600,000 but I reckon it was the best fifty grand I ever earned.

The players still needed to be paid. Susan said the players would understand that the sponsor had gone bust and that I should do a deal and pay them less than agreed. I could not do that. I have always believed I must pay my way at any cost and never endanger my reputation. I went to the players, explained the situation and agreed with them and their managers that they would all be paid in instalments over the following six to twelve months. Every player agreed to go along with this, and every player received 100 per cent of his prize money.

Soon after that, I was on holiday in Miami when I had a call from Steve Dawson, my right-hand man. 'Are you sitting down, Barry? StormSeal have gone bust with debts of over a hundred million pounds. We have no chance of getting any money from them.'

With my bank borrowing high, interest rates high and business at a low ebb, you can imagine what this news did to me, but I decided we just had to live with it. There was nothing we could do about it except work and work, so I started to get very positive. Now, at this time I had a deal with Continental Airlines. In exchange for some sponsorship rights, they gave me free airline tickets, always subject to available space. I usually managed to go first class. Having had the news about StormSeal, I queued up with my family and in-laws at the Continental Airlines first-class check-in at Miami only to be told, 'I am awfully sorry, Mr Hearn, but first class is full.'

Oh well, I thought, we'll have to live with business class. 'I am afraid, Mr Hearn, business class is also full.'

There we were at the back in economy with other people's kids running up and down the plane, and my wife turned to me and said, 'I suppose I had better get used to this.'

It was a wonderful line and, by the way, I made sure she never did have to get used to it.

I have no doubt that, during this difficult time, some of our detractors and rivals were thrilled. Flash Barry Hearn and his Matchroom empire get their comeuppance. The *Sunday Times* ran a long piece in April 1993, with the headline: 'Hearn and the fall of Matchroom'. Several of the Matchroom snooker players complained that their tax affairs were not up to date and that boxing had become my consuming interest. Tony Meo, Neal

Foulds, Dennis Taylor and Willie Thorne were all quoted, having a pop at me. Cliff Thorburn and Terry Griffiths were loyal. 'I was eleven years with Barry, and I wouldn't criticise anything he has done for me,' Griffiths was quoted as saying. 'My tax is up to date and my financial affairs are in order.' It was true, though, that we had moved on and snooker was no longer our core business. Steve had won his sixth and final World Championship in 1989, slaughtering John Parrott eighteen frames to three, and Stephen Hendry had taken over, the king of the 1990s.

I was well aware of Hendry's potential when he first emerged in the mid-1980s. His manager, Ian Doyle, called me up and suggested a weeklong series of matches between Steve and Hendry up in Scotland. I sent Steve up for seven matches in seven days with strict instructions: destroy this kid; take away any thoughts he has that one day he might be a great player. Steve duly obliged with seven nights of slaughter upon slaughter, trapping Hendry with safety and clearing up, time after time. But we soon knew that Hendry would become a threat, and a great player, because he took it on the chin and came back stronger and more determined. He looked like an angel or a choirboy in those early years but, like Steve, there was a killer within.

Boxing had become my principal passion but establishing myself as a successful boxing promoter proved a lot more difficult than I thought it would be. I had the enthusiasm but lacked the knowledge, and that could only be gained over time and with a lot of hard work . . . and I was learning too slowly.

In the early days of my boxing promotion career, I was looking to put on big fights and make a name for myself. Bruno versus Bugner did that, all right, but I still needed more domestic success with fighters who had underachieved but could be made into champions, with the right matchmaking.

One such fighter who came to mind was Jim McDonnell, a caretaker from Camden who had been an excellent featherweight, becoming European champion. In 1988 he moved up to super-featherweight and went in against the legendary South African

Brian Mitchell for the WBA world title; he was comfortably defeated in the first loss of his career.

It was at that time that Jim, who boxed for the Astaire-Duff-Barrett-Lawless cartel, was probably questioning why he wasn't earning decent money for the type of fights he was taking on. We met, got on well, and he decided to join our stable of fighters. After a warm-up win, his second fight for Matchroom was against Barry McGuigan at the G-Mex Centre in May 1989, which I promoted in association with my pal, Jack Trickett, from Manchester.

I thought McGuigan was coming to the end of his illustrious career and that Jimmy would be too hungry for him. So it proved: McGuigan was stopped in the fourth round with a cut, giving McDonnell his biggest win. That was excellent matchmaking: the right opponent at the right time.

After that, all Jim wanted to know about was fighting for a world title, but it was tough to get him in with anybody of merit. Everyone knew that Jim was a very capable fighter with great technique. He wasn't near the top of anyone's shopping list. I spoke to Don King, who was promoting the legendary Azumah Nelson, the WBC world super-featherweight champion, and managed to extract Nelson from his clutches for one fight at an exorbitant cost of £300,000, to fight Jim McDonnell at the Royal Albert Hall.

Jim was a terrific kid who trained to a level I hadn't encountered. We had become close and he lived at Mascalls with me and Susan as he was preparing for his fight. Susan cooked him the proper food and we worked out a lot together. With my marathon running, I was fit, but Jim was a different class. He was so fit he had to carry a certificate in case he had an accident because his pulse rate was so low.

But he was up against a quality champion in Azumah Nelson and, despite giving everything, he was stopped in the twelfth round. The damage that Nelson inflicted round after round on Jim and the heart that Jim demonstrated left a deep impression. I felt guilty about not pulling him out towards the end of the fight because he was taking so much punishment, until word came through that one of the judges actually had Jim in front. I couldn't bear the thought of pulling him out if there was any possibility of him winning because I knew how much it meant to him.

He needed a long recuperation after that fight and I think I have to take the blame for his comeback fight when we put him in with Kenny Vice from South Africa in September 1990, nearly a year after his defeat to Azumah Nelson. It was bad matchmaking on our part. Kenny Vice was a puncher and the last thing that Jim McDonnell needed after the beating that Nelson had given him was to be put in with a puncher. It was no great surprise when Vice knocked Jim out in the fourth round.

It was a bad knockout, and it took Jim some time to recover. He had one more fight some years later and then never put on the gloves again. He became a top trainer, working with Danny Williams, James DeGale and others. Jim remains as fit as a butcher's dog. I still look back on our relationship with a smile and I hope he has forgiven me for that terrible bit of matchmaking.

From childhood, I wanted to be the heavyweight champion of the world. My first sporting love was boxing. I'm not sure why, for no one in the family had boxed. Watching Pathé News in the cinema and short clips on TV inspired me to follow some of the great fighters in the 1950s and I can remember as a very young boy listening to fight commentaries from America on a small transistor radio underneath the bedclothes. Rocky Marciano against Archie Moore at the Yankee Stadium in 1955 is my first recollection. I was seven. I loved Marciano's style of fighting. He could take a punch but always moved forward with one intention, which was to knock out the other guy as quickly as possible. Moore, called the Mongoose, was a clever fighter and he survived until the ninth round. That was Marciano's last fight. He retired with the perfect record: forty-nine fights, forty-nine wins.

In common with countless millions, my greatest boxing hero was the Greatest himself, Muhammad Ali. I watched him, when he was Cassius Clay, win the gold medal in the Rome Olympics in 1960 at light-heavyweight. When he turned professional as a heavyweight, he was lighter on his feet than any of the big men, before or since. He had a fluid, dancing style that made him very hard to hit, and he could punch as well. Brash, outspoken, very funny, he was one of the game's great self-publicists. He boasted like no one else, but he always backed it up in the ring. Strangely enough, the first fight I remember listening to after the Olympics was Ali against Archie Moore in 1962. In those days, old fighters like Moore went on for years and years and they never got the financial rewards they deserved.

I never gave up on my dream of becoming world heavyweight champion until I tried boxing properly in my late twenties and reality intruded. That was when I was trained by Freddie King and ended up in hospital with a broken shoulder. Once again, I concluded that I might not be a sporting champion, but I could help to make one, or more than one. And in time the idea of helping to take someone to the heavyweight championship itself was even more enticing.

The first heavyweight I managed, Jess Harding, was not world class. British and European title level was his ceiling, but what a top bloke, still one of my best friends. As a middle-class boxer, he was unusual. His dad was smart, a director of a car-leasing company; they were well off. Jess had played some rugby; he was a tough fellow who fancied the fight game. He joined us in our Romford gym and Freddie King trained him.

Those were the days when I was still working out and sparring as well as getting serious about my running. I had a circuit, running around the woods near Mascalls. It was two-and-a-half miles and I used to go round five times, sometimes ten, when I was training for a marathon. I took Jess round one day and after the first circuit he stopped and threw up on the side of the path. I told him straight up he was nowhere near fit enough for a professional boxer and I took him under my wing. We did regular circuits and I put up a bar in the forest so he could do chin-ups on the way round. I had him chopping wood with an axe as well, just like Jack Dempsey and the old-timers.

Jess became super-fit, built up a decent record and I reckoned he was ready to challenge for the British heavyweight title. The champion was Gary Mason, who was being groomed by his manager, Terry Lawless, as the successor to Frank Bruno. Mason was a big lump and punched like a mule. He had thirty wins from thirty fights at the time, with twenty-nine stoppages. But I knew he wasn't too keen on training and his stamina was suspect. I told Jess, and kept telling him, that he could beat Mason. Just use your southpaw stance, Jess, stay out of the way, keep moving, and after six rounds you'll be able to do what you like with Mason.

We offered Mason £50,000, which was gratefully accepted, and put it on at the Brentwood Centre, broadcast by ITV. Jess had a big following and sold £20,000-worth of tickets. That was his purse as well. I might as well have saved my breath giving Jess all that advice, explaining how he could win. Perhaps he took the advertising slogan on the fight posters too literally: 'No Retreat, No Surrender'. As soon as the first bell rang, he went in for a tear-up. He was pumped up, believed he was invincible and felt obliged to give his fans thrilling value for money. Halfway through the first round, Jess's gumshield flew out as Mason caught him with a right hook. Then he got caught with a heavy shot and might have gone down except that he bounced off the ropes, straight back into trouble. Mason caught Jess again and he went down, hurt, but was saved by the bell. I was in the corner, though not as one of the official cornermen, and I could see that Jess had not fully recovered when he went out for the second round. Mason soon hit him with another big punch and Jess fell backwards, pole-axed, hitting the back of his head on the canvas with a thud. His head bounced and hit the canvas again as his gumshield flew out once more.

Jess lay still, spark out. I thought he was dead. The doctor was quick into the ring and put Jess on his side. He didn't move for what seemed an age but after a few minutes Jess was able to sit up, stand up and leave the ring. He had a few more fights and retired at the very young age of twenty-six, investing his money in a flat, a yard and a pallet business. Jess did not win the British title, but his boxing career was a huge success. He became a successful businessman, and he's a happy man. He's one of my frequent fishing companions and a very close friend.

My next heavyweight, Lennox Lewis, had huge potential; he was clearly destined for greatness. Every four years, fight fans, managers and promoters keep a sharp eye on the Olympics. We all watched with interest as Lennox won the gold medal in the super-heavyweight division in the 1988 Games, stopping Riddick Bowe in the second round. A massive man at 6ft 5in, and well educated in the pugilistic arts, Lennox was bound to turn professional. But where? He had Jamaican roots, was born in West Ham, London, and had grown up in Canada, the country he represented at the Olympics.

Every big-time promoter in America and the UK wanted Lennox's signature on a contract. But it was a small-time and small-in-stature fight man from south London, Frank Maloney, who managed against the odds to secure it. Maloney had been scuffling about with mixed success for some years. He didn't appear to have the front to be a major player, but he was a persistent little sod. He pursued Lennox all over the place until he got him cornered and offered a deal to be financed by a fast-talking entrepreneur named Roger Levitt.

Levitt started a financial services company in the 1980s and attracted a lot of attention with some big-name investors and because he was such a magnificent salesman. With his deep-green eyes, bow tie and persuasive patter, he could have sold sand to the Arabs.

It was all enough to turn Lennox's head and he returned to Britain, managed and promoted by Maloney and Levitt. Four easy fights and wins ensued, but these were small-hall affairs. Maloney was not delivering the glitz that Levitt craved. Levitt called me and asked if I would be interested in being his partner, fifty-fifty, on the promotional side of Lennox's career. Yes, I would. What I didn't know, but maybe should have guessed, was that Levitt's extravagant investments and lifestyle were funded by using other people's money.

I spent time with Lennox and found him a sensible, serious person. He knew his own value and was clearly going to be in charge of his career. That meant no tough fights until absolutely necessary. Lennox had an image problem. His Canadian background affected his commercial appeal in Britain, and he had been subjected to booing more than once. I came up with an ingenious plan, designed to make him popular in the way that Frank Bruno had been. The idea was to avenge the defeats that Bruno had suffered so painfully. Bruno's first defeat was against James 'Bonecrusher' Smith; then he was badly beaten by Tim Witherspoon at Wembley in his first attempt at the world title; finally, he was stopped by Mike Tyson. I suggested to Lennox that he should go on a campaign to avenge the three defeats suffered by the nation's hero. Lennox was not interested. Those were not the kind of fights he wanted early in his career. He passed. In fact, he only fought one of those gentlemen, Tyson, and that was later on, when the time was right for Lennox. I couldn't blame Lennox. He ran his career for his own benefit and, while that might not have suited the fans, if any of us were getting punched in the face, we would surely follow his cautious example.

Lennox had ten further fights with Matchroom involvement, winning the European heavyweight title against Jean-Maurice Chanet at the National Sports Centre, Crystal Palace. Chanet, who had been beaten by Jess Harding two years earlier, was a French fairground operator, not the most stylish fighter, but as game as they come, and he rumbled forward constantly until he was stopped in the sixth round.

Every fight in which we were involved had made a loss because Maloney had done a good job for Lennox in demanding generous purses and Levitt, whose ego was bigger than the Empire State Building, paid him more and more, irrespective of whether the show turned a profit. All very well, but I was beginning to think it was about time we made some money.

Three fights and a year later, we needed a well-known, competitive fighter to sell some tickets and improve the TV ratings. Glenn McCrory, a British fighter who had won the world cruiserweight title and was happy to campaign at heavyweight, was the choice. This was where my serious problems with Levitt began. I valued McCrory's purse at £40,000. He wanted double that, but I wouldn't budge and negotiations stalled. I wanted to finally make a profit on a Lennox fight and I knew that Levitt would give in to anything Lennox wanted. By this time, it was also becoming clear that Levitt's 'investment' business was sinking into oblivion.

Levitt phoned to say he had good news: the McCrory fight had been made. When I said I couldn't agree terms with McCrory, Levitt said that was no longer a problem. He had agreed to pay McCrory £80,000.

The fight turned out to be a mismatch as McCrory was battered into submission in the second round. He got his money; Lennox got his money; and, glory be, the show just about broke even. But I'd had enough. I phoned Levitt the day after the fight and told him it had been a pleasure being involved in Lennox's career – not a profitable pleasure, but a pleasure. And he could have his 50 per cent share of Lennox Lewis back.

Lennox went on to win the world title and became a great fighter. Levitt was convicted of fraud, banned from doing business in Britain, and moved to New York. I was well out of it.

There was an unusual postscript to Frank Maloney's story as well. During a fishing trip to British Columbia in 2014, with no phone signal in the wilderness, I finally got through to the UK and spoke to my son, Eddie. He asked me if I had heard the news about Frank Maloney – that he was now a woman, Kellie Maloney. I was standing on some mountain at the time and nearly fell off. I had known and worked with Frank for thirty years and had no idea at all that he was going through the kind of torment he described before undertaking gender reassignment. I admit I wondered at first if it was one of his publicity stunts. How wrong I was, and now that she is established as Kellie Maloney, I cannot do anything but wish her the very best in her new life.

Matchroom had a good stable of boxers, mostly trained by Freddie King, and we were putting on dozens of shows a year. Unfortunately, most of them lost money and, although I had reserves, my income was lower than expenditure. Not a happy state of affairs. Susan was not aware of just how dire the situation was. I did a good job of hiding it from her and outwardly I remained as positive and energetic as ever. There was only one way to turn it all around, and that was to roll up my sleeves and get stuck in. There wasn't a day, an hour, a minute when I wasn't thinking about how to make money, how to get myself out of a terrible hole.

In retrospect, this hard, frightening time was good for me. I learned more than I ever did when profits came easily, lessons that would be invaluable whenever tough periods returned, not least the challenges presented thirty years later by Covid-19.

My business affairs were at a low ebb in 1989 but that didn't mean life was dull. In fact, one of my many trips of a lifetime began in July of that year, when Steve Davis and I were sitting in the British Airways lounge at Heathrow Airport, waiting for a flight to Nashville, Tennessee, where we were to represent Riley Leisure's pool tables and cues at a billiards and snooker trade show. The plane was delayed and we were pondering whether we should just go home and try again the next day when I had a flash of inspiration. I put it to Steve: Mike Tyson is fighting in Atlantic City this Saturday and Don King is promoting the show. Why don't we fly to New York instead of Nashville, get a limo to take us to Atlantic City (about three hours), take advantage of Don King's legendary hospitality, watch Mike Tyson demolish another

My mother, Barbara Winifred Hearn. Her values and determination
to succeed were my life's foundations.

Family of four: Mum, Dad, Christine and me in the back garden, 135 Chequers Road, on the Debden Estate, 1951.

Fancy dress for the Coronation street-party, 1953. I won first prize.

Autumn term report, 1955: promising, and note the number of kids in the class, 47.

Smiles all round. We may not have been well off financially, but my childhood memories are warm and happy.

Since age 12 I have had a life-long love of cricket. I'm in the front row, second from the left. Credit: Old Buckwellians Association.

Football for Buckhurst Hill Grammar School. I'm front row, third from left, a centre-forward with limited skill, but very aggressive.

Dave Mackay, the Spurs iron man, lifts the FA Cup in 1967. It took me forty years to get his autograph. Credit: Douglas Miller/Stringer.

Young love: Susan at 16, me at 18. The moment I saw her
on the platform at Bank tube station, I was smitten.

Wedding-day, July 1970. Susan's parents on the right;
my mum and Grandad Will on the left.

Snooker royalty in Romford: Joe Davis's widow, June, holds the Joe Davis Memorial Trophy with Fred Davis beside her. Joe Coral and yours truly in attendance.

Matchroom masters: Ray Reardon (far right) and Steve Davis (far left) look superior among the greats, and no wonder: each won six world titles.

Me, Susan and Bill Davis – the team behind the main man.
Credit: David Muscroft.

Welcome to Thailand: our first foray into the Far-East.
We were greeted and treated like rock stars.

The Hearns: nothing in my life has been as important or rewarding as raising our beautiful family.

opponent, drive back through the night to our hotel next to the airport in New York and get an early-morning plane to Nashville? No problem! We changed our tickets and off we went. We touched down in New York and, as arranged, a limo was waiting to drive us to Atlantic City. I told the driver to park up by the Convention Center and we'd find him after the fight. I managed to track down Don King and Steve was super-impressed when Don, in his usual style, greeted me like a long-lost brother. I introduced Steve as the world snooker champion and King, who had probably never heard of snooker, greeted him in the same manner.

'Any chance of a couple of tickets for tonight's fight?' I asked King, hoping for a freebie.

'For you, my brother, anything you need.' He handed us two tickets marked A1 and A2, which I thought looked good enough for anybody, front row.

'That will be two thousand dollars,' King said.

I paid up, managing to keep a smile on my face.

'And here are two tickets for the after-party,' King said. Once again, Steve was super-impressed. The after-party had to be something special.

When we arrived at the arena we saw that seats A1 and A2 were actually twenty-six rows back, with all the seats in front us occupied by VIPs, hotel guests and Don King's friends. Still, we could see the ring, Tyson knocked out Carl Williams within a round, and we reckoned it was $2,000 well spent. Steve was desperate to go to the VIP party to experience something special but as we were leaving we noticed that the floor was littered with VIP tickets handed out by Don King. Undeterred, we walked to the address of the VIP party. It was only a few blocks, but in Atlantic City a short walk can take you into an unfriendly neighbourhood, which was exactly where the VIP party was being held. We walked in, looked around and walked straight out again. This was not a party for a snooker player and his manager.

So, back to the limo. We woke up the driver and he drove us to JFK, where we caught a flight to Nashville. All in all, pretty exhausting, and in Nashville we had to go straight to work on the Riley's trade stand. That lasted all day, but I had a stroke of luck when I managed to wangle two tickets for the Grand Ole Opry, the global centre of country and western music. I sat there in awe as Loretta Lynn and the others performed. Steve, not a country and western fan, slept through most of the show.

For me, it couldn't get better . . . but it did. On getting back to the hotel, I discovered that the greeter, the guy who is paid to chat and make sure you are happy with everything, was none other than Minnesota Fats, one of the great pool players of all time and one of the world's great raconteurs. For many years on American TV, he had a weekly show in which he would play against Willie Mosconi (whom we would honour in Matchroom's Mosconi Cup). Minnesota Fats would break the balls and tell a story about some game he had played in the past, then he would take his shot, miss, and Mosconi would usually clear up because he was a far better player.

Minnesota Fats never kept much of the money he earned, which was why he ended up as a hotel greeter in Nashville. We chatted for hours and he asked me if I would like to go to his room for coffee at the end of the evening. All I could see in his room were pictures of gorgeous women with Minnesota. 'You know, Fats,' I said, 'when you were a young man you must have been something of a stallion.'

His reply will live with me forever: 'Barry, when I was your age, women used to follow me with a mattress tied to their back.'

Despite such wonderful experiences, I was finding it hard to stay positive in the face of recession. My lowest point came at the end of 1989. I had an event, the European Snooker League, starting in January and on Christmas Eve I went to make one final pitch to try to get a sponsor. My last chance was Trusthouse Forte and at four o'clock in the afternoon I was shown in to see the managing director, a guy called Alan Hearn (no relation). I made the worst pitch of my life because, in truth, my heart wasn't in it. I was just about beaten, as close to throwing in the towel as

I had ever been. I was even thinking about going back to work as an accountant.

Once I had made that dreadful pitch, Alan Hearn looked at me and said, 'It's Christmas Eve; you must really want this.'

'Yes, I do,' I said.

'Well, I've got no money,' he said.

That was like getting kicked in the nuts, but I thought I would go out with dignity. 'Mr Hearn,' I said, 'I hope you and your family have a lovely Christmas.'

'. . . but I have got hotel rooms.'

'What do you mean?'

'You want £300,000 from us to sponsor this event. I've got no money, as I said, but I will give you £300,000-worth of hotel rooms instead, if you are interested.'

That may have been the best Christmas present I ever had. By the time I had walked back to the station at Slough, I had used my early-model mobile phone to talk to a few friends in the travel business and had sold the £300,000-worth of free rooms at a 40 per cent discount – £180,000 in cash. That cash didn't just save my business, it saved me. I believed in myself again, believed that I could overcome any obstacle. From that day, that belief has never left me.

For years I'd had a notion, which became a conviction, that sport on TV would be the key to everything I wanted to develop. Back in 1980, on one of my trips to New York for Deryck Healey International, I went down to Bristol, Connecticut, to visit ESPN (Entertainment and Sports Programming Network), who were just starting out. In fact, they were still operating out of temporary huts, broadcasting basketball matches. They had vision and plenty of ambition and soon grew into one of the world's biggest broadcasters. I was looking for a chance to get involved in something similar in the UK and thought I had found it in the late 1980s when a guy called George Black, who was the director of sport for a small satellite and cable outfit called Screensport, in which ESPN had a stake, invited me to his office.

Straight away, Black came clean. 'I am the director of sport, but I know nothing about sport. Can you help me?'

I could. I helped him by producing event after event, snooker, pool and boxing, anything he wanted. Unfortunately, he didn't have much budget and every event lost money.

Promoting events for Screensport gave me invaluable experience and helped make me the promoter I became. Working for George Black was great because he was always straightforward, and you could not meet a nicer man. One day he called me into his office and told me he was dying, that he had cancer of the blood and had to take several tablets every day to balance his platelets. He told me he had six months to live. Of course, I said, don't be silly, fight on, you'll be OK – but he knew he wouldn't and he said he wanted to get all my contracts up to date because I had done so much work for him and he wanted to protect me. His condition deteriorated rapidly and in just a few months he went from taking a few tablets a day to taking dozens. Eventually, six months later, he called me at home to say goodbye and I cannot tell you how difficult it was to have that conversation with someone who believed in me and had supported me through thick and thin. He died the next day and I lost a true friend.

ESPN took a controlling stake in Screensport, but with competition from Eurosport and then Sky, Screensport was in financial trouble and ESPN decided to halt the operation. That left me with a host of events that needed broadcasting. At least I had the long-term contracts George Black had signed before he died, so I thought I was in a strong position – until I met one of ESPN's top men, who had come to the UK to supervise the winding-up of the operation. His name was Rick Spinner.

The first time I met Spinner he was everything you would imagine an aggressive businessman to be. He was the hatchet man who had come to make sure ESPN could walk away with as little pain as possible. And part of that plan was eliminating my TV contracts. When we sat down to negotiate my exit, I was given a clear ultimatum: accept the offer I am going to make, or we will wind up the company and you will get nothing. I was between a rock and a hard place and suddenly the contracts George Black had given me to protect my position didn't look so good.

There was nothing to lose, so I decided to appeal to what seemed in short supply: his sense of fairness.

'Mr Spinner, you have me in a very difficult position. You have made up your mind and I have to say I find your tone and your suggestion offensive. I have worked diligently for this company over a number of years and have lost a huge amount of money because I believed in what we were doing. I liked the people and I always gave my best. I have produced innumerable events to a high standard but unfortunately you and your fellow directors have decided you are not prepared to continue to support this enterprise.'

He nodded and I carried on with my speech.

'This is my suggestion. I want you to spend the weekend sitting in my seat. Think about what I have said and what we have done and what you have offered and ask yourself as a man if that is fair. You may be in a position of strength, but I will find out what type of person you really are. Please think about your offer and on Monday morning phone me with your final offer. I can tell you now, I know that I must accept that offer, whatever it is.'

I stood up, shook his hand and left the building. On the Monday morning, Spinner called. 'Mr Hearn, you have given me the worst weekend of my life, but I have done as you asked and my revised offer is twice my original offer, and I trust you will find that acceptable.' I did and we parted friends. I was paid £600,000, which was a lot more than I would have made if I had been kept on and fulfilled the contract.

Screensport could have been a great business with the right owners, but they couldn't be found. I phoned Greg Dyke to suggest London Weekend Television should invest, but they didn't. Greg later put this decision down as one of his biggest mistakes.

Eventually, Screensport's business merged with Eurosport and we worked together for several years, mainly on boxing, so in a way I got paid twice, which is never bad.

I had another massive piece of luck in 1989, that year of troubles, one that elevated me to the top of the pile in the boxing business.

'Mr Hearn, I am an athlete and I know what I am worth.'

Those were the first words said to me by Christopher Livingstone Eubank after he came swanning into the lounge of the Grosvenor House Hotel in Sheffield, a little-known fighter with a million-dollar swagger, a peacock in full plumage. I knew, therefore, from the very first, that this would be no ordinary, feudal-type relationship between a boxing promoter and his tongue-tied pug.

Eubank made the initial approach through Len Ganley, the renowned snooker referee, suggesting a meeting while I was up at the World Snooker Championship. Eubank was undefeated as a professional after thirteen contests and wanted me to guide his career, so long as the terms were satisfactory. His terms included three unusual demands concerning opponents: no undefeated fighters; no southpaws; no one under twenty-five years old.

The financial deal was that I would pay him £2,000, £2,500 and £3,000 for his next three fights, plus £300 a week living expenses. He said I could stop paying him if he got beaten and I responded by saying I would stop paying him if he got beaten twice. After all, he might get cut or lose by a bad points decision. There was no point wondering whether he would be 'a good ticket-seller' as boxing promoters used to say. In those days, and still today to some extent, boxers were expected to sell tickets to family, friends and acquaintances, but Eubank refused from the start. He said that selling tickets was my job; his job was fighting.

Eubank's first fight for me, at the York Hall, Bethnal Green, against an American journeyman named Randy Smith, was a stinker. The First Division title-deciding match between Liverpool and Arsenal (this was before the Premier League) had been rescheduled for the same night, and we had about ninety people in the famous old arena. They endured a boring contest that Eubank won on points.

Next up, Eubank beat Les Wisniewski, a Canadian, at the Brentwood Centre. Wisniewski was dispatched in great style, and we managed to sell out the place and make money. I reckoned Eubank deserved a treat so I suggested he should have a nice weekend on me. Take your girlfriend to Paris. I'll book you a nice room at the Hotel George V, five-star. All fine, until the bill arrived. It came close to £20,000. When I confronted Eubank, he said I had only booked a room and he liked to stay in the best suite. I had not arranged a car, so he had hired a white Rolls-Royce with a black driver to be at his disposal twenty-four hours a day.

'It's not on,' I snapped. 'You were supposed to have a nice weekend with your girlfriend, and you've ended up spending twenty grand, which it is impossible for me to pay.'

'Bazza, you gave me the rope and I hung you,' Eubank said.

This was such an hilarious statement that my anger turned to laughter and in the end we agreed to go fifty-fifty on it. I had learned a lesson: give this man rope and he *will* hang you; also, he has no idea how to save money but is awfully good at spending it. Still, I could not help admiring this extraordinary character and as time went on I became almost as attached to him – and as committed to our mutual cause and adventure – as I was to Steve Davis. Passion had taken me over once again and I would do anything to protect and promote Eubank. I once said that Ronnie Davies, his loyal trainer, and I would both take a bullet for him on the way to the ring, and that is true.

There were no bullets but every sort of aggravation when it came to the famous first contest between Eubank and Nigel Benn. The battle inside the ring has gone down as one of the most thrilling in the long history of British boxing; it was pretty tasty outside the ring, too.

Eubank had built a record of twenty-four fights, twenty-four wins, but he hadn't taken on any really big names and he had not fought for a world title. Benn had lost once in seventeen fights, to Michael Watson, but had since won the WBO world middleweight title in America and defended it with a sensational knockout victory against another tough guy, Iran Barkley, in Las Vegas. What's more, Benn and Eubank loathed each other and made no secret of it. They both had ancestors in the Caribbean, but they were chalk and cheese. Benn had been in the army and was a no-frills warrior who tried to knock his man out with every punch. Eubank had taken to wearing a monocle, jodhpurs and calf-length boots. He strutted around like some plantation owner, belittling Benn at every opportunity. Benn, the Dark Destroyer, wanted to take Eubank's head off every time he saw him; Eubank was arrogant, goading Benn continually. At the press conferences, they were virtually spitting at each other.

Benn was represented by Bob Arum, the veteran American promoter who had been involved with Muhammad Ali in his glory days, and Ambrose Mendy, a wheeler-dealer on the fringes of the British boxing scene. They had negotiated a good deal for their man and we paid Benn £300,000 to put his WBO world middleweight title on the line. Eubank, the challenger, was to receive £100,000. Tickets sold out almost immediately, but it didn't really matter because in those days, before pay-per-view, there was little chance we would make a profit. But ITV came up with a decent sum and we looked set to break even. In my optimistic world, that was a great result because all I foresaw was a win and stardom for Eubank.

Although I was the promoter, I was so anxious to secure the fight that I had conceded almost every demand made by Arum and Mendy for Benn. They would choose the dressing-rooms, they would enter the ring second and so on. They refused every request we made, and I just had to sit there and bite my tongue. I did this for a reason: although Benn was the defending champion, his team had not insisted on options in the contract should Eubank be victorious. Eubank was not even a mandatory challenger, so we were in no position to refuse options.

Options are standard practice in big-time boxing. If your man loses, you have an option to force a rematch or take a percentage of the purse from the winner's next contest. Arum and Mendy had either forgotten to insist on an options clause or suffered from the greatest sin, complacency. It was a schoolboy error that amuses me to this day, especially since Arum, who graduated with honours from Harvard Law School, is reckoned to be as savvy as they come. Not always the case, I'm afraid.

But conceding all those demands brought problems. I had heard rumours that Benn was having trouble making the weight and his team was desperate to mentally upset Eubank. On the day of the fight, they allocated us a tiny, scruffy dressing-room, including the worst thing they could have done to Eubank, who was always fastidious in his preparation – dirty towels.

All through the day of the weigh-in and the day of the fight I was waiting for a knock on the door to say 'the fight doesn't happen unless we have options on Eubank', but that knock never came. On the night itself, I was desperate to hear the sound of the first bell because then it would be too late for them, and control of our future would be down to what happened in the ring.

The mind games didn't stop there. Eubank always walked into battle to the sound of Tina Turner belting out 'Simply the Best'. This was thanks to my wife, Susan, who turned round to him one day and said, 'Eubank, this is your walk-on music.' He knew better than to disagree, so he said, 'OK, Susan, that is now my walk-on music.' He had his signature tune.

At fight-time, Eubank, myself and Ronnie Davies entered the packed NEC in Birmingham, the sound of Tina Turner echoing around the packed arena, but it just stopped after a few seconds. I went crazy – mind games and underhand tricks don't usually get to me, but the fact that they had done everything to upset us in the lead-up to the fight and had now ruined our walk-on music was a step too far.

The music control centre was high up in the arena. I flew up the stepladder to see a guy with a ribbon of tape in his hands.

'The tape just broke,' he said.

I went crazy, completely losing the plot. Chaos ensued until I got dragged off by a couple of security people, which is just as well because I might have killed him. Freddie King, who was in Eubank's corner along with Ronnie Davies that night, dragged me downstairs.

I was still mad as hell when I returned to Eubank's side.

'Bazza, they gave me a shitty dressing-room, they gave me dirty towels and now they have ruined my walk-on music,' Eubank said. 'Can you please calm down and let me go and spank this geezer.'

I felt about two inches tall. I simply said to Eubank, just go to work, son, and teach him a lesson. He proceeded to enter the ring looking every inch a warrior. Benn came into the ring with a full army squad drumming him in. There was no mistaking the hatred and violent intent on Benn's face. Eubank was calm, self-possessed as ever. The awful suspense felt by most before a big fight seemed to pass him by.

I was sitting in the front row, next to Bob Arum who was next to Ambrose Mendy, and I was still thinking, please, please, don't give me an option agreement to sign now. And when the bell rang at last, I couldn't resist it.

'You do realise you're completely fucked, don't you?' I said to Arum.

'Why?' he said, taken aback.

'Because you have no options and there is no way we are going to lose this fight.'

Arum turned to Mendy. 'Haven't we got options?' he said.

'We don't need them,' Mendy said.

Big mistake. The fight went completely to plan. Benn attacked, slugging, and Eubank countered with a strong defensive guard. When a punch got through, he took it, because he had the best chin I've seen in boxing. It was punch and counterpunch, hurt and be hurt, a thriller that came to an end when the referee, Richard Steele, jumped in and stopped it in round nine. Benn was a mess and Eubank, who had taken considerable punishment himself and was almost sold-out physically, was WBO world middleweight champion. Rarely in my life have I felt such wild excitement.

Now we were up and running properly, with a charismatic world champion whose record was twenty-five wins and no losses. Even my dog could have promoted that.

Early in 1993, I was promoting a world-title fight between John Davison and the WBO featherweight champion, Rubin Palacios from Colombia. It was a co-promotion with my friend Tommy Gilmour, to be held in Washington, Tyne and Wear. When Palacios arrived two days before the bout, he failed an HIV test and was immediately stripped of the title. That left Tommy Gilmore and me scratching our heads with a sold-out arena, a TV date to fulfil and no top-of-the-bill.

I had a brainwave and phoned Steve Robinson, a journeyman fighter from Cardiff whose record was thirteen wins, nine losses and a draw. Steve was not even a full-time professional; he also worked as a storeman in Debenhams, Cardiff.

'Steve, what are you doing Saturday night?' I asked.

'I'm going to sit at home and watch the fight with my girlfriend.'

'Well, how would you like to be in it rather than watching it?'

Steve was flabbergasted and most enthusiastic, but the most important thing was that he could make the weight. He might not have been the best featherweight around, but he was always in top condition, ready to take any fight at the drop of a handkerchief.

Tommy Gilmour was a brilliant operator in such situations, and he persuaded the WBO to sanction a fight between John Davison and Steve Robinson for the vacant title. Without even asking me how much he would be paid, Steve told me he was 100 per cent ready and I told him to get on a train the following day.

It was a classic fight. Davison, a strong favourite with a much better record, was cheered on by the home supporters while Robinson, realising that fate had given him a chance he might never get again, boxed quite brilliantly. Just before the bell went for the final round, I managed to sneak a glance over the supervisor's shoulder at the scorecards, which showed that the fight was locked as a draw, with everything dependent on the final round. I ran over to Robinson's corner and screamed at him to get the job done and just throw punches for what was going to be the most important three minutes of his life.

In the opposite corner, Tommy Gilmour, who managed Davison, was giving his man exactly the same advice. Robinson gave everything in the final round and emerged a split-decision winner of the contest.

Steve Robinson, who became known as the Cinderella Man, had become world featherweight champion.

I would like to tell you the story had a really happy ending and that Steve and I continued with his career until he eventually retired with a pile of money, but that wasn't the case. Just before that famous fight, Steve and his management signed a promotional agreement with Tommy and me, but somehow or other he then signed a deal to fight with Frank Warren on his shows. It was hurtful but far from unusual in the boxing business. We were protected by the contract Steve had signed and which was eventually upheld in the High Court. Steve had to pay us damages of over £100,000. I just hope he didn't have to pay it himself, and that the promoter who lured him from us gave him some kind of indemnification and covered his losses. All I know is that we gave Steve his big chance and it was a shame that we didn't stay together for the rest of his career. Steve eventually lost his world title to Frank's latest prodigy, Naseem Hamed, after which Steve, surprise, surprise, came back to us.

With Eubank as our number-one attraction, the Matchroom Boxing stable was firmly established. My involvement in snooker had diminished. In fact, I was just about back where I started with snooker: looking after Steve Davis. But when the most talented of them all, Ronnie O'Sullivan, emerged from east London, I wasn't going to let that opportunity pass me by.

We first heard of Ronnie when he was about twelve. There were stories coming out of Gants Hill Snooker Club, not one of ours, about this amazing kid. You get those stories a lot, but with Ronnie they kept coming. He paid the odd visit to our Romford club, playing a few frames with Steve and Vic Harris.

His dad, Ronnie Senior, was always with him. They were as close as I am with my boy Eddie. Ronnie made his first maximum break in competition when he was fifteen. By that time, he was already more than a match for just about any professional, except Steve and Stephen Hendry.

Ronnie was still an amateur when I became his manager and we had great plans for him, but when his father was locked up for murder in 1992, I could see those plans, and Ronnie Junior's world, falling apart.

To keep him occupied and on the straight and narrow, I was sure he should turn professional straight away, but he was only sixteen, a few months too young to turn professional according to the rules of the World Professional Billiards and Snooker Association. Now, I was not in the least popular with the WPBSA. Matchroom had 'gone East', to the land of milk and honey, and I withdrew Matchroom players from various WPBSA events, for which we were fined. I was on and off the WPBSA board like a light switch. And it was true that, when I was on, I just looked after the interests of my own players.

So, when I went to a WPBSA meeting in Coventry to argue the case for Ronnie to be granted professional status, I wasn't expecting any favours. I put the case for Ronnie and could tell it was not going down too well. Then I took extreme action, action of which I am not proud, though it was effective.

'We all know what's going on here,' I said, standing up. 'It's not about Ronnie O'Sullivan. It's about you not liking me, which I can understand. Well, I've got some advice for you . . .'

I undid my belt and trousers and let them drop to the floor. Then I took off my underpants, turned round, leaned over a chair and stuck my arse towards the board members of the WPBSA.

'If you've really got to fuck someone, fuck me, don't fuck the kid,' I said.

'P-p-p-pull up your trousers,' Geoff Foulds, one of the board members, stuttered. Five minutes later, they let Ronnie in. They didn't want to see my hairy arse again.

Ronnie found solace in snooker, as I hoped he would. He wanted his dad to be proud of him, to be able to take trophies to the prison to show him. I went to see Ronnie Senior twice, in Gartree high-security prison. He was serving a life sentence for murder. He had pleaded not guilty and got hammered. He didn't get out for eighteen years.

Ronnie Senior had a reputation inside as a hard man and seemed to have everything organised. He was working out in the gym, playing football, and was in great shape. He looked ten years younger than when he went in. While we were talking, this little fellow came over and asked Ronnie if he wanted a cup of tea, a sandwich or a cake. Ronnie told him to fuck off. He told me the fellow, who he called Deirdre, had been getting grief and Ronnie had looked after him, and now Deirdre sorted everything out for him, cleaning, ironing and so on.

'What's he doing in here? He's harmless,' I said.

'He got home early from work one day and found his missus in bed with another fellow. They told him to get lost, they were busy, so he went downstairs and came back up with two jugs. What's that, they said. He poured the contents of the jugs over the pair of them, struck a match, and bosh, he's done them both with petrol.'

Not only did Ronnie Senior have Deirdre waiting on him hand and foot, but he could inform the cook what he wanted to eat and got it. I believe he also had control of the phone cards, so he was top dog.

With Ronnie Senior inside, Ronnie's mother took over the family business, porn shops and some property, but she got into trouble with the Inland Revenue over tax matters. Ronnie phoned me up and asked a favour. Would I stand bail for his mum? At the Old Bailey.

I do well in court cases; I'm credible in a suit and tie.

'Are you good for a million pounds?' the judge asked.

'Well, I have a three-million-pound house, I am a fellow of the Institute of Chartered Accountants and I have a business which turns over twenty million pounds a year.'

Bail was granted. My relationship with Ronnie may have deteriorated over the years, as he increasingly bucked authority in his sport, which I later represented, but he has always been grateful to me for helping his mother. Ronnie would go on to dominate the game, and I rate him the greatest player of all time.

Like all geniuses, Ronnie is not a normal person. If he was, I don't believe his snooker would be so sublime, nor would his career have lasted so long. He can be a pain, but that seems to go with such out-of-this-world talent. We've had many public disagreements but I know deep down he likes and respects me as much as I like and respect him.

Don King was difficult to do business with because he always wanted all the money, but as a boxing promoter and self-promoter he was unsurpassed.

8

No Sleep for Don King

The mutual animosity between Chris Eubank and Nigel Benn was far from settled and the first fight had been so dramatic that the clamour for a rematch grew until, three years later, we fixed it for 9 October 1993 at the Old Trafford stadium in Manchester.

The hype and build-up were just as crazy as the first time. Both fighters had gone up in weight and had won world titles in the super-middleweight division. Benn had gone back to America and had been very successful. He returned to Britain swearing vengeance, his aggression and hatred of Eubank as violent as before.

Once the contracts were signed, I kept looking at the numbers for the promotion and became more and more concerned. Benn, who held the more prestigious WBC world title, was to receive £1m and Eubank £900,000. But I didn't have a TV deal, tickets had not gone on sale and the overseas revenue was not promising. It was looking risky.

Out of the blue, I had a phone call. 'Hi, Barry, Don King here, I'm going to be your partner on the Benn–Eubank fight.'

I asked him what he had in mind.

'I will pay you two million dollars for your overseas TV in exchange for 50 per cent of the show. But I want both fighters under contract after this fight is over, the winner and the loser. I'll give them the best deals they've ever had.'

Well, normally I don't like partners in any business because I don't trust anyone, and I certainly didn't trust the electric-haired former felon and number-one hustler, Don King, but this was too good a deal to turn down. It guaranteed me a profit when I was worried I might lose a bundle.

I didn't in fact have a written contract with either Benn or Eubank and I thought I should let them know about King's offer. I sat down with each of them and spelled it out. They were excited about the thought of being promoted by King, so they both agreed to go along with it. King had promised both of them huge purses to fight the biggest names in the USA. I knew I couldn't compete with those numbers, even if they weren't real, especially against one of the best salesmen who ever lived. So, it was total transparency: tell the fighters the truth and let them decide.

A few weeks after King and I had done our deal, he phoned me to say that his friend Frank Warren was having a tough time financially and he would like to involve him in the show. He suggested giving Frank 10 per cent, 5 per cent from each of us, as a sign of goodwill, and for some daft reason I agreed to go along with it as a favour to King. I had no problem with Warren. He was a decent boxing promoter, and he knew the sport, but he couldn't add much to this show. He just got a nice handout.

A word here about Warren, a major player in the boxing world in the 1980s and beyond. He started out as a solicitor's clerk and moved into boxing promotion when his second cousin, Lenny McLean, was looking for a promoter to arrange a fight on his behalf. Warren became an unlicensed promoter.

In those days, boxing was effectively controlled by the Cartel – Jarvis Astaire, Mickey Duff, Terry Lawless and Mike Barrett. With their connections at the British Boxing Board of Control and an exclusive contract with the BBC, they had a monopoly of big-time professional boxing in Britain. The policies of the British Boxing Board of Control gave them a huge advantage in sole access to the main venues and fight dates. Warren challenged and eventually overturned those policies and the door to fair competition was opened. Everyone involved in the sport should doff their cap to Warren for those early efforts, and that includes me.

Warren and I are two very different characters and over the years we have had our ups and downs. We have been partners on occasion, but primarily fierce competitors. Over the years he 'stole' a lot of fighters from me, and I 'stole' a lot of fighters from him, so we ended up about even.

Be it administrations, liquidations or creditors' voluntary arrangements, Warren has encountered them all in his very chequered financial career, but you have to congratulate him as one of the world's great survivors. He even survived an assassin's bullet in Barking, east London, in November 1989.

The day after the shooting, the police came to see me at my offices in Romford to ask where I was the night before. As luck would have it, I had the perfect alibi: I was watching snooker at Preston Guildhall, seeing my friend Steve Davis play in the UK Championship, live on the BBC.

Our paths rarely crossed once Matchroom became a global operation and boxing was only a marginal part of our business. That changed when my son Eddie took over the boxing and expanded it hugely. But the strange thing is that, at the time of writing, Eddie has never met Warren.

For my part, I must say that while we have had our disagreements and many of them have been public, Warren was always great company socially, a pleasure to be with. I can only wish the very best going forward for him and his family and hope that all turns out well for him. It's a tough business and it takes its toll.

Back to that second Eubank–Benn fight. You could tell how massive a promotion it had become. The press conference was held at the Waldorf Hotel. As well as King and Warren, Bob Arum was there to protect his interests in Benn. Arum and King were sworn enemies and rivals going right back to the Muhammad Ali days. Warren and I were hardly best buddies either. But money can be a great healer of rifts. Mind you, it was Matchroom that did the work. Warren likes to make out he was deeply involved, especially with the broadcasting deal with ITV, but I closed that deal, which was worth £1m. That sum went straight onto the bottom line as profit. We all made money.

Financially, it was the biggest promotion staged in Britain up to that point. We sold 45,000 tickets and the TV ratings were off the scale – somewhere around 18m viewers live on ITV. We made a pile of money.

The fight itself, however, was a big disappointment and nowhere near the intensity of the first contest. It was close and difficult to score but frankly, as I said in my interview in the ring immediately afterwards, I could not separate them. I had to give it as a draw. Most ringside observers had Benn winning and he was convinced he had done enough. But since one judge gave it to Benn, one to Eubank and the third made it a draw, the result was indeed a draw. Some people criticised the fact that the last judge whose score was announced was Harry Gibbs, who happened to live in Brentwood, just a few miles from my office. He gave the fight to Eubank by 115 points to 113 – but I can assure you there were no favours done. Gibbs just scored it as he saw it.

When the result was announced, Eubank came over to me in the ring. 'A draw, a draw, what does that mean?' he said.

'It means we can do it all over again!' I said.

But we didn't and it remains one of my major disappointments in boxing that we never got to see a third instalment of Eubank versus Benn. With pay-per-view, which soon came in, it would have been huge and made many millions for both boxers.

We were having a small drinks party after the fight when it suddenly occurred to me that Don King had not paid me my $2m. I walked after him all night like a little lamb, following him around the building trying to get his cheque, but with no success.

About four in the morning, my wife Susan had already gone to bed and it was just me and a few people with King.

'Don, can I please have my two million?' I said.

'Don't worry, Barry, about your two million. I'll give it to you in the morning.'

I was getting seriously pissed off and tired and the words that came out of my mouth were: 'Don, for you there is no sleep tonight until I get paid.'

King gave me an old-fashioned look, because I think it's the kind of line, the kind of thinly veiled threat, he might have used himself a few times. He instructed his lawyer to write out the cheque, which I took to bed with me. I slept with it under my pillow, and I slept well.

The real barney came in the morning when I came down to breakfast in the hotel to see Don King holding court with a cluster of newspaper and media people. I could hear King exclaiming in his loud voice that he was now the dominant factor in British boxing, that he had Benn and Eubank and he was going to move a sizable part of his operation to the UK and take over.

He looked at me and said in a rather patronising way: 'And here is Barry Hearn, the greatest promoter in the world and, don't worry, Barry, there is a part of this show for you.'

That pissed me off again. He was making out he was the guv'nor, and I don't work for anybody except myself and my clients.

'What are you talking about?' I said.

'Well, you know our deal, Barry. I've got Benn and Eubank so I'm going to be taking over the place.'

'I don't know what you are talking about, Don, but I do know that I wrote the contract. Win or lose, you had Benn and Eubank, that is for sure, that is in the contract I wrote and the contract you signed, but the fight was a draw, so I suggest you fuck off back to America!'

King, a big man who can turn very aggressive, went ballistic. What he wasn't going to do to me hardly bears thinking about, but I felt reasonably safe because I was in England, and he was out of his normal environment. So we had a slanging match but, when he read the contract, he knew I was correct. He had no rights over either fighter.

Draws are not common in boxing, but they happen more often than many people realise. And funnily enough, when I wrote the contract originally, I remembered that King had once had a similar problem with a world-title fight between Jeff Fenech and Azumah Nelson in Australia. That fight ended in a draw and he was left with no contractual rights, so I thought, what the hell, let's leave the draw out of the contract and see if he notices. He didn't and he paid the price. Eubank stayed with me out of loyalty, but Benn did in fact sign a contract with King, probably because he was so annoyed that the result had been a draw when he believed he had won. King was never one for crossing the t's and dotting the i's. I am. That was part of my accountancy training and has always been a strength.

Let me, however, give an example of how clever and persuasive King could be. I was sitting in his outside office once, talking boxing with Al Braverman, an old-school pug who became a cornerman, trainer, manager and aide to King. The door opened and a huge black man asked, in a very menacing voice, where King was. Underneath his jacket, this guy had a very obvious shoulder holster and gun, so we just pointed down the corridor to King's office. The fellow went in that direction, clearly with bad intentions. Al and I looked at each other, wondering what might happen next. But we heard no shots, no noise at all, and eventually the door opened and Don King came out with the black guy, all smiles and pats on the back. 'You are going to be the next great heavyweight champ!' King told the guy. I have no idea who that fighter was, but I know he never won the heavyweight title.

Eccentric, controversial, avaricious beyond measure, King was also a brilliant communicator, a man from the streets who learned Shakespeare in prison and could quote the Bard at will. As many boxers testified, and as I discovered myself, he was difficult to make a deal with because he always wanted all the money. But his ego meant that he was always great to put in front of the press and the cameras because he could sell tickets to anybody.

These days, in his nineties, he still has occasional dealings in boxing, but does not have the power he had in the days when he controlled the heavyweight division. That is as it should be, but I still miss his press conferences.

As far as the second Benn–Eubank fight was concerned, King had messed up, just as Bob Arum had messed up over the options for the first Benn–Eubank fight. I may have been quite new to big-time boxing, but I had got one over on each of the top two promoters in America and the world.

But let's be honest. It wasn't so much that I had been clever; Arum and King had fallen victim to their own complacency; they had failed to observe my Principle Number Five, to think poor however rich you might become. And of course, since they were both very rich and had been successful for decades, they were especially vulnerable to complacency.

Don never forgave me for his contractual slip. His alliance with Frank Warren became stronger and for two or three years they colluded to try to put me out of business. It made for an interesting period; they failed. Before long, King and Warren fell out over Naseem Hamed's contract. King sued and won a judgment worth $12m in his favour.

The other problem that can crop up when you have success is that vermin comes out of the woodwork, and that's what happened when Eubank fought Dan Sherry in Brighton, Eubank's home town, in 1991, after the first Benn fight. Howard Kruger was a young impresario and sports manager who had some experience in snooker, managing Alex Higgins and Tony Knowles among others. When we announced the fight, Kruger, who also lived in Brighton, asked me if I needed any help locally. I said it would be handy if he sold some tickets and I would give him a commission. He jumped at the chance.

Eubank employed some strange antics against Sherry. At one point, with his back to Sherry, he executed a backward headbutt. It caught Sherry, who went down dramatically. For a moment, I thought we might get disqualified, but the referee was having none of Sherry's antics and Eubank went on to win by stoppage.

Within a week, I had a letter from Kruger's solicitors asking me when I would be accounting for Kruger's 50 per cent share of the profits from the show. I could scarcely believe my eyes, as I had known Kruger in the snooker world for years and he seemed a reasonably decent guy. It appeared he was struggling and had decided to pretend that our telephone conversation was the basis of a partnership agreement. No paperwork, of course; purely his word against mine.

My lawyers told him to get lost. His lawyers insisted their client had a case, but he would settle for £20,000 compensation. This was a red rag to a bull. There was no way I was going to give this man £20,000, and he was told so. Next, Kruger issued a writ claiming aggravated damages for the money he claimed to be owed. Unbelievably, this spurious action ended up in the High Court in London. After three days of evidence, the judge stopped the case to say to Mr Kruger that he had no case whatsoever and that rather than waste the court's time any further he was throwing the case out and ordering all costs to be paid by Howard Kruger personally.

Kruger argued that in bringing the action he was representing his company, not himself. The court accepted that argument and awarded costs against his company, which of course folded immediately, leaving me stuck with all my legal bills. The costs came to £80,000, four times the £20,000 he wanted to go away, but there is no way you can give in to such bullies, so I was relatively happy to pay the bill. After the verdict, Kruger had the nerve to stretch out his hand to shake mine and said, 'No hard feelings.' Needless to say, he didn't get his handshake.

After beating Sherry, Eubank outclassed Gary Stretch, a British fighter with a fashionable following, and then took on Michael

Watson, one of the greatest middleweights Britain has produced. It was Watson who had spoiled Benn's unbeaten record, so it seemed natural that he and Eubank should meet to determine domestic supremacy at middleweight.

Watson was a marvellous guy but quiet and reserved. Unlike Eubank, he didn't go in for the bullshit banter that sells tickets. Never mind. We sold out the Earls Court Exhibition Hall with 10,000 seats. It was a classic fight and many experts thought Watson won it. I didn't: I thought Eubank won a very close decision and it is always a principle that a challenger has to take the title off a champion, not just be involved in a close fight.

There was a good deal of controversy in the press and a huge clamour for a rematch. It took place at White Hart Lane stadium three months after their first contest and it ended up being by far the worst night I have had in boxing.

We only sold 11,000 tickets when we needed 20,000 to break even, but that was beside the point in view of the tragedy that unfolded. Watson dominated the entire fight and actually handed Eubank a boxing lesson. Miles ahead on points, Watson dropped Eubank for the first time in his career in the tenth round. Eubank sank to his knees after taking a barrage of punches. But as a true warrior, he climbed to his feet. Showing unbelievable bravery after the battering he had taken, Eubank beckoned Watson forward as if to say, 'Come on and finish the job.'

As Watson went forward to do just that, Eubank hit him with an uppercut that put Watson on the floor himself. It did not seem possible that anyone could summon such a punch after being out-boxed for ten rounds, but Eubank had managed it. It was Watson who went back to his corner looking as if he couldn't continue.

I left my seat and rushed into Eubank's corner, screaming at him to just go out and throw punches because they would have to stop the fight. Watson was in no position to defend himself. Then I looked into Eubank's eyes and saw a boxer who was also absolutely exhausted. I shut up and went back to my seat.

Eubank went out for the next round and threw a flurry of punches, none of which landed conclusively, and the referee stepped in to stop the contest. Watson slumped to the floor in distress and was escorted from the ring to go straight to hospital. Unfortunately, the ambulance service took him to a hospital that wasn't a neurological centre, which meant that by the time he did get to a neurological hospital the so-called 'golden hour' had passed and Watson was engaged in a fight for his life.

I went to see Watson in hospital the following day and what I saw still distresses me to this day. He'd had two brain operations already and the surgeon, Peter Hamlyn, told me it was fifty-fifty whether he would survive; and should he survive, he would live the rest of his life completely incapacitated.

Thankfully, that prognosis proved pessimistic and, although Watson has had to live with disabilities, his condition over time has greatly improved. I think it was his belief in God and the fact that he accepted whatever challenges God gave him that has enabled him to live as normal a life as possible.

Watson is a remarkable man. To complete the London Marathon in 2003, walking two hours each morning and afternoon over six days after being told he would never walk again, is just a miracle, and the contribution he has continued to make in his local community and within the boxing world defies belief. He is the bravest man I have met and the uncomplaining way in which he carries himself is commendable. I am proud to call him a friend.

Eubank went straight to hospital as well after that fight but not before he did everything to avoid going. I remember he went to the toilet in his dressing-room and was in such a terrible state that he couldn't get off the seat. He refused to use a wheelchair to take him to the ambulance. He wanted to walk but found he was incapable of standing up. Fortunately, he suffered no lasting physical effects from the battering he took, but his mental attitude to boxing changed.

That extraordinary fight, which is very rarely shown on TV because of its dreadful conclusion, shows how fickle boxing and life can be. Everything changed that night for both men. Watson was cruelly injured, and Eubank was never again the same fighter. I doubt that he felt guilty, because everyone accepts there are risks when you enter a boxing ring. I think it more likely that it made him a more cautious fighter, because he was acutely aware that such an injury could happen to him. In my view, he was never remotely as good a fighter after that contest. That, for me, explains why the second fight with Benn, compared with the first, was such a tame affair, and explains why Eubank did not win and win well.

That didn't mean, of course, that life would be uneventful with Eubank involved. After he had moved up to super-middleweight, he still struggled to make the weight and it was no great surprise two days before his fight with Juan Carlos Giménez in Manchester when a very weak-sounding Eubank phoned me to ask if I would come and see him. I drove straight down to Brighton, unprepared for one of the strangest incidents in my career.

As I walked into Eubank's study, he asked me to lock the door behind me, which I did. He then proceeded to drop his trousers and drop his underpants, and I have to say I have never seen someone's manhood quite that size.

'Good God!' I said.

'It's not normally this big, you know,' he said, which reassured me.

Eubank explained that normally two weeks before a fight he didn't have any sex and he thought he would take the opportunity, as he had been experiencing some problems, to get circumcised. Circumcision for a man later in life is extremely painful. Nevertheless, he went through with it and was showing me the effects it had had on his nether regions. I couldn't believe he had done this just a few days before a major fight, but he seemed to think it made sense.

'I know what you're thinking, Bazza,' he said. 'You're worried about the drugs that may be in my system. But rest assured, I wouldn't let them give me anything.'

He had only had a local anaesthetic. He told me he had taken his trainer, Ronnie Davies, with him, under instructions that no matter how much he cried out he was not to be given any form of drugs in case he failed a test before the fight.

Before the fight itself, I spent most of the evening stuffing paper tissues down the front of his protective cup to give him some form of cushioning, but every time Giménez punches strayed below the border I winced. After Eubank had won easily, I asked him what on earth he was thinking of, having this operation done so soon before a fight, and, by the way, what was it like to go twelve rounds with this tough fellow from Paraguay?

Eubank's response was classic: 'Bazza, for what you are paying me, I would go in there and fight with one arm.'

He might have lost his edge as a boxer after the Watson fight, but Eubank remained as brave and cool under fire as anyone in the world. A good example came when he defended his WBO world super-middleweight title in Berlin against Graciano Rocchigiani. It was the most racist, hostile atmosphere I had encountered. On the walk to the ring, accompanied by Ronnie Davies and me, Eubank seemed to be enjoying himself. I was watching out for trouble and saw someone in the tiered seats trying to grab Eubank. I swivelled round and managed to get a little bit of head on his head. The Romford kiss, if you like. Quite a smacker, actually. Eubank turned round with a smile on his face and just said, 'Nice one, Bazza.'

When we arrived at ringside, Eubank at first refused to get into the ring. Instead, he walked around the perimeter, snarling at the German fans, goading them. I thought a riot could break out any second and the fight would be cancelled, so I told Eubank to get in the ring.

'Bazza, I'm just eating up the hate,' he said. He proceeded to out-box Rocchigiani for twelve rounds, leaving the German fans silent and dumbfounded.

Another paradox in boxing, and probably many other professions, is that once you've made your reputation, your best work may be behind you, but you can earn a lot more money. So it proved for Eubank, thanks chiefly to the advent of Sky TV, which was known as BSkyB at the time.

Early in 1994, Sky were making a big push for subscribers and had decided to feature two sporting acts: Torvill and Dean, the skaters, and Eubank. At that time, the former editor of the *Sun*, Kelvin MacKenzie, was Sky's head of sport. He asked for a meeting in his office at Isleworth and I insisted on taking Eubank with me because I knew it was going to be something he had to be involved in from the beginning.

MacKenzie looked us straight in the eyes. 'I want you on Sky,' he said, 'and I am prepared to pay you five million pounds to fight eight times in one year.'

Bear in mind that Eubank's purses had mostly ranged between £200,000 and £300,000. I was gobsmacked. It wasn't just a massive offer, but boxing eight times a year meant there would be no need to go into training camp because Eubank would virtually be in full-time training. It would be all income and little expenditure.

I kicked Eubank under the table to keep him quiet, because I wanted to close this deal pronto and take the £5m, but Eubank, as ever, insisted on saying his piece.

'That is a very upsetting offer,' he told MacKenzie.

MacKenzie found it more than amusing that someone was calling an offer of £5m upsetting. But it worked.

'You're right,' MacKenzie said. 'But I won't give you more than six million.'

From then on, we knew we had Mr MacKenzie where we wanted him and there wasn't a problem in getting the deal done. He said yes to virtually everything. We wanted all the sponsorship money, the overseas rights, copyright ownership etc. MacKenzie just repeated the same word over and over again: yes, yes, yes.

I will always remember MacKenzie's final words after we closed the deal. 'Now Barry, these fights will be proper fights, won't they?'

'Of course, Kelvin.'

'But just don't get him beat.'

The great Sky adventure was under way. We had a massive contract and Eubank was earning several times more than he had made in previous fights. Now we had to work out how Eubank and I were going to split the proceeds.

When we sat down in his house in Brighton, Eubank wanted to know how much he was going to earn, as simple as that. I told him his basic would be £800,000 a fight plus the promotion's profit, all subject to a deduction for me. I asked him what percentage he was happy for me to have and he said he would be delighted still to give me 25 per cent. I would have taken half that and told him so, but he insisted on 25 per cent because he felt we were in this together. That was the mark of the man.

I was delighted. When he asked me what he would earn in total, I told him he would probably be looking at ten million, gross. I pointed out that we would need to have decent opponents and he would need to remain undefeated. From his point of view, the old rules concerning opponents that he had laid down the first time we met remained: no one under twenty-five, no southpaws and no one undefeated.

The first four fights under our eight-fight deal with Sky were straightforward enough and Eubank was in no danger of defeat. But we were coming under pressure to come up with better contests. Frankly, we were struggling to find decent opponents. I had the brilliant idea, which turned out to be not so brilliant, that Steve Collins, the reigning world middleweight champion who was also under our promotional banner, should move up to super-middleweight to fight Eubank. We were struggling to find a decent opponent for Collins at middleweight anyway and I explained to him that there was no downside for him. Eubank wasn't a concussive puncher who came forward and beat up people; he was more of a technical artist. I thought Collins would be too weak at super-middleweight to win the fight but he could at least make it competitive.

Eubank was happy to take the fight and Collins was very happy to get a great payday when he wasn't putting his world title at risk. Sky were happy to have a big fight to broadcast.

The build-up was good, the atmosphere was great, but the fight, at the Green Glens Arena in Millstreet, Ireland, was really strange. At the press conference on the day of the weigh-in, Collins announced that he had been hypnotised into believing he would not suffer pain when hit or hurt. I thought this was laughable because you can't hypnotise a chin, but it certainly got to Eubank. It did his head in. He thought it was some kind of black magic.

After the weigh-in, at which Collins looked extremely confident, I went back to Eubank's room, where he told me he was going home. I was sitting there with a sold-out arena and Sky saying thank you for a great fight in prospect, and my main man wanted to go home. Ronnie Davies and I sat up with him until one in the morning, trying to put his mind at rest, and eventually he agreed to take the fight. It may be a decision he regretted.

The fight illustrated more than ever the effect of the Watson fight on Eubank. He didn't really engage, and Collins, cheered on by the Irish crowd, was clearly ahead in the contest. Even when Eubank came forward and put Collins on the floor, he stood still and posed when Collins got up, which gave him a chance to recover. Eubank didn't want to commit himself to finish the job, perhaps for fear of walking on to a punch like the one he'd delivered to Watson. Collins grew stronger and it came as no surprise when he was awarded the decision on points.

Eubank had suffered his first defeat, which was to have major repercussions for our relationship. It was a big blow to his ego; he was no longer world champion and his money from the Sky contract was reduced. For Collins, now super-middleweight and middleweight champion, the world was his oyster. I had taken Collins on a couple of years earlier, when he had nowhere to go, no friends in the business and no money. We had built him up to become a world champion and for the efforts I made on his behalf he should have had a framed picture of me above his mantelpiece.

As I went to climb into the ring to congratulate Collins and commiserate with Eubank, Barney Eastwood, the Irish bookmaker and boxing promoter who had previously managed Collins, told me my problems were just beginning. How right he was. Collins told me straight after the fight that he wouldn't pay me the percentage we had contractually agreed. This led to a protracted legal dispute which, according to the contract, had to be settled under Irish law. I spent twenty-four days in the High Court in Dublin and lost. Halfway through the case, Collins came over to me and suggested we settle. I told him it wasn't the money I wanted. In his verdict, the judge decided that since I had both fighters in the fight, I had a conflict of interest and therefore the contract was void.

I had lost about £600,000 and Susan, who had lost her husband for twenty-four days while the case was going on, was philosophical and typically blunt. 'Surely you didn't expect to win in Ireland against an Irish boxer?' she said. Well, I did expect to win, and it remains one of the worst days of my promotional career.

After two more fights, both knockout wins, Eubank asked me to come down to Brighton to have a meeting with him. Eubank was dead straight with me. 'We have had a great run,' he said. 'I appreciate everything you have done but it is time for me to move on. I am no longer world champion and I'm afraid to say that this is the end of our working relationship.' He held out his hand and I shook it. Two proper men came to a proper understanding and walked away, which is probably why we are still friends today.

When he became a free agent, Eubank's record stood at forty-three victories, one loss and two draws. A rematch with Collins was lost on a split decision before he decided to promote himself around the world, which was a financial disaster. That forced him back into taking the type of fights I would have shied away from. His last three fights were a loss to Joe Calzaghe, the brilliant super-middleweight world champion (Eubank broke his own rule: that he would never face an undefeated fighter), and then at cruiserweight he lost twice to Carl Thompson, who inflicted such damage on him that I was close to tears watching on TV.

Eubank will always hold a high place in the history of British boxing. He was one of the most significant characters in my life, helping me to save and rebuild my business financially and to deliver an unforgettable level of excitement. He could also be a pain in the neck and worse, which brings me to the strange story of two prima donnas, Eubank and Barbra Streisand.

I was staying at the Hotel Plaza Athénée in New York and happened to be travelling in the lift from the twelfth floor, when it opened around the tenth floor and Barbra Streisand stepped in, with a dog she was trying to get into a carrier bag. She asked me if I could help. I was starstruck but managed to stutter the dumbest words imaginable: 'I would be honoured.'

Recovering somewhat as we descended, alone together in the lift, I told her that the last time I had been so close to her, it had cost me twenty thousand dollars. She asked how that could be and I said that my wife and I were huge fans of hers and I had bought four front-row tickets when she performed at the Wembley Arena. What I didn't say was that Eubank and his wife were our guests. Eubank was never on time and the show was about to start when the stage manager noticed the two empty seats next to ours and asked if it would be all right if he put two of his people there, because Miss Streisand would not come out to sing with empty seats on the front row. I said all right, but just as I said it, I heard a roar going through the arena. I thought that must be for Barbra Streisand, walking out to begin her performance. But no. It was Eubank making his entrance at the back of the hall, complete with monocle, jodhpurs, hacking jacket and swagger stick. With his wife on his arm as well.

'Evening, Bazza,' he said as he took his seat.

'Eubank, where have you been? Miss Streisand will not come out if there are empty seats in the front row.'

'Tell Miss Streisand I have arrived, and she may begin.'

I wish it had all ended better for Eubank. At the top, he told me he had a recurring nightmare, that he would end up on the kerbside, drinking red wine. In a way, he encouraged that possibility by the way he spent money. He spent a fortune on clothes, never wearing a shirt twice. He bought a worthless title, Lord of the Manor of Brighton, for £90,000, and his attempt to promote himself was a failure.

Eubank is no down-and-out, but I can't help comparing his somewhat straitened circumstances with the examples of Jess Harding and Francis Ampofo, who both saved their money from the ring and established successful businesses. Ampofo, who won the British and Commonwealth flyweight titles, saved every penny and bought some land in Norfolk. He is now Marks & Spencer's biggest egg supplier. Francis drops in at Mascalls from time to time and always brings a few dozen eggs. Jess Harding used his final purse to set up a pallet business and became a successful businessman. I'm proud of them and the other fighters who made something of themselves after boxing. I hope I educated them a little along the way.

It's great now to see that, following my career in boxing, Eddie's principal fighters are making enough money to launch business careers. Carl Froch is a property developer, Tony Bellew seems to own half of Liverpool and of course Anthony Joshua is setting up a complete business plan, en route to becoming a billionaire post-boxing.

As for Eubank, he may have squandered a great deal, but he was irresistibly brilliant. I was best man at his wedding and although we have had disagreements, particularly over his promotion and management of his son, Chris Eubank Jnr, I will never have a bad word spoken about him. Mad as a hatter he may have been, but he gave me some of my greatest boxing experiences and was as loyal and honest as any man I've met.

Crazy as almost every Eubank promotion was, the strangest boxing promotion in which I was ever involved was the one that never happened, the one known as High Noon in Hong Kong.

In 1994, I met John Daly, a Londoner based in Los Angeles who had made a name for himself in the movie business, particularly with the film *Platoon*. Apparently, he had also been involved in the early days of the classic George Foreman vs Muhammad Ali promotion in Zaire. But halfway through his involvement the whole show was hijacked by Don King, who established a relationship with the Zaire government and ended up as the principal promoter, much to John Daly's chagrin.

Daly never lost his love for boxing and told me he wanted to promote a mega-show in Hong Kong. He wanted me to provide Herbie Hide, the WBO world heavyweight champion, to fight Tommy Morrison, and Steve Collins, the WBO world middleweight champion, to fight Lonny Beasley. No problem. He also persuaded Bob Arum to provide Tommy Morrison to fight Hide and to be involved in promoting the show. Mickey Duff was also invited to the party and came up with Frank Bruno, who was going to be involved in a non-title fight with Ray Mercer, as well as Billy Schwer to fight for the IBF lightweight title against Rafael Ruelas.

It was a huge card, put together by me and Arum. As ever, Bob, with his massive ego, wanted to be the main named promoter. I didn't care so long as we all got paid. I also believed my fighters would both win. Herbie was never quite big enough to be a mainstream player in the heavyweight division, but I reckoned he would box the ears off Morrison. Steve Collins was desperate to get some work as the new middleweight champion and Lonny Beasley was an ideal opponent for him. I was very gung-ho and especially pleased when John Daly sent us a deposit of around $500,000 to cover all our expenses to get over there and set up our training camp in Hong Kong.

The problems began as soon as we arrived. Everyone was caught up with the hype of the fight and the interest it was generating around the world, but no one was making any decisions and there was no cash flow. I believe John Daly was just gambling that there would be a huge walk-up of spectators on the night to pay the bills he had incurred.

Daly never seemed to come up with the money to meet his contractual obligations, while Arum was pacing up and down in his room all the time wondering what was going to happen because he realised that as the main headline promoter it was going to fall on him to provide the cash, which he didn't fancy one little bit.

I was on to John Daly every hour of every day to find out where the money was. At one stage he said to me: 'Don't worry, you will get paid immediately after the fight.'

I replied: 'But if I don't get the money before that, there won't be a fight.'

As the clock ticked down, I became increasingly concerned. In the early part of the week prior to the fight, I told Daly I wouldn't take cheques or cash, and I needed cleared funds in my bank or in the WBO's bank before the weigh-in on the Friday evening.

Perhaps Daly thought I was bluffing. Not so. At six o'clock on the Friday, when the officials called the fighters to the scales, I told them to put their tracksuits back on as we were all going home. And go home we did. It was a fiasco, with around 2,000 fight fans in Hong Kong who had bought tickets never getting a refund.

John Daly said it was Bob Arum's fault but Bob and I both agreed that it was John Daly's fault. Writs were soon flying around right, left and centre and, inevitably, as the one who had pulled out his fighters, I became involved. I went to Las Vegas to give evidence in an action brought by Tommy Morrison against Bob Arum. I told the judge exactly why I wouldn't let my fighters fight, explaining that it was my responsibility in a sport as dangerous as boxing to ensure my client was going to be paid. In this case, I couldn't be sure, and I had no choice but to remove my boxers from the card.

The judge agreed with me and gave me an exemplary report in his judgment. But that show was one that got away, a great card that would have been a fabulous night of boxing. Fighters in the ring are told by the referee to protect themselves at all times; and for managers and promoters, the right thing is to protect your fighters at all times.

Catching carp: my passion, my own lake and a whopping old friend soon to be returned to the water.

9

Six Hours Drowning Maggots

Sky Sports, which began in 1990, transformed the coverage of sport on British TV and enabled Matchroom to expand from a minor player promoting snooker and boxing into one of the world's biggest sports promotion companies.

Sky's first head of sport was David Hill, a man I soon came to admire. He is one of life's crazy characters, an innovator, risk-taker and near-genius. He may have nine ideas that fall flat, but his tenth will change the way sport is broadcast.

I took David my idea for a Snooker World Masters, similar to the Wimbledon tennis fortnight, with men's and women's events, pairs and juniors, to be held at the NEC Birmingham. David liked it but I needed £2m, which represented £1m in prize money, £500,000 to stage it and £500,000 in TV costs. David said that sum was beyond his remit, and I would have to sit down with the man himself, Rupert Murdoch. David arranged the meeting and Murdoch arrived with six lieutenants, each representing a separate territory in his global interests.

I've never experienced anything like it, before or since. Murdoch reminded me of a schoolteacher, diminutive of stature but demanding respect. I felt like calling him 'sir'. Stone-faced, Murdoch listened to my pitch.

'Why should I buy this?' he said when I had finished.

'Mr Murdoch, at this stage of your career, you may be successful, but you do not own very much. This you can own.'

'I like to own things,' he said. He turned to his lieutenants and gave them their orders: you take care of this in the US; you sort out Japan, get it on in Australia, and so on. They all nodded. The meeting had lasted exactly seven minutes and the deal was done.

Soon there was trouble. Sky were not happy with the way their business costs were spiralling out of control and wanted to renegotiate the contract downwards. This time I had to deal with Sam Chisholm, the pugnacious New Zealander who was Murdoch's hatchet man. Murdoch owed money all over the world and Chisholm was brought in to cut rights fees across the board.

David Hill was still head of sport when Chisholm arrived with his hatchet. I was in Hill's office when he said that the new guy was down the corridor and would love to meet me.

'Fine,' I said. 'Let's go and see him.'

I suspect David knew what was coming. 'No, you go on your own,' he said. 'He's just round the corner, second office on the left.'

Chisholm turned out to be a short, very aggressive Antipodean who seemed incapable of forming a sentence without swearing. He waded into me straight away about my refusal to cut my rights fees. I believe I was the only operator at that time who would not budge. My point was that I wasn't making any money with the deal at £2m; I was doing it because the sport needed such an event and I wanted to forge a relationship with Sky, but only on the right terms.

I thought he was going to start throwing punches as he waded towards me, shouting and swearing. I gave it to him straight: 'If you don't stop swearing at me, I'll knock you spark out, and by the way, when Barry Hearn signs a contract, he lives with that contract, and I expect you to do the same.'

That hardly improved our brief relationship, but I will not be bullied. Chisholm had no choice but to honour the contract, but he also told me we would never work together again. The event went ahead and was a great success, but it was too expensive and was never repeated. Chisholm issued instructions that Barry Hearn was not to be allowed into the Sky building and approached Frank Warren, offering a huge deal to screen his boxing shows. I was out in the cold, my relationship with Sky worse than non-existent.

A couple of years later, Chisholm became ill and was waiting for a double lung transplant. That gave me the chance to renew my acquaintance with David Hill. I went to see him with an idea that most people thought was off the wall: live fishing. The idea had come to me when I was fishing for carp in a lake in Ockendon, Essex. I had watched *Wrestle Mania* on TV the night before and I suddenly thought what fun it might be to do a fishing show and call it *Fish'O'Mania*.

My pitch to David Hill started slowly. More people go fishing at the weekend than watch professional football. They are passionate and are not well served by TV. Fortunately, he got the point, but he didn't yet know quite how ambitious and serious I was.

'Yes, Barry, I see that,' Hill said. 'Fishing can work, but we have to be careful not to lose the attention of the viewer. Thirty-minute programmes might be possible, but I like the idea of fifteen-minute programmes, round-ups with loads of action.'

'Not what I had in mind, David. I want a massive national campaign to find sixteen anglers to battle it out to be king of the water. We'd have women's events, junior events. We'll call it *Fish'O'Mania*, and for that I want six hours of live TV: half an hour build-up, five hours' live event and half an hour close-down.'

'Fuck me, are you mad? You want six hours' live TV on a Saturday before the football season starts, showing people drowning maggots?'

'David, you've got it in one.'

'I'm not going to even consider it. It's madness.'

'David, why are we in this business? To go through the motions and follow what other people have done, or to do something different, something amazing, maybe something mad – but we are mad, that's what gives us the edge.'

'This is the craziest idea that I ever heard in my broadcasting career. It's so crazy, we are going to do it.'

That was in 1993. The following year, David Hill had gone to America to become a legend on a third continent and Vic Wakeling, a dour Geordie, had taken over at Sky Sports. I went to see him and told him about my conversation with his predecessor. He held up his hand to tell me to stop talking.

'I'm not saying I like it, and I'm not saying I don't like it,' he said. 'But when I first sat at this desk, I opened the right-hand drawer and saw a note from David Hill. It said, *Fish'O' Mania*, we are doing it. Now, I'm not going to take responsibility for this, but we will not walk away from a commitment we have made.' When Vic Wakeling said that, I knew he was my kind of man: hard but straight.

The first *Fish'O'Mania* took place in 1994. It is still running in 2022 and is the only live fishing event in the world on TV. It involves thousands of anglers and the five-hour live final has been preserved. I have fished in two qualifiers myself, without success, just to experience the excitement and imagine what it must be like for those who get through to the big lake for the final, the chance of glory and the first prize of £50,000. I know some people just don't get fishing. Dr Johnson defined it as a stick and a string with a worm at one end and a fool at the other. In that case, I'm a fool, but a passionate fool. Following my passions rather than just following the money has brought me wonderful times, and money as well.

I can't overstate the importance of fishing in my life. When things are going badly, when you just want to get away, there is nothing quite like having a rod in your hand and sitting quietly by a stretch of water. I have fished on and off all my life and, although I have never come close to winning *Fish'O'Mania*, I am certainly a good amateur and as I get older fishing seems to become more and more important to me as a release. No texts, no emails, no aggravation, no one except yourself and your thoughts. It's a brilliant way to pass time and pass my time I do. Whether it is going to my favourite fishing place in the world, Nimmo Bay in British Columbia, Canada, where you can fly by helicopter to the mountains and take out a hundred salmon in three or four days, or whether it is going down to France to fish for giant carp at Domaine de la Ribière, near Limoges, fishing brings me closer to nature and gives me a chance to be reflective. I have taught my grandchildren how to fish, and hopefully to appreciate the environment in which they live and to reflect on how fortunate we have all been.

Beside my lake at my house in Essex, I have built a small two-bedroom cabin. My lake, which Steve Davis insists on calling a pond, is stocked with carp who have become great friends. They are all barcode tagged and each time I catch one, it is weighed, logged in my notebook and returned to the water. Trying to catch them is not just an escape, because without the ideas I've had with rod in hand, I would not have been as successful or as happy as I am. With so many of my best business ideas coming while waiting for a fish to take the bait, the lake has turned out to be highly profitable.

I still haven't ticked my bucket list for a 50lb carp, missing out by a few ounces at Domaine de la Ribière. As Arnold Schwarzenegger says, I will be back.

By the mid-1990s, my involvement in snooker had diminished so much that it basically entailed managing Steve Davis when he was no longer a major force as a player. That was easy enough. Steve was always Mr Sensible, Mr Reliable. But then he phoned me early one morning in 1995. 'I've got a problem,' he said.

He had met a woman when playing an exhibition in Devon. He had never messed around during his marriage to Jude. She was a lovely girl and they had two lovely kids. But as he entered middle age at thirty-nine, he had been tempted. The young woman had pursued him, and he had stayed with her overnight in a hotel after filming *A Question of Sport*. When he went downstairs in the morning, there were two photographers from the *Sun* sitting on the bonnet of his Porsche. 'And they don't want my autograph,' Steve said on the phone.

'Don't panic,' I said. 'Nothing will happen until they speak to me. I know everybody at the *Sun* and no one's come on to me yet. Just keep calm. I'll get back to you soon.'

Five minutes later, the phone rang again. Paul Ridley, sports editor of the *Sun*.

'Morning, Paul. How's it going?'

'It's not a good day, Bazza.'

'What are you talking about? The sun is shining. It's a beautiful day.'

'We've got Davis.'

'What do you mean, you've got Davis? You've kidnapped him?'

'No. Seriously, this is a horrible phone call to make, but it's my job. A couple of months ago we were approached by this girl and had a meeting with her and her mum. She said she was going to sleep with Steve Davis and what was it worth? Well, he shagged her last night in a hotel and we had cameras set up in the room. Before we publish, I want to give you the opportunity to give Steve's side of the story.'

There it was again. The opportunity to put his side of the story . . . I wasn't falling for that. It was entrapment, of course. These days, we would mount a massive court case against the *Sun* and we would win. But back then, it was commonplace, the 'public's right to know' as the tabloids put it with brazen hypocrisy.

'Print anything and I'll sue you,' I told Ridley. 'There is no comment whatsoever. You do what you've got to do, and I will too.'

I rang Steve. 'It's going to be all over the papers tomorrow,' I told him. 'Go home and tell Jude about it.'

The story ran for three or four days. Seven-times-in-a-night romp, the lot. The day the story broke, Steve rang and begged me to go round to his place. There had been tears and tantrums and twenty journalists were camped outside Steve's gate. Steve and Jude had been up all night.

I was there for two or three hours, and I left telling them to sort it out, even if they had to talk all night again. 'Jude, he's been an idiot,' I said. 'But don't let this spoil what you've got. Don't let this tramp who has sold herself be the winner.'

As I drove out through the gates, I had the window down. 'Can we have a quote?' came the chorus.

'You can have a quote, you scumbags. Look at my face. I'm looking at yours, and I'm remembering every one of you.'

I drove straight to Brentwood police station. 'I want to report a felony,' I said.

'What felony?'

'It hasn't happened yet, but my pal, Steve Davis, has twenty scumbags outside his gate upsetting his kids, and they're upsetting me. If you don't do something about it, it won't be pretty.'

The sergeant consulted a couple of colleagues and they said they had to allow one of the journalists to stay there. They got rid of the rest.

I don't think women ever forgive betrayal, and eventually Steve and Jude did break up. Thank goodness, it all ended up all right. Jude is happily remarried; Steve has a long-term partner; the kids are both doing well.

Steve's obsession with winning snooker matches declined. He pursued his interest in music and became an accomplished snooker commentator. He played on until he announced his retirement from competitive play at the Crucible on 17 April 2016. I shed a tear and the audience gave him a standing ovation. He might have carried on, but his dad, Bill, had passed away. I suspect the only reason Steve carried on as long as he did was that his dad loved the game so much and loved travelling with him. It gave Bill an interest.

When Steve retired, I told him I was going to give him the best retirement present I could give him.

'But we don't buy each other presents,' he said. 'We never have.'

'I know, but this is a special occasion,' I said. 'I have managed you for forty years and I am going to manage you for the rest of your life, but from now on I will never take another penny in commission.'

We both reckoned that he wouldn't be doing very much in the future, so my generosity would not be too costly. A few weeks later, he was wanted by the TV show *I'm a Celebrity, Get Me Out of Here!* I negotiated his fee, a cool £250,000. My cut? Zero.

If the crown fits: I play kingmaker with two monarchs of the oche, Phil Taylor (left) and Raymond van Barneveld at Alexandra Palace. Credit: Lawrence Lustig

10

Darts, Glorious Darts

I played club cricket for South Loughton for close on twenty years. For the record, I bowled 1,473 overs, took 334 wickets at an average of 11.65 and took 76 catches. My batting was all right, no better. My top score for South Loughton was 87. I never made a century until I was in my mid-forties, not for South Loughton, but opening the batting for the Matchroom team in July 1992, somewhere down in Kent. I made the century, stumped for 102 to be precise, was man of the match and arrived home absolutely pissed. I went into Eddie's bedroom and woke him up. He was thirteen at the time. I gave him a thirty-minute lecture about never giving up, about keeping your dreams alive, fighting and fighting. It had taken me over thirty years to make a century, but I had done it. Yes, yes, Dad, he said. Let me sleep.

I assumed he hadn't taken a blind bit of notice of his sodden old dad. But a few days later he came up to me with a smile.

'That talk you gave me made a lot of sense,' he said.

'What talk are you on about?'

'About never giving up on your dreams. I made a century against Middlesex today.'

That was for Essex under-fourteens. Eddie was an opening batsman, with a load of ability and an attacking game. Three years later, he was in the Matchroom team for the Courage Six-a-side National Championship. We made it through to the final stages at the Oval, involving eight teams. Every team had five of their own players, plus one from the Surrey staff. We played one match where our opponents had a quickie who had played for Australia. He was bowling off a six-yard run-up to start with but was still lively. He bowled an over-pitched ball to Eddie and Eddie smashed the ball out of the ground. The Surrey players in the pavilion couldn't stop laughing.

Then Eddie got cheeky. 'Is that the best you've got?' he said to the Aussie.

'No, son.'

He went to his full run and slung down a really fast ball. Eddie did it again, hit him for six. And again, making three sixes in the over. Eddie tended to wind people up, but he could back it up. At Brentwood School he was the best cricketer by a country mile. Frank Lampard, in the year ahead of Eddie, was the best footballer. Eddie got slung out when he sixteen because he was trouble; plenty of mouth and aggravation. But they were gutted to lose him from the cricket team.

Susan went to every game to watch young Eddie. She used to hide behind the sightscreen and say a prayer. Please let him get to double figures; please can he make fifty. As often as not, her prayers were answered. Eddie played at every age level for Essex and even toured Hong Kong and Barbados. But like me, he knew he wasn't quite good enough to play regular county cricket, especially when it was for about eighty pounds a week.

I loved playing with Eddie, but my own cricket was becoming less dynamic, more social. Steve Davis and I were invited to play for the Lord's Taverners one day and we went for it. We got there and the organiser asked me if I could keep wicket. Their usual wicketkeeper couldn't make it.

'Who is your usual keeper?' I asked.

'Godfrey Evans.'

At the mention of one of the greats, one of those we used to imitate in our street games all those years earlier, my ego kicked in. 'Sure,' I said.

Then I discovered our opening bowlers were also former Test players: John Snow and Fred Rumsey. It was an education. Rumsey swung the ball all over the place while Snow was brutal off a six-yard run. Even with wicket-keeping gloves I ruined my hands and I said to Steve, 'I think I've broken my thumb and several fingers.' But there was no way I was coming off the field.

Mick McManus, the wrestler, was fielding at first slip. He was much smaller than I expected. In the third over, someone snicked a ball from Snow. It hit McManus on the finger and flew away for four runs. McManus started crying. 'That really hurt,' he blubbed.

'Mick, I thought you were a hard man,' I said. 'I watch you every Saturday, bashing people up and throwing them out of the ring.'

It was great fun playing regularly for the Taverners and other celebrity teams, mixing with the game's greats. I batted once against Richard Hadlee (he didn't get me out) and I hit Rumsey for three fours in an over. I bowled against Graeme Pollock and Barry Richards, two of the all-time greats, and met so many of my heroes. These matches also raised huge sums for the benefit of youth cricket, as well as paying for coaches for disadvantaged kids. I am still proud to be a Lord's Taverner today. I opened the bowling for Courage Brewery against Old England – the opening batsman were Colin Cowdrey and Tom Graveney. Old, overweight and less than agile they smacked me all over the ground – and I loved it.

I always had a hankering to get involved with pool and once my dealings with Sky had become amicable it was time to make my move. I became pretty decent at snooker, and a decent snooker player is likely to be a good pool player. I was aware that pool had become really popular in the pubs around the country, and I played myself, especially when I went over to America in the 1980s, working for the Deryck Healey International fashion business. I'd attend a trade fair or meet some manufacturers or retailers in Los Angeles, San Francisco, wherever, and then search out the local pool hall.

In New York, I had done a presentation in a white suit, very dapper, and wandered into a shabby old pool hall looking for a game. One of the patrons got quite abusive and I ended up whacking him. We had to be separated by the management. This could have turned ugly but when I said I was just there for a game of pool, the atmosphere improved and I was made welcome. I played one-pocket pool for about four hours. It's a very specialised game and I lost every rack, which was expensive but educational.

I began by inventing and promoting the European Pool Masters, held in Plymouth in 1993. Two years later, we made it the World Pool Masters and invited the best sixteen players from all over the world. We have held it in Las Vegas, Poland, the Philippines and lately in Gibraltar. No one had properly promoted pool before, so the players had one thing in common – they had very little money. But they had the desire to be recognised as the best. There was pride and technical brilliance, so it made very viewable TV.

I knew I could go further with pool and I decided to borrow an idea from another sport I love, golf. By the 1990s, the Ryder Cup, which had started out in 1927 as a friendly challenge match between the top players in the US and those from Britain, was on its way to becoming one of the world's premier sporting events. I wanted to stage a Ryder Cup of pool.

In 1993, Willie Mosconi, the greatest ever pool player, had just died. He had won the world title fifteen times between 1941 and 1957 and played many of the shots for Paul Newman and Jackie Gleason in the film *The Hustler*. I wanted to honour his legend but also to give my Ryder Cup idea credibility. Mosconi had been managed by Bill Cayton, a New York boxing promoter who controlled all the pool players in America with his partner, Jimmy Jacobs, via their company Big Fights Inc., under a very brutal management contract. I went to see them in New York and explained my idea. Cayton didn't seem to think it had much mileage, or he would have asked for some money, but he did say I would have to clear it with Flora Mosconi, Willie's widow. Cayton got her on the phone and handed the phone to me.

I told Flora Mosconi that I wanted to preserve her husband's name by staging a Mosconi Cup involving the best players in America and Europe, playing nine-ball pool. She was thrilled and gave me permission straight away, over the phone.

We held the first event in a bowling alley in Romford as an exhibition, broadcast by Sky, to raise the game's profile in Britain. It soon became a serious event, but in the first few years the Americans almost always won. They were just better. They started sending over their best players and we were using too many snooker players, as much for their high profile as anything else, rather than experienced pool players. The worst drubbing was in 2001, 12–1 at the York Hall in Bethnal Green. But the following year gave me my best memory of the event, involving a showdown match between Earl 'The Pearl' Strickland and Steve 'The Nugget' Davis. Strickland, another legend, was clearing up in the final rack. But inexplicably he missed a cut-back into a pocket – rather similar to the one Steve missed in that 1985 World Snooker Championship final against Dennis Taylor – and Steve was left with a chance to take the game. He got out of his chair looking as unflappable as ever, but he has since admitted he'd never known tension like it. The hairs on the back of his neck were solid, sticking straight up, and the atmosphere in the York Hall was electric. Steve managed to control a shaking arm and pot the final few balls to win. From that year on we had a really thrilling, well-contested event on our hands. These days, the Mosconi Cup is a huge, global event. The venue alternates between Las Vegas and the Alexandra Palace in north London and we sell broadcasting rights to over a hundred countries.

With *Fish'O'Mania* and the Mosconi Cup established, I was now most welcome at the Sky offices. It may not have quite been the red carpet but at least I wasn't barred, as I had been by Sam Chisholm. I also had any number of snooker events, and boxing was pretty much flat out with Chris Eubank our star attraction. With the darts phenomenon and big-time boxing, particularly with Anthony Joshua, the relationship with Sky was to get much bigger and much more mutually beneficial, until, inevitably, with the world changing, our relationship changed as well.

The Mosconi Cup was a good idea that worked, so I repeated it with ten-pin bowling. This was yet another sport I tried in my youth only to discover I was reasonably good without being spectacular. I believe my highest game was 226, which is respectable but way short of the 300 maximum. Ten-pin bowling alleys were great meeting places in the 1970s and 1980s and had a surge in popularity in Britain. In America, the sport remains the most participated in of all, with over 39 million people visiting an alley at least once a year.

I was already advising America's biggest bowling operator, AMF, on the sponsorship of their World Cup and I was out in Thailand, at Pattaya, where the event was being held, when I got to know one of the sport's legends, perhaps the best ever, Dick Weber. He was there as an ambassador. I went for a walk along the beach with Dick and told him I was going to do him the biggest favour anyone had ever done for him. I said I was going to start an event that would carry his name so that he would be remembered in perpetuity. It will be the Weber Cup and will be like the Ryder Cup, I told him. Dick was delighted and gave his permission, wishing me every success.

The Weber Cup hasn't yet taken off as I had hoped. It is a long haul but, as always, we take the long-term view and good events tend to develop their own history and status, which the Weber Cup has started to do. It was wonderful in 2008 to see Pete Weber, Dick's son and another bowler of the highest class, representing his country in an event named after his father. We now alternate the match between England and America. The 2019 edition was held at the Mandalay Bay Hotel, Las Vegas.

Thanks to my enthusiasm for golf, I had shamelessly borrowed the Ryder Cup format for pool and ten-pin bowling. As a player, with a handicap of a pretty consistent eighteen over the years, I was no threat to the big boys on tour, or even a handy amateur, but naturally I wanted to be involved in the sport, so when I was approached and asked to take over the EuroPro Tour, the starting point for all young pros in Europe, I seized the chance. I have always said there is no point in having a beautiful flower if you don't water the roots and I knew that developmental tours were important. I was able to bring some television to the table through Sky, but there was something missing, and that was credibility among the game's decision-makers. I therefore approached Sandy Jones, the chief executive of the Professional Golfers' Association, and put to him a rather novel idea. The PGA ran the Mastercard Tour, and we ran the EuroPro Tour. Why not combine the two?

I do not like partnerships or committees, so the idea was that the newly formed PGA EuroPro Tour, run by us, would pay a sanction fee to the PGA. They would allow us to use their highly regarded initials and they would provide officials and administrative staff for our events. It was a masterstroke and I have to thank Sandy for having the vision to join forces with us. The tour may not have been my greatest financial success, but we made it the biggest developmental tour in the world, with over five hundred members, and provided a springboard for a host of great players, including Louis Oosthuizen and Charl Schwartzel, both Major championship winners, and several European Ryder Cup team members, such as Jamie Donaldson, Tommy Fleetwood and Tyrrell Hatton.

My entry into the world of darts was altogether different. From the moment I walked with curiosity into the Circus Tavern to be hit for the first time with the full-on, raucous madness of a big-time darts event, I felt at home and sensed the potential.

It must say something about me. When I walk into Wembley Stadium or Madison Square Garden or the Great Hall of the People in Beijing, I'm impressed. But when I walk into a snooker hall, or Brisbane Road, or that day in 1998 walking into the Circus Tavern, I'm at home.

On this occasion I was flanked by Dick Allix and Tommy Cox, two stalwarts who were running the Professional Darts Corporation, the organisation that had broken away from the tired, traditional British Darts Organisation. The PDC, which was formed in 1993 when players such as Eric Bristow and Phil Taylor realised they were being undervalued and under-rewarded, had all the top players, but they were struggling. A long-running legal battle with the BDO was draining their resources and ambitions.

You wouldn't know it from first impressions at the PDC World Championship. The joint was jumping, as they say. Eight hundred people crammed into the low-ceilinged, shabby venue in Purfleet just off the M25, all roaring, pints in hand as up on the stage two players threw their darts at the board. You'd need to have had twenty-twenty eyesight and be in the front row to see where the darts landed, but it didn't matter. They all loved the theatre, the ritual. One hundred and eighty!

My first remark has gone down in darts folklore. I turned to Dick Allix and said: 'I smell money.'

Dick and Tommy wanted me to explore and expand the PDC's commercial income and I resolved straight away to help as much as I could. I liked them. They were not 'blazers'. Dick was a grammar-school lad who had been the drummer for Vanity Fare, a 1960s rock group of some renown. Tommy was a traditional darts man through and through.

They were fortunate that Sky TV had supported the PDC from the beginning. But Sky was famous for not being particularly generous if they could possibly avoid it (unless Kelvin MacKenzie was in charge). Vic Wakeling, Sky's head of sport through most of the 1990s, was a northern lad who loved his darts, but he always wanted the best deal he could get for his employers – quite rightly.

Vic was a brilliant administrator and organiser but if you broke his arm he had Sky TV written through the bone. I once said to him that we had done hundreds of deals together, but he had never done me a favour. Vic's reply was classic: 'I may never have done you a favour, but we have done an awful lot of business, haven't we?'

That summed up our relationship, because you don't expect favours from people in business and you shouldn't ask for them. Favours don't last; good deals do. That was Vic's mantra and it worked.

During one contract renewal discussion, I said to Vic: 'It's tough to negotiate with you as I always feel you have one of my testicles in your safe.' Vic's reply was priceless: 'Barry, I've got both your testicles in my safe.'

Sky were paying £100,000 a year for all their darts coverage and there was zero overseas interest, so my task was quite clear. It was to boost the Sky contract and look at the overseas market to begin to export this great British sport.

I had some success on both fronts and for the next couple of years I did my best to make the PDC a little more profitable, or at least reduce their losses. Eventually their legal battle with the BDO was resolved: a draw, with both sides having spent too much money on lawyers. The acrimony, however, would last for years and years. When I took over the PDC later on, I wrote to Olly Croft, who ruled the BDO like a private fiefdom, and tried to make peace, suggesting a meeting. The reply from Croft was a one-liner: 'I see no point in a meeting.'

I wrote back and told him I found his attitude disrespectful, and that I would do my best to destroy his business. It took a while, but in 2020 the BDO went bust and ceased to exist. Mission accomplished.

The PDC directors appreciated what I was doing and came to a very brave admission and decision. They admitted that they required better management to go to the next level and asked me if I would consider becoming the chairman of the PDC. As usual, my response was: 'I don't do chairmanship; I do ownership.'

Still, I could see that a business that was making some progress but losing £200,000 a year needed an injection of some serious funds. I suggested to the directors that although the business was losing money it was still valuable. I put a notional figure of £500,000 on the business and proposed they should organise a rights issue to existing shareholders of another £500,000 to give them some much-needed working capital. Should any shareholder not take up their option to buy shares from the new issue, then I would underwrite the £500,000 and buy any shares left over.

This was a neat solution. It put a value of £500,000 on a company that wasn't worth £500,000 and it offered existing shareholders an opportunity to maintain their share of the company should they have the funds to take up their entitlement to new shares. In the event, £360,000-worth of the £500,000 in new shares was not taken up, so I paid the money in 2001 and became the owner of 36 per cent of the PDC.

I thought it would be a good idea to get Sky involved, with a stake in the PDC, so I went to see Vic Wakeling. I offered him 10 per cent of the PDC for £100,000 and told him he would get a seat on the board. He was not impressed. 'It's a bit small for us to consider,' he said.

That was a major error. Indeed, Vic later admitted it was the biggest mistake he ever made. He had been offered an acorn that grew into an oak. Remember Rule Number Five: always think poor. Today, the market value of the PDC has gone through the roof. I bought up further shares whenever I could and Matchroom's holding is now around 70 per cent. At the beginning of our adventure, PDC stock was £25 a share. The last offer to existing shareholders was £4,000 a share. Eric Bristow had 150 shares, which, I believe, when he died in 2018, were a substantial part of his estate, inherited by his children – and they deserve every penny.

As the principal shareholder and chairman, I had control of the PDC and my real darts adventure had begun. My aim was to turn the game into a world-class sport played in a party atmosphere, giving a unique experience for fans and viewers alike.

It took us from the Circus Tavern to Alexandra Palace, from Purfleet to Las Vegas, Tokyo, Prague, Berlin, Copenhagen, Sydney, Auckland, New York, in fact all around the world. I saw darts as working man's golf. The main difference was that there were no barriers to entry. You didn't have to buy an expensive set of clubs, pay green fees and join some country club. It offered a level playing field independent of sex, colour, religion or class. All that counted was ability on the oche. You just needed a set of darts and a nearby pub. Or you could hang a board in your bedroom, as Eric Bristow did when he spent hours every day turning himself into the best player the world had seen – until Phil Taylor came along.

I knew that what darts players, like all sportsmen, needed more than anything else was activity. The top players needed regular tournaments to make a decent living, so we made a tour of it, like golf, with 128 players on the tour and a Q school, just like golf, where hundreds of players from all round the world came to win their golden ticket, their PDC tour card. We also created a Challenge Tour for those players who had been to Q school but had not won their tour card, a developmental Youth Tour for sixteen- to twenty-two-year-olds, and a Women's Series.

I borrowed some grand titles, such as the Las Vegas Desert Classic, the World Masters, World Matchplay, the Premier League. The idea of the Premier League came to me while I was fishing in my lake. It has grown from small-hall rounds to crowds in excess of 10,000 all around Europe. Our record attendance is 21,000 for a World Series event at the Schalke football stadium in Germany. We hold the annual PDC awards dinner in the Dorchester Hotel, Park Lane. All a long way from the Circus Tavern.

Never too proud to copy a good idea, I saw how World Wrestling Entertainment Inc. built up their wrestlers' personas and ramped up the atmosphere. We made sure every player had their own nickname, their own walk-on music, character and personality.

A good example is Peter 'Snakebite' Wright, the world champion in 2019/20 and 2021/22. Peter was an average player with little or no personality who set about rebuilding his whole persona with outrageous hairstyles, coloured clothing and a walk-on that defied imagination. His game also improved as he rose to the challenge of becoming a superstar in his sport. Peter developed a fan base and also a stage presence that built his reputation and changed his life financially.

The World Championship, held at Alexandra Palace over Christmas and New Year, has become one of the great sporting shows on earth. Where else would a young plumber or banker rub shoulders with Stephen Fry and Alastair Cook, Prince Harry and Zara Phillips? Zara and Mike Tindall regularly attend at Ally Pally. Prince Harry came along one year with three mates from the army. They proceeded to consume dozens of pints of lager and merged in with the crowd rather well. Harry was like any ordinary bloke on a night out with his mates. Eddie and I joined them on a table of six and it was clear they were on a bender. I reckon sixty pints of lager went down, and I didn't have much of it.

At one stage a chant went up: 'Harry, Harry, give us a wave!'

I looked at him and said, 'If you stand up and wave back, your street credibility will be cemented for a lifetime.'

Harry smiled. 'I do not think I am allowed to,' he said.

At the end, Harry announced they were going on to a nightclub and would we like to come? Not us, I said. You guys are too dangerous.

Over many years, TV viewers had a bonus in the commentaries of Sid Waddell, one of the greats of any sport. He was the oracle of the sport, with an understanding of the players, a great knowledge of darts history and records, and a broadcasting style that was deadly serious, scholarly, wildly enthusiastic and hilarious.

At the moment that Bristow won his first World Championship in 1980, Sid told viewers: 'When Alexander of Macedonia was thirty-three, he cried salt tears because there were no more worlds to conquer . . . Bristow's only twenty-seven.' Sid was the son of a Northumberland miner. He won a scholarship to St John's College, Cambridge, where he founded the inter-college darts championship. As well as being vital to the sport's development, he was wonderful company.

Stephen Fry loves his darts and he loved Sid's commentaries. In 2010, at the finals night of the Premier League, he joined Sid in the commentary box. What a combination. When Phil Taylor won his match, Sid waxed lyrical: 'Once upon a time he was breaking all records, now he's breaking all hearts. Nothing you can do, total eclipse of the dart.'

A great line, instantly matched by Stephen: 'Ah, Bonnie Taylor.'

I asked Stephen if he was enjoying himself. 'I feel like a pig in Chardonnay,' he said.

It was a terrible blow when Sid died in 2012. We commissioned a new World Championship trophy, the Sid Waddell Trophy, so that his name will live on. It was the least we could do in recognising his enormous contribution.

Two months after Bristow won his first world title, *Not the Nine O'Clock News*, the BBC's hugely popular comedy sketch show, screened their famous/infamous darts sketch. It featured Dai 'Fatbelly' Gutbucket, played by Mel Smith, versus Tommy 'Evenfatterbelly' Belcher, played by Griff Rhys Jones. Commentary, in the manner of Sid Waddell, was provided by Rowan Atkinson. Rather than hitting singles, doubles and trebles on the dartboard, they went up to the oche and sank single pints, double and triple vodkas.

Opinion in the darts world was divided. Sid Waddell thought it was funny; Eric Bristow and most of the players believed it would damage the game. It certainly held darts up to ridicule and damaged its sporting pretensions. Broadcasters, including the BBC and ITV, didn't listen to their audience and lost interest.

That may have had an influence a few years later when the PDC broke away and Sky began to broadcast darts.

Funnily enough, we had a case of life imitating art some years later when we put on a pay-per-view event featuring a showdown between Phil 'The Power' Taylor, the PDC world champion, and Andy 'The Viking' Fordham, the BDO world champion. Pay-per-view on darts; we had 60,000 buyers. it seems unbelievable, doesn't it?

We held it at the Circus Tavern and sold out the place instantly. Andy Fordham, who weighed over thirty stone at the time, used to drink twenty-four bottles of lager before playing and he had certainly drunk so much that night that when he went under the TV lights he suffered serious dehydration. Taylor was ahead by five sets to two (best of thirteen sets) when it became clear that Andy could not continue. He was rushed to hospital where he was told he had to go on an immediate diet.

Andy was a great lad. He won the 2004 BDO World Championship and the Winmau World Masters in 1999, so he was no pushover, but I'm afraid his dietary habits did not bode well for his long-term future. After our pay-per-view semi-disaster, he had a gastric band fitted and went on a weight-loss campaign, but he never settled to a long-term commitment to become healthier. Sadly, in July 2021 Andy died in hospital from organ failure – he was fifty-nine years old.

It was easy for snobs to sneer at darts, and the challenge has always been to present it as a legitimate sport while having a great time. In that regard, you need unquestioned excellence just as much as characters for the soap opera. That was why Bristow and Phil Taylor were so important to the game's credibility.

Everyone, just about, has thrown darts in a pub or club, so they have some idea how difficult it is to play even reasonably well. Phil Taylor's mastery was easily appreciated by everyone. The world's greatest ever player has been the best ambassador for darts and managing his career has been one of the highlights of my sporting life. As a bloke, he is very basic. He understood he had God-given ability and he knew he needed to put in the hard work, just like Steve Davis. For both of them, it was all about applying work ethic to maximise natural ability. I asked Taylor once, when he had been the dominant player for years, how he managed to keep driving himself forward when he was slaughtering people week in, week out, and hitting three-dart averages that no one had seen before.

'Simple,' he said. 'I get up in the morning and go to work. I clock in at nine, play four hours of darts, break for lunch between one and two, clock back in again and play darts for another four hours. If you do that every day you will definitely get better. But you have to do it properly. You mustn't be lazy.' My Principle Number Three in a nutshell.

Phil left school when he was sixteen and was employed in a variety of jobs, including making ceramic toilet-roll handles, for which he was paid fifty pounds a week. In the late 1980s, with a £10,000 sponsorship from Eric Bristow, who saw his potential, Phil started playing full-time and achieved almost immediate success. He won the BDO World Championship in 1990 and 1992 before the seismic split from the governing body. He also won fourteen PDC World Championships, making sixteen, as well as sixteen World Matchplay titles, eleven World Grand Prix titles, six Grand Slam titles and six Premier League titles. No wonder some people thought PDC stood for Phil's Darts Club. In 2002, he produced the first UK live-televised nine-dart finish, for which he was paid £100,000. As money improved and more and more players were able to make their living from the game, the nine-dart finish became more common. These days, we get dozens a year. Taylor raised the bar; others followed; Taylor kept raising it again.

In the end, however good you are, the pack will close in on you. It happened to Steve Davis, to Stephen Hendry and in the end to Phil. Michael van Gerwen and a host of other great players were hunting him down and putting in the hours that Phil used to put in, and as Phil got older, he found it harder and harder to put in the same number of hours. The inevitable decline happened and suddenly there was a new kid on the block – van Gerwen.

Michael started playing darts when he was thirteen and quickly became a teenage prodigy. At seventeen, he won the World Masters and threw a televised nine-dart finish at the 2007 event the following year.

He struggled for a while and was only ranked thirty-eighth in the world at the start of the 2012 season. By the end of 2013, he had started winning events again and from that point on never really looked back. At the age of twenty-four, Michael became the youngest winner of the PDC World Championship. He holds the record for the highest three-dart average in televised darts with 123.4, an unbelievable figure when you consider that Eric Bristow was winning BDO World Championships with averages in the high 80s. That is a testament to the improvement in standard at the top, thanks largely to the great flag-bearer, Phil Taylor.

Michael is living proof that if you have the ability, you can achieve your dreams. He is one of the darts players currently capable of annual earnings in excess of £2m. The other figures relating to the darts boom are equally impressive. Prize money when I took over the game was around £500,000 per annum. It rose, pre-Covid, to some £15m. The Sky contract when I was originally brought in to renegotiate it has increased from £100,000 a year to £10m. Darts has become the second-highest-rated sport on Sky after Premier League football. Our overseas TV sales, which were zero when I was first brought in by Dick Allix and Tommy Cox, are well beyond £10m annually.

I said that I smelled money when I first saw big-time darts at the Circus Tavern back in 1998. You could say I smelled it and I made it, and along the way we changed some lives, and had some fun.

For me, the best aspect of my darts adventure is the opportunity it has offered aspiring players who have the chance to change their lives. With few barriers to entry, and with ability as the only requirement, darts players are real working-class heroes. Look at the emergence of Gerwyn Price, the Iceman, as he has moved from professional rugby, playing both codes, to become the world number-one darts player. The lives of Gerwyn and his family have been transformed and he has helped inspire the next generation. Darts has never been in a better place and I consider the growth of the sport to be my finest career achievement.

King of Orient. My heart told me to take over Leyton Orient
as chairman and benefactor. My head warned me against it.
For once, the heart won. Credit: Lawrence Lustig

Charming Charles (horse in the centre) was an unlikely present from a snooker fan, and my first racehorse. Credit: Mirrorpix.

Charming Charles jumping clear on his way to his only victory. The bookmakers of Market Rasen were not best pleased. Credit: Michael Haslam.

Trio of relentless fistic legends (from left): Jim McDonnell,
Jack 'Kid' Berg, my son, Eddie Hearn.

Matchless Matchroom: (left to right) Tony Meo, Terry Griffiths, Willie Thorne,
Cliff Thorburn, Yours Truly, Steve Davis, Neal Foulds, Jimmy White,
Dennis Taylor. Credit: Bob Thomas/Getty.

Deryck Healey ADF (Manc) FSIA   Chairman

Deryck Healey graduated from Manchester College of Art and specialised in textile and fashion design. After a couple of years as design manager for a group of print studios in South Africa he returned to a design Fellowship at Manchester College of Art. During this fellowship year Deryck Healey worked on environmental design and colour projects and on the basis of this worked freelance for a leading wall-paper manufacturer and received the Council of Industrial Design award. He was invited to become design Manager and co-ordinator for W.P.M. and subsequently accepted a challenge to work on several design and colour projects for ICI Fibres under the direction of Elsbeth Juda. As a result of this work the D.H.I. Studio was founded in 1966.

Having started with a small group of six designers, the Studio gradually expanded as international contracts were taken on. The D.H.I. Studio moved in 1971 to an early Victorian building where over seventy resident designers work with clients in Europe, America, South Africa, Australia and Japan.

Deryck Healey's aim is to provide a total design and colour service to industry and the Studio is now a recognised international colour and fashion authority.

Bob Learmonth M.A. B.Com.   Managing Director

Bob Learmonth graduated from Edinburgh University having specialised in French, German and Italian. He was for ten years with B.N.S./ICI Fibres in their sales and marketing department and lived in both Germany and Italy working mainly on knitwear and print.

He joined D.H.I. in February 1972 to deal with day to day Studio management and has travelled to U.S.A., South Africa, Japan and Europe co-ordinating D.H.I. contracts

Tom Blyth LL.B

Tom Blyth is the director of D.H.I. responsible for the Company's legal affairs and providing general business advice. He is a qualified solicitor and a senior partner in a London firm of solicitors.

He has been involved with D.H.I. since its incorporation and has travelled extensively for the Studio negotiating overseas contracts.

Barry Hearn ACA   Company Secretary

Barry Hearn qualified as a Chartered Accountant in 1970 and then spent three years with a major firm of international accountants based in London.

He joined D.H.I. in June, 1973 and is responsible for day to day financial control and long-term monetary planning aimed at co-ordinating the Studio's expansion both in the U.K. and overseas.

Marathon man and mentor: Sandy Risley was my trainer, my inspiration and a great friend.

Father and son, master and pupil: Eddie turned out to be a better boxing promoter than his dad.

London Marathon 1987. I ran my personal best. It was the achievement of a lifetime, and all the training was worth it.

When Romford HQ became Aladdin's cave: Steve Davis ruled the snooker world for a decade, the 1980s. Credit: The Sun/News Licensing.

Promoting snooker was a breeze with such characters and entertainers: Alex 'The Hurricane' Higgins and Jimmy White, 'The Whirlwind'. Credit: Mirrorpix.

Jess Harding, my first heavyweight, was game and capable. He never reached world level, but he kept his money and remains a close friend.

Freddie King with the heavy brigade: Herbie Hide and Frank Bruno both won world titles in boxing's most compelling division.

Matchroom boxing team: (from left) Tony McKenzie, Errol Christie, Johnny Nelson, Me, Jess Harding, Carl Crook, Jim McDonnell, Chris Eubank.
Credit: Michael Fresco/Evening Standard/Shutterstock.

Superfight: the first grudge match between Chris Eubank and Nigel Benn is rightly considered one of the greatest contests in the history of British boxing. Credit: PA Images/Alamy Stock Photo.

11

Orient forever

In January 1995 I received a phone call from Tony Wood, chairman and owner of Leyton Orient Football Club. He wanted to come over to my office for a chat. Sure. Why not? He turned up with a couple of fellow directors. His purpose, as I knew it would be, was to sell me the club.

I liked Tony, admired him and felt sorry for him as well. He had become a very wealthy man thanks to a joint venture with the Rwandan Government to establish coffee plantations. At one time, his fortune was valued at £200m, and his pet project was Leyton Orient. Every year, he kept the club afloat by writing a cheque to cover the losses, which was generally in the range of £300,000 to £500,000. But civil war in Rwanda brought disaster. His plantations were burned, his staff murdered and his business ruined.

Around the time when we sat down to talk, Channel 4 were filming a fly-on-the-wall documentary at the club that would be called *Leyton Orient: Yours for a Fiver*. The title came from a throwaway remark Tony had made in an interview when he said the club could be bought for a fiver if anyone had a fiver spare. The documentary brutally exposed the club's plight. They were going bust fast and could not even pay their milk bill. On the field, they were losing game after game and looked a certainty to be relegated from Division Two.

Tony soon twigged I wasn't keen to buy the club. As an accountant, I could see they were losing some £500,000 a year and were in dire straits. He gave up on his selling pitch and came up with a masterstroke: he invited me to go over to the ground at Brisbane Road to see the 'potential'.

That was the word he used. Potential. A wonderful word that is meaningless or can mean anything to anyone and something else entirely to someone else. I raised my eyebrows, but I went.

I stood in the directors' box and looked around the dilapidated property with few facilities but a nice, green pitch. At least the groundsman was doing a decent job. I reminded myself that the club as a business was a disaster matched only by the team that was propping up Division Two.

Then Barry the accountant switched off. His wallet and his heart merged. He was a boy again, watching from the terraces as Tommy Johnston scored goal after goal. And he remembered that old fellow with a cloth cap who had spun a yarn, telling him to watch the credits at the end of the film he was going to see that night, *Cleopatra*, and to spot the name of his daughter, Edith Head, the great costume designer. In the absence of the accountant, the romantic had taken over, all misty-eyed, and the romantic saw nothing but potential.

I bought the club. It only cost £2.43. That's right, £2.43 with no noughts missing, to acquire the 243,000 shares Tony owned, a huge majority stake. But then there were £2m of unpaid debts.

Our first home match after I became chairman was the semi-final of the Auto Windscreens Shield against Birmingham City. With the excitement of my taking over and the fact that it was a semi-final for a reasonably big competition, we had a massive crowd there that day of 10,830 despite the fact that we were propping up the division and looked certainties for relegation.

There were lots of Birmingham fans as well because they fancied the job, but it seemed that the main purpose of the evening was for the Leyton Orient fans to welcome me and their dreams of a new future under our stewardship. I took young Eddie and Katie to the match and as we walked up the stairs and entered the old directors' box, all you could hear was thousands of voices chanting, 'Barry Hearn's red-and-white army.' Katie loved this and couldn't stop grinning. 'It's like having your own Subbuteo team, isn't it, Dad?' she said.

'Don't get too used to this, Katie,' I explained. 'This is the euphoria of the dreams of a new future but if we don't deliver the results this friendly atmosphere will change very quickly.' Football is not a sport so much as a religion and the affinity each fan feels for their local club is the reason that no other sport in the world can match it for passion. It is a national obsession, but also a local obsession, and this can produce some of the greatest and worst days of your life. All you can do is sit back and hope to enjoy.

Birmingham duly knocked us out of the cup, and in the programme for our league match against Crewe Alexandra three weeks later, I outlined a kind of mission statement for the fans. I told them that the financial bleeding, losses of £10,000 a week, had to stop. I committed the club to a community-based policy. Children under sixteen were to be able to buy a season ticket for ten pounds. We would campaign against drugs, crime and racism. We would not be buying big-name players in the transfer market or splashing out on overseas players. We would create a London club for Londoners, investing in a youth policy and developing our own players. Some of those ideals proved unrealistic.

If I had any illusions about the size of the task, they were soon dispelled. We lost that home match against Crewe 4–1, in front of 2,797 spectators.

Steve Dawson, who had been my right-hand man for ages, put it bluntly: 'Barry, you told me for years, don't ever buy a football club, it's a licence to lose money. The next thing, you say you've bought a club.'

Every week, I'd walk past Steve's office at Matchroom headquarters and he would call out, 'forty grand' or 'eighty grand' or 'sixty grand'. That was what we had lost that week. We had Leyton Orient for nineteen years. We made a small profit twice, broke even twice and did our bollocks for fifteen of those nineteen years.

I tried to treat Orient as a business and made sure I never lost more than I could afford. My rule was that it should never cost me more than £1m a year. But the truth is that it remained an affair of the heart, not the head. The board of directors and management, like me, were diehard Orient fans.

I loved the club and always wanted people who would be equally loyal to Orient, which was the key to the appointment of Matt Porter. When I first came across him, he was still at university in Norwich, writing reports of Orient matches for the *Waltham Forest Guardian* and *Hackney Gazette*. Soon after I took over as chairman, he applied for the job of press officer. I liked the look of him and could see he was Orient-mad and dead keen. 'Go and see Steve Dawson, our chief executive, and sort it out,' I said. That was the only job interview he ever had. Matt did so well that a few years later, when he was driving me over to a media conference, I asked him how he would feel about becoming chief executive himself. I needed Steve Dawson, my marvellous right-hand man, at the Matchroom head office. 'I'd be honoured,' Matt said, and thus he became the youngest chief executive in the Football League. He and I shared all the emotions, the disappointments and occasional triumphs over the years. A little later, I made him chief executive of the Professional Darts Corporation as well, and then a main board director of Matchroom. Matt, like Frank Smith in our boxing division, is a great example of the benefits of finding people with talent, giving them opportunity and a better life. My benefit was staff loyalty. Most of the key people at Matchroom have been with us for decades.

It was while I was wrestling with Leyton Orient that I came across Max Griggs, who was chairman of Dr Martens, the boot manufacturer. He turned out to be one of the most extraordinary people I have ever met, and I've met a few. The Dr Martens business had been handed down to him by his father. It was profitable but not huge, making air-cushion boots mostly for policemen and postmen, but when Naomi Campbell wore a pair at a catwalk event, they instantly became fashionable. Before long, Madonna, Elton John and the Pope, yes, His Holiness in the Vatican, were wearing them. Dr Martens took off, big-time.

Max Griggs died in July 2021, aged eighty-two. He was one of life's gentlemen and a homebird. Despite his wealth, his favourite night out was to take his wife in his Range Rover to a local fish-and-chip shop and to eat it with a flask of tea, sitting in a layby close to his house.

When I asked Max if he would like to become a shareholder in Leyton Orient, he looked at me in horror. And not for the usual reason. 'Goodness me, no,' he said. 'I'm from Rushden near Irthlingborough and I wouldn't invest in Northampton Town, which is only seven miles away.'

Instead, Max built up his local club, Rushden & Diamonds, as a hobby, with great success. He eventually sold it to the fans for a pound, but our business connection began when he had built a new stand and office complex at Nene Park, their stadium. Max said he wanted to make the club more famous, and I suggested he could sponsor Matchroom's Premier Snooker League, which was screened all over the world and would give him good value. He loved the idea, in part because he loved snooker. In fact, he was already sponsoring a young local lad, by putting a snooker table in his house as well as meeting some other expenses. That lad, Shaun Murphy, went on to be a world champion.

Max wanted Rushden & Diamonds to host the Premier Snooker League, with Dr Martens sponsoring it. He asked me to attend the next Dr Martens board meeting to convince his fellow directors. Naturally I did, but when I walked into the boardroom, I felt a wave of negativity coming across at me from a sea of gloomy faces. I pitched it as best I could but after twenty minutes explaining why snooker was a great investment for them, I hadn't even raised a smile. It was time to exit with honour.

'Gentlemen, I appreciate this is a big venture for you and no doubt you will want to consider it, so I look forward to hearing from you in due course.'

I thought this was my exit line. But as I stood up to go, Max Griggs, the chairman, said, 'Oh no, Barry we want to do this.'

Then the managing director spoke up: 'Mr Chairman, have we made up our minds on this?'

'Yes, we are going to do it,' Max replied. 'I like him, and he will do a good job for us.'

The board was clearly vexed that they had no part in the decision, but it had been made.

As I left, I turned to Max and said, 'Max, we haven't discussed money.'

'Well, what's fair?' he said.

'Well, I was going to ask for £500,000 a year but I will actually take £300,000 for the first year, then £350,000 and £400,000, for a three-year deal.'

'That's fine,' Max said. 'When do we pay this sponsorship?'

'Well, normally it's half on signing and half at the end of the sponsorship.'

'No, I'm awfully sorry, I can't do that.'

I began to worry that they had cash-flow problems, until Max explained: 'I don't like to owe people money, so I'd like to pay you all of it up front.'

I had never heard anyone suggest that and I accepted straight away. We had three years of sponsorship, but the board still showed no interest and when the time was up, I thanked Max Griggs for his support.

'Well, you know the directors never wanted to do it,' he said. 'But I have enjoyed it and thank you for providing it for Dr Martens. By the way, who is your next sponsor?'

'We don't have one,' I admitted. 'But I'm sure we'll get one shortly.'

'Well, let's do one more year to give you more time to find a replacement,' he said.

What a man. With someone like Max, you could shake his hand and take that handshake to the bank. He was so straight he couldn't walk round a corner.

In March 1999, when I was fifty years old and on top of the world, I had the shock I had been dreading for most of my life. It was five in the morning and I was in bed at Mascalls with Susan.

'Wake up, Susan.'

No response. 'Wake up, please.'

I had a terrible, bursting pain in my chest. I wasn't surprised because I had been waiting for this moment all my life. My father had died from heart disease in his mid-forties; his father and grandfather had also died young from the same condition. It seemed the male Hearns were not designed to last long.

'Please, call an ambulance.'

'Are you sure?'

'Yes. I can't breathe.'

'Why not give it ten minutes and see how it goes?'

'Just get me an ambulance.'

'I can't dial 999.'

'Why not?'

'It's just for emergencies.'

I cannot repeat the expletives with which I tried to get her to make the call, but she really couldn't and went to wake up Eddie, who dialled 999 and asked for an ambulance, thank heavens.

It came quickly and I was taken to Oldchurch Hospital, Romford, where I was put on medication, wired up to monitors and given an oxygen mask to breathe through. Word soon got round. The nurses were impressed when Steve Davis telephoned, and very impressed when Michael Flatley, the dancer who wanted to be a boxer, telephoned. But then, to their amusement or horror, Chris Eubank arrived in person, in full regalia: waistcoat, riding boots and jodhpurs, carrying a silver-topped cane and a gentleman's handbag by Louis Vuitton.

'Bazza, I thought you might appreciate some poetry,' he said, and began to recite verses from memory. Kipling, I think, and some other stuff. I let him go on for fifteen minutes before removing the oxygen mask.

'That's really kind, Chris. But I think I ought to get some rest now.' Chris left to spend a couple of hours on the children's ward, entertaining them with his thoughts – no media, just the actions of a good man.

My consultant, John Stephens, diagnosed a blockage in the main artery, arranged the surgery and talked me through the procedure, which took place at a private hospital in London. John instantly became a friend and is to this day. I was awake during the operation and watched on a monitor as a device was inserted into a blood vessel near my groin and manoeuvred towards my chest. It was fascinating, like watching a surgeon operating on someone else on TV. The surgeon was a boxing fan and he asked me for Naseem Hamed's autograph. I told him to concentrate on what he was doing.

'There's your problem,' he said, once he arrived up near the heart. He blew out the blockage with a blast of air and inserted a tube to strengthen the artery. The post-op advice was predictable: take it easy, no late nights, be careful with the booze, no smokes, diet, exercise. Fair enough, but there's a quality of life I refused to give up. I did not change my workload that much, or pass on full English breakfasts, lobster and chips. I took, and still take, medication to lower my cholesterol, including two aspirins a day. I jog on a machine and get in the gym most days. More than anything, the heart attack crystallised everything for me. I stopped getting uptight too often. I began to laugh rather than get angry. And when anyone invited me for a game of golf, my first reaction was to say, yes, lovely, instead of finding a reason not to. Turnberry? No problem. I'll get a flight. I did not know how long I would live, but I knew I would make the most of every minute. That attitude has stayed with me and will for the rest of my life.

After I got home from the hospital, I asked Eddie how he felt about it. Eddie didn't say he felt sorry for me or anything like that. He just said he had been worried he'd have to take over the business. In time, son, in time.

Twenty years later, on Sunday, 5 April 2020, I had another heart attack. This happened during the Covid-19 lockdown. Stuck at home, I was exercising in my gym every day rather than a few times a week. Bored, I did a two-and-a-half-hour session on the Saturday and must have overdone it. The next morning, I had chest pains and, on the advice of the marvellous John Stephens, on whom I can always rely, I went off to hospital. The surgeon at the Basildon Cardiac Centre put in two stents, gave me a clean bill of health and discharged me. It was almost routine. My lasting memory was an apple crumble and custard that was out of this world. After this episode, I began to think it might soon be time to step aside, that Eddie should take over as chairman of Matchroom, and I would be president.

It was not long after my first heart attack, around the turn of the Millennium, during the internet.com boom, that I was approached by some Americans who wanted to buy Matchroom Sport, the whole company. They were talking about a lot of money, far more than I thought the company was worth at the time and far more than I had seen in my life – in excess of £30m. And I would be kept on.

At that time, I knew that Susan really wanted to move houses because she had fallen in love with breeding and racing racehorses. We had eleven acres at Mascalls but she wanted to build a much bigger operation and we had been looking for somewhere more suitable for years.

At first, I kept the Americans' offer for Matchroom to myself, following my principle that I make the final call on anything business-related and on anything else Susan is the guv'nor. Then we were walking in the garden one evening and I asked Susan if her quest for a house with more land, stables and so on, might succeed if she had a bigger budget to play with. She said she did not want to spend more than the budget, which was £3–4m, and asked where I would get the extra money anyway.

I came clean and told Susan about the deal on the table from the .com youngsters in the States. She seemed very unimpressed with the amount of money involved.

'What about you?' Susan said. 'What would you do if you sold your business?'

'Well, I would have to stay on for three to five years as a consultant and management adviser.'

'How do you feel about that?'

'OK. The problem I have is I do not like these people. They are young and aggressive; they bang the table a lot; they shout and holler and they are probably going to drive me crazy. But it's a lot of money and if that's the price I have to pay to do the deal, then I am prepared to pay it.'

Then Susan, as usual, nailed the point. 'You've been successful. You've had some ups and downs, but our life is sweet now. How can you even think about doing business with anyone you don't like? Surely that's the independence you have worked for. Why throw it away for the sake of a few million pounds?'

The following week the two young guys I was dealing with were in the UK and I asked for a meeting. They came over.

'This deal is not going to happen,' I said.

They had done a good bit of due diligence and were sure the deal was in the bag, so my opening remark did not go down very well.

'Why? What do you mean?' they screamed. 'We've come all this way and done all the work and now you change your mind?'

'It's really straightforward, gentlemen,' I said. 'I do not like either of you.'

'What's liking us got to do with it? This is business, man. Liking us has nothing to do with the deal.'

'That's it, exactly. The fact that you can think like that is the reason I'm pulling out. Sorry, guys, this is not going to happen.'

They had never come across anything like it. It was the true beauty of being independent, of being able to tell the truth, no bullshit. A perfect example of my Principle Number Two: Tell the truth – it is easier than telling lies.

It was back to business, my business, and a surprise phone call from Naseem Hamed, the world featherweight champion. He wanted to discuss something with me and asked if we could get together, at the Dorchester Hotel.

There was some history to me and Naz, going back eight years to the time when he made his professional debut. His manager and trainer, Brendan Ingle, told me in 1992 that he had a precocious talent on his hands, the real deal, and wondered if he could be included on some of our shows. Naz duly appeared on 14 February 1992, vaulted the ropes as he made his ring entrance and easily dismantled one of our Matchroom fighters, Ricky Beard. Three more appearances and three stunning victories followed. All was going well, but Brendan Ingle then informed me he had done a deal with Mickey Duff and that Naz would henceforth be fighting for Duff and his partners in the Cartel. I was furious. Ingle had not told me he was unhappy with our arrangement, or that he was thinking of taking Naz elsewhere. I never forgave him and never spoke to him again.

The deal with Duff didn't last long and Frank Warren took over as Naz's promoter, taking him to European and World titles and stardom.

Eight years on, I went to meet Naz and his brothers at the Dorchester. Naz asked the first question: 'Would you like to promote me again?'

I told Naz that was just about the most exciting question I had been asked. I told him how much I admired him as a fighter and a showman. For me, it was also an opportunity to get back into big-time boxing, which I missed.

Naz explained that he wasn't getting the kind of money from Warren he felt he was entitled to, and that he was going to take over his own career. He wanted someone he knew could do a good job to promote him, but he didn't want to work for a promoter, he wanted a promoter to work for him. He suggested a fee of £100,000 for each fight. I would have to take care of the promotion and all the venue arrangements. Naz and his team would be responsible for the purses, TV contracts and sponsorship. For me, that was easy money, easy work and no risk. Done deal.

Naz's first fight under our banner was against Vuyani Bungu, a South African, on 11 March 2000, a sell-out at Olympia in Kensington. Bungu was a decent fighter but Naz destroyed him in round four with a devastating knockout. Naz was happy, I was happy, Naz made a fortune, I got paid and so the relationship seemed to be working well. Next up, in the States, Naz took on Augie Sanchez at Foxwoods Resort, Connecticut. Naz sparked him in four rounds for another devastating knockout.

By now the TV companies around the world were in love with Prince Naseem Hamed and he delivered some great ratings and started to make some serious money on both sides of the Atlantic. But the pressure was building for him to take on one of the greats rather than just keep knocking people out. The name that kept cropping up was Marco Antonio Barrera, a Mexican legend who had been in with everybody and was as tough as hell.

Unfortunately, Naz had such self-confidence, such belief in his ability to knock out anyone put in front of him, that he completely underestimated Barrera. I went to see Naz training in Palm Springs and was horrified that he spent more time talking about the sound system and the colour of the cloth on his pool table than getting down to serious sparring.

As ever, complacency is a killer; as far as Naz was concerned, as he told me on several occasions, all he had to do was just turn up and he would knock Barrera out. While Naz was idling around in Palm Springs, Barrera was up in the mountains running through the snow.

The bout took place at the MGM Grand, Las Vegas, on 7 April 2001. Naz vaulted into the ring and looked supremely confident but Barrera was a different class. He out-boxed Naz and won a clear points decision.

During the fight, I sat next to Naseem's dad, Sal Hamed, who had his prayer beads and was praying throughout the early rounds of the fight, in a language I didn't understand as they were a Yemeni family. At the end of round three, his dad turned to me.

'How are we doing?' he said.

'Just carry on praying,' I replied.

Naz never got over that loss. It shattered his confidence and once that confidence had gone he was never again going to be the same fighter. The bubble had burst.

Naz did come back for one more fight when he took on the European champion, Manuel Calvo, at the London Arena in May 2002. From the first bell, it was clear that the old Naz just wasn't there; no sharpness and no intent to go forward and finish off an inferior opponent. The crowd were brutal by the end of the fight. They were booing as Naz won a points decision. Naz was realistic enough to know that his career had been brought to a sudden conclusion.

One of the all-time great British fighters started with me and finished with me, but it was sad that it ended on a sour note. He was an amazing fighter and could punch harder than any featherweight I had seen, but of course the noble art is about more than just punch power.

Matchroom led the way during the poker boom and I admit I was hooked. Not quite the Cincinnati Kid, but I had my moments. Credit: Simon O'Connor

12

Tonight I Feel Unbeatable

With a new millennium on the horizon, I was running a football club as well as working in many other sports when I was seduced, big-time, by poker. It all started when I was in Atlantic City to watch Lennox Lewis defend his world heavyweight title against Andrew Golota. After the weigh-in, there was very little to do and I wandered around the boardwalk, popping into the odd casino just to while away the time; I ended up at Trump Casino, where I saw a queue of people. Being English and inquisitive, I asked one guy what he was queueing for. He said they were all registering for the poker tournament. I asked him what it entailed, and he said that about five hundred people were going to play; they would all put down $1,000 and the prize money would be $500,000. Here was a game where for once the prize money was put up by the players, not the promoters. I loved that idea.

Lewis made short work of Golota and I went straight back to the Trump Casino to see what all the fuss was about. I enlisted in the game without knowing the rules and sat there for about eight hours, learning, laughing, exploring, wondering. When I was back in England, I went straight to see Vic Wakeling at Sky and told him I had something new for him: the biggest poker event in the world. We could be the first people to go live with poker, as every other poker programme I had seen – and there weren't many – just showed recorded highlights. We could do something much more exciting, especially with a first prize of £1m.

My Life: Barry Hearn

Sky had a limited budget and I knew the costs, especially the prize money, would be huge, so at first the numbers did not add up. Eventually I came across Ian Payne, who was chief executive of the Reo Stakis Casino Group. They were keen to sponsor the event, but just when I thought the deal was in the bag, Reo Stakis were bought out by Ladbrokes. I thought that was another good idea gone to waste, but six months later Ian Payne rang me. He had been made managing director of Ladbrokes Casinos. Was I still interested? You bet. We agreed a sponsorship fee and when I was trying to think up some clever name for the event, Ian said keep it simple: it's poker, the first prize is a million, let's call it Poker Million.

Recruiting players was not as difficult as I anticipated. We managed to get 176 of the best players in the world signed up, and we charged a $10,000 entry fee. That paid for the first prize, but players did not like the idea of coming from all round the world with no prize money going beyond the winner. I thought I was going to have a rebellion or a boycott, so I phoned Ian and told him the situation. He asked what it would take to cure the problem. I said I needed another £250,000 sponsorship. He instantly made a gut decision. 'You've got it,' he said. 'Carry on and have a great event.'

Saved by one man's instinct and belief, and he did not regret it. Poker Million first took place on the Isle of Man and was an instant TV hit around the world. Within a few months of Poker Million airing on Sky in the UK, Fox Network around America and on other Murdoch channels around the globe, poker became hot. Within two years, Matchroom had become the largest poker producers in the world, establishing Premier League Poker, the World Poker Open, the UK Poker Open, Sports Stars Challenge Poker, and on and on. We had a queue of customers wanting to pay us to produce poker programmes and our in-house TV directors, led by my daughter Katie, had the best team of poker production staff in the world. Hundreds upon hundreds of hours of televised poker were produced and broadcast everywhere. On the back of that exposure, we helped to build any number of internet poker sites. Matchroom also had a joint venture with Ladbrokes for an online Poker Million as well as Party Poker and Poker Stars.

Everyone made a load of money. And now that I was providing Sky with pool, ten-pin bowling, fishing and poker, they really should have rolled out the red carpet on the frequent occasions I visited the Sky headquarters. They didn't, but they certainly paid me well.

This was the time when Katie really came into her own. She is quite different in character from Eddie, her brother. Katie is a worrier, a details person. She has the same work ethic as Eddie as well as the stroppiness of her mother. Once she has an idea in her head, it is very, very difficult to shift it. Katie's early life was all about studying and being smarter than everyone else. When she was a teenager, I made the rash promise that I would give her £500 for every A grade pass she had in her O levels. She came home with the results and announced that she had passed all thirteen that she had taken.

'How many As?' I enquired, a little anxiously.

'All of them.' That cost me £6,500. She went out and bought her first car.

Katie went on to Bournemouth University and was awarded first-class honours in marketing. She joined Sky Sports as a junior and after six years became the first female producer of Premiership football. She joined Matchroom in 2005. I always knew she would be successful, but her talents are quite different from mine and Eddie's. She is not into sales or business, but she is super-creative in TV production. Her TV direction of poker was astonishing. Poker is one of the most difficult sports to broadcast properly. You have to marry the play, from any number of cameras and angles, with all kinds of graphics and information, to make it intelligible. If you don't pull it together live, the edit can take months. Katie was so good at directing poker and adding the graphics at the same time that her live programme was almost ready for syndication as a highlights programme. I have never seen another TV poker director get anywhere near her standard. She did it with her special combination of hard work, command of factual detail and creativity. She also became a very capable, rock-solid, poker player.

I've always said I only promote sports I love, and I had fallen head over heels with poker. It started with that first game of Texas Hold'em No Limit in Atlantic City, when I made an idiot of myself but learned a lot. The mind games, the one-on-one challenges that keep coming up, appealed to me. There is also a percentage of luck involved, which was good for me because I could never match the very best players, the calculators, over time. Poker is about 80 per cent skill and the rest is luck. That suits a passionate player like me. I began to play every day, mostly online but also in tournaments. At least in tournaments I knew exactly what I was in for. Ten grand in the hole: I could afford to lose that. Or a hundred grand in the hole: that was as much as I ever lost, and it hurt. All right, it became a bit of an addiction, but I was having a ball.

The short TV formats we put on suited me. I badly wanted to play but I always asked permission because I was the promoter and realised it might look bad, especially if I won. I asked the sponsors of the European Open and they said it was fine, good publicity. I reached the final table, six players left. Channel 5, the broadcasters, were now worried. So were the sponsors. They said, you're not going to win, are you? I told them I would try my nuts off. I came second, won £100,000 and everyone was happy. That year, 2004, I made five final tables on TV. I came second, third, fifth, whatever, but never won one. It was good money, but I was gutted. I wanted a trophy.

I always wanted action and could be impulsive. Katie was much better, a proper player. She played in the World Series and for three days hardly played a hand. That's the patience and discipline the top players need. She was the highest-placed woman in a field of 9,000 players but slow-played aces and was beaten by a flush draw on the river. (That's poker talk.)

Whenever I went to Las Vegas I played, usually in cash games. I never had much success in tournaments over there until I played in the Bellagio Cup, when I concentrated and played a much more traditional style. It started at ten in the morning with 120 players. By three the next morning, there were just three players left on the final table, including me. I was quite happy to come third. I'd had some fun. Actually, I wasn't that happy. I knew the other two were professionals, both sponsored by the same poker company, Full Tilt. They were both wearing Full Tilt shirts, and I knew they were in league against me. It was their living, after all.

The first bloke went all in with his first bet, over $300,000, and the second bloke folded straight away. I had a king and a ten, different suits, not a great hand. The bloke who had gone all in was looking at me, quite aggressively.

'I must tell you a story,' I said.

'I don't want no fucking story,' he said. 'You fold or you call.'

'Excuse me, the cards are with me, it's my turn and I'm going to tell you a story. This is my favourite hand, and I'll tell you why. Three months ago, I was playing in the semi-finals of the UK Open . . .' (by now they were both going to sleep) '. . . against my son – it was on TV, so you can find it on YouTube – and I had this exact same hand. Well, he bet first and went all in, and he had ace-jack, which is probably what you've got, and I called him and the first three cards on the flop gave me the winning hand, so there's no way with this hand I should be calling you, but I'm going to, I'm all in.'

Would you believe it, he had ace-jack as predicted and the flop went ten, ten, three, so I won it with three tens.

'You motherfucker,' he said, 'there's no way you can call me with that hand.'

'Fuck off,' I said. 'That's my lucky hand. Do yourself a favour, don't slam the door on your way out.'

He got up and told his mate: 'Kill him.'

In the very next hand, with two of us left, the other fellow went all in. I looked at my cards: king, three, suited. Terrible hand.

'I've got to tell you,' I said, 'my name's Barry Hearn and I feel unbeatable tonight, even though you probably have a high pair.

You're going to be sick because I shouldn't be calling your bet but I'm going to call it. I don't think you can beat me, whatever you've got.'

I called him and he turned over a pair of jacks. On the flop, it looked bad for me until the fifth and final card brought another king and I won with a pair of kings.

He went ballistic. I just said: 'Welcome to poker.'

I had a trophy, and I have it now in my office, the only one I've ever won at poker.

Fortunately, I didn't get carried away by believing I could really succeed at the top level. I remember playing one match, England versus the Rest of the World, on the same table as Phil Ivey, one of the game's legends. I had the feeling he knew every card I had in my hand, which was very unsettling.

Before long, the game changed. Some very bright boys, many of them Scandinavian, came in, brilliant calculators; the tournaments were played over longer formats and the better players won more often. It was time to get out.

At one stage, poker contributed 40 per cent of Matchroom's pre-tax profits, but when online poker was banned in the United States, the bottom fell out of it. It came on the last sitting day of Congress in December 2006. There was a defence bill to make it illegal for foreign companies to buy US maritime ports and they tagged another bill on to it, which they can do, to make online poker illegal. It passed. Party Poker, for example, which had a market capital of about $5bn, dropped to $1bn overnight. That's a serious loss and while the game has recovered somewhat, it's a long way from its heyday. At Matchroom we may well get involved again, bringing back Premier League Poker, my favourite poker event of them all. Perhaps it's time to deal the cards again.

In 2004, after a search lasting eight years, Susan and I at last found the property for which she had yearned, one with enough land, 150 acres, to allow her to expand her stud farm. I remember the estate agent telling me as we drove to East Hanningfield, near Chelmsford, that the estate included a cricket ground and a fishing lake. Sold, sight unseen, as far as I was concerned, and it was perfect for Susan as well. The elegant house was much smaller than Mascalls but there was far more land for Susan's horses.

For over thirty years, Susan has been in love with horses and horse-breeding. She has worked tirelessly to master her science and craft and I'm sure she found it frustrating that it took her so long to become an overnight success, which is what happened, gloriously, in 2021.

She had some success on the way to her year of years. Red Carpet, for example, was fifth in the 2000 Guineas Stakes in 2001 and Urban Fox won the Group One Pretty Polly Stakes at the Curragh in 2018. But the highlight of her breeding activities was when she purchased a mare called Reckoning in 2014. She paid 160,000 guineas, which may not be a king's ransom in horse racing but was significant for her since she always likes to get value.

Well, value is what she got with Reckoning, as she has thrown winner after winner. Most notably, Subjectivist won the French St Leger, the Dubai Gold Cup and the Ascot Gold Cup. Reckoning also threw a horse called Sir Ron Priestley, which won two Group Two races in the same year as well as finishing third in the Group One Goodwood Cup. Alba Rose, the next baby in line, has already been placed in Group races and we are all waiting to see how World Without Love, a horse Susan has kept in training herself and is now with the renowned Mark Johnston yard, will fare.

Of course, it is all very well winning races with horses you have sold. You still want to create a successful business and in October 2021 Susan achieved that when she sold a colt from Reckoning sired by Roaring Lion to David Redvers Bloodstock for 450,000 guineas, comfortably beating her previous best, 160,000 guineas. That capped a magical year, and I could not have been prouder of her.

Susan, who has a strong sense of duty, also remains the family matriarch. When she was approaching seventy, it was suggested that instead of Susan cooking Sunday lunch for ten people each week, we should all take turns. No chance. Susan said that was her job.

Mascalls remains of huge, emotional importance to me. My children grew up there, my business developed there and today it is the head office of the Matchroom Group.

When we changed its use from a family home to an office, we had to get Brentwood Council to grant planning permission. They did me an enormous favour by granting it. I seem to remember telling them there would be about a dozen people working there. At the time that was accurate, but these days there are at least sixty.

I like to think Mascalls, as our working hub, has added some prestige as well as employment to our area, but more important than that is the atmosphere of the place. All I hear, all day long, is the sound of laughter. All I see is people smiling. We must be doing something right.

Mascalls sits on a bend at the top of a hill just outside Brentwood, Essex. It is an impressive building as you approach it and equally impressive as you enter through the great oak doors.

Come on in. Let me show you around. The area on the left inside the hall used to be my study when we lived here. As a kid, Eddie used to spend hours and hours in here, listening to me on the phone as I did deals with the likes of Don King and Bob Arum. Now it is home from home for Michelle Wassell, my long-standing, long-suffering, ever-dependable PA. Straight ahead is the lounge where we spent years as a family watching TV and socialising together. That lounge, which has a view over the back garden and beyond to the City of London, was my office for twenty years. I have now been kicked out because it has been taken over by the new guv'nor, Fast Car Eddie Hearn.

Needless to say, Eddie has put his own style and imprint on this part of the building. Over-flash, if you ask me. And if you turn left from the hall, down the corridor, the walls are festooned with pictures of the memorable moments from my forty-year career. But I have noticed recently that my pictures seem to be disappearing and are being replaced by pictures of Eddie and his career. Surely, that's a kind of constructive dismissal. I must speak to my lawyers. At the end of the corridor, you throw a little left to descend slightly into the ballroom where, in the olden days, they used to have tea parties and afternoon dancing. As one does . . .

Matchroom Multi Sport is now based in this room, with Emily Frazer and her team organising everything from *Fish'O'Mania* to the Weber Cup as well as dominating the world of nine-ball pool with the Mosconi Cup, the World Championships and the World Cup. It is always a hive of activity, one of my favourite rooms in the building.

If we go back to Eddie's office, the room to the right is what I call the posh dining room. As a family, we usually ate in the kitchen and the posh dining room was only used for the occasional (very occasional) dinner party and Christmas. Christmas was always a joy at Mascalls. Presents would be opened in the lounge and the turkey served in the posh dining room. That room did not get used more than six times a year, but that made it special.

The posh dining room is now my daughter Katie's office and the centre of Matchroom Media. There is great change afoot here, as Katie's department became a fully fledged company in its own right on 1 July 2021. What used to be a fairly simple production unit is now syndicating somewhere around 40,000 hours of TV programmes globally. Katie is a great mother to her twin boys Sam and George; she also has that Hearn trait of working hard, not leaving the desk until the task is finished.

Further along to the right, we come to the old housekeeper's quarters, which is now a fitness area, where fighters such as Anthony Joshua and Jim McDonnell have worked out, along with Orient players and many guests. These days, it's reserved for the grandchildren and staff to use. The indoor swimming pool is fabulous, the sauna great and the jacuzzi top drawer – what else could you want for an early-morning workout? We are a sports company, after all, and if you work for a sports company, you should live the life, keep yourself in shape. The gym and swimming pool are open to anyone who works at Matchroom whenever they wish.

Let's go upstairs. The first room on the left used to be Eddie's bedroom. Now it's the office inhabited by Steve Dawson, our chief executive. Steve has been my right hand now for thirty years-plus and I trust him implicitly. Further down the corridor, the room on the left was once the main bedroom, for me and Susan. That's where I had my first heart attack, but let's pass over that. At one stage it was the accounts department but now, with the huge expansion of darts, it has been taken over by the Professional Darts Council. Matt Porter runs that very well and his team are absolutely brilliant to a man and woman. Matt has come a long way since starting off as press officer at Leyton Orient. He is a now a Matchroom main board director, at the top of the tree.

Opposite the PDC is the accounts department, somehow crammed into what used to be Katie's bedroom. There are six people working in here, which is really far too many. As the business expands, it is only a matter of time before we are going to have to reshuffle the space. Further down the corridor we come to various meeting rooms, edit suites and TV offices.

Outside, the old stable block, for most of three centuries, was for horses, coaches, carts and, later, automobiles. It has had a lush transformation into Matchroom Boxing headquarters. Led by Eddie, the boxing department has a wealth of talent, including social media and digital staff, matchmakers, publicists and organisers. They report directly to Frank Smith, who is a success story in his own right, having joined us at sixteen years of age. He is in charge of the day-to-day running of Matchroom Boxing globally, and reports direct to Eddie. Ten years on, Frank is living proof that we seldom take on the finished article; we prefer to grow our own. Frank is also a main board director now, which is a hell of a compliment to a really capable young man.

The gardens stretch to about eleven acres, occupied by four alpacas and a couple of peacocks, which provide a touch of eccentricity and fun. Those exotic animals were birthday presents for me from the Matchroom staff. They clearly have a sense of black humour as well, because my 2020 present, after my second heart attack, was a defibrillator.

In the summer, our garden is a great place to relax or hold meetings and, just in case you need to impress someone, the helipad is there to fly in the wealthier guests. As a tight bastard, I do not own a helicopter. I would rather rent someone else's. As I've tried to instruct Eddie, when it comes to aircraft and boats, it's best not to buy but to rent.

The gardens hold lots of memories for me with the fun I had when the kids were growing up, bowling to Eddie as he learned to bat so well, watching Katie develop into such a wonderful human being. Where else could you sit on the balcony with a bottle of champagne and watch the most amazing firework displays all over London on New Year's Eve, and where else could you arrange birthday parties and celebrations on a scale beyond your wildest dreams for friends and family to enjoy your success? The best of all was my seventieth birthday extravaganza in June 2018. Principally organised by Eddie, Michelle, Emily Frazer and Katie, no expense was spared. Champagne all the way, every kind of cuisine and they even flew in Michael Buffer, the famous ring announcer, first class from Las Vegas, to make the announcements. No wonder that party put a dent in our profits for the year.

All in all, it makes Mascalls a special property, a happy and lucky house from the day I bought it in 1982. I'm honoured to own it.

Poker was a relatively brief but colourful and profitable excursion. Owning Orient was a long sentence, a heavy ball and chain, but I like to be positive so let's concentrate on my happier times as a football chairman. Two games stand out, and to such an extent that they are both included in my Top Ten Sporting Moments, which you'll find towards the end of this book. The first was played at Oxford's Kassam Stadium at the conclusion of the 2005/06 season. Martin Ling, our first-rate manager, had assembled a squad of triers, a real team who worked for the collective cause to a man. We needed to win to be sure of automatic promotion to League One (which was the same division, after a name change, that we'd been relegated from just after I became chairman). If we drew or lost, and Grimsby won their final game, played simultaneously, they would be up and we would have to face the play-offs. It was a nail-biter, with all eyes on the pitch and most ears to the radio to hear what was happening at Grimsby. One moment we were up, the next we weren't, until, with seconds to go, Lee Steele scored, and the celebrations could begin.

That occasion took some beating, but perhaps it was surpassed by the FA Cup campaign of 2011. The FA Cup seems to have lost some of its glamour in recent years but, as an old-fashioned football fan, I love it. To my mind it is the most prestigious cup in the world and embodies everything that is right about sport — everyone has a chance and it's all about ability on the day.

Over the winter of 2010 we had a dream start with wins in the first and second rounds, highlighted by a match against non-league Droylsden where, in the second-round replay, we trailed 2–0 but managed to score six goals in extra time.

In the third round, when the top two divisions come into the draw, we were treated to a day at Norwich City, where the wonderful Delia Smith was chairman. The welcome we had, the hospitality, and the congratulations from the chairman herself when we had upset her club 1–0, were the warmest I ever received in football. It left a lasting memory and confirmed the importance of the FA Cup and the marvellous personality of Delia Smith. Great cook, too.

In the fourth round, we drew another useful team, Swansea City away. Somehow or other we beat them 2–1 and, as luck would have it, and I always think the draw for the FA Cup is the most exciting thing in football, we drew Arsenal, the Gunners, at home, with a sell-out guaranteed.

That match, on 20 February 2011, gave me one of the best moments of my life. The atmosphere was fantastic, but our intrepid team didn't really do anything dramatic and it was no surprise when Arsenal went one up. Fortunately, Arsène Wenger, the urbane Arsenal manager, was guilty of failing to observe one of my great principles in life. He allowed complacency, that deadly disease, to creep in. With his team leading away from home, he assumed they would win and move on to the next round. He had four or five of his best players on the bench but didn't want to risk them. He was sure he didn't need to. Fate, however, doesn't work like that and in the eighty-eighth minute Jonathan Téhoué, our French striker and super-sub, jinked his way through the Arsenal defenders and from the edge of the penalty area smashed the ball underneath the hapless Arsenal goalkeeper to equalise.

The place went mental and the front row of the directors' box was the most mental of all. Me and Susan, Eddie and Katie were all going crazy. We had two minutes plus injury time to hold on to give us a replay at the mighty Arsenal's home ground – and well over a million pounds in ticket income as well.

The tension was unbearable, and Eddie and I both lost it. Eddie kept shouting at the referee (using extremely abusive language) to blow his whistle. Susan turned to Eddie, her son, and said: 'Edward, stop that language, sit down and behave yourself.' Eddie did exactly as he was told.

When the final whistle blew, the place went crazy. We had earned ourselves a visit to the new Arsenal Emirates Stadium. A special bonus was the fact that Susan's dad, Fred, who was in his eighties, had been an Arsenal fan since he was seven. It was the treat of a lifetime for him to go to watch his second team, Leyton Orient, play his first love, Arsenal, and to watch it from the boardroom of the mighty Gunners.

The replay went much as expected – we got totally outplayed and lost 5–0. Still, our compensation was £1.4m, our share of the gate money. For the first time, we actually made a profit for the season. Fred, my father-in-law, also did rather well. I said to him that this will probably be the first and last time we will ever be here, so steal everything you want as a memento of the day. Anything with an Arsenal logo ended up in his pocket.

That was our longest run in the FA Cup since 1981/82, but we missed the League One play-offs by just one point. I was becoming disillusioned, mostly because I was putting money into the club month by month, but we did have one further exceptional season in 2013/14 when, through good management, we had put together a squad capable of promotion, with one of the smallest budgets in the league. We were so fortunate to have Russell Slade as our manager – he was without a doubt my best appointment.

Despite such wonderful, if sporadic, moments, I had come to the conclusion, confirmed by bitter experience, that there was no potential in football as a proper business. It used to be said that if you want to own a football club you have to be a millionaire. But in today's world you have to be a multimillionaire to have any chance and a billionaire to have a good chance of success. I decided during the season of 2013/14 that it was time to go. I wasn't prepared to put my personal wealth or my family's welfare at risk. I had set a limit of a loss of a million pounds a year and I was happy to cover that, but I knew it wasn't enough to achieve what I really wanted.

I began to look around to see if there was any chance of finding someone who would have the resources and desire to make the club successful. I had plenty of interest from people with no money, the fur-coat-but-no-knickers brigade. Football is awash with such people. Then along came a very strange individual – Francesco Becchetti. His interest emerged through a variety of people who claimed to represent him. Becchetti was an Italian businessman, supposedly a billionaire who had made his money in waste disposal, largely in Albania. Make of that what you will, but it was surprising that this rather flamboyant character brought his mother to every meeting of significance. She was clearly the boss, although I never heard her say a word. Eventually, Becchetti came up with the deal I wanted and convinced me he was going to put in as much money as was necessary to take the club to the next level.

To sell or not to sell was a big decision and that meant it would be made by our family as a whole, and over Sunday lunch. Susan cooked, of course, and when we sat down I announced that I had found a buyer for the club who would take over all the aggravation, but I wanted to know what everyone else felt about it. Eddie said it was always a great day out when the club won and, although it was costing us money, we were doing OK, so let's keep it. But the vote went against him and I must admit that after nineteen years I had had enough.

The final deal for the sale of Leyton Orient was for £4m plus bonuses if we were promoted to the Championship and the Premier League during the following five years. I retained ownership of the ground and entered into a rental agreement with the club so that the ground was safe and no one could develop it. This was the security I wanted to deliver to the Orient fans.

I paid the club approximately £7m for the ground and leased it back to them on a twenty-year lease with a twenty-year extension. The rent was reasonable, around £180,000 per year.

Negotiations for the sale were difficult because Becchetti was a very loud, aggressive person who was clearly used to getting what he wanted. There were times when he was so annoying, I could have whacked him, but every time I got upset, I had my right-hand man, Steve Dawson, next to me quietly saying, 'This is your exit chance, don't mess it up.' I bit my tongue several times and we signed the deal, but the most important thing was that Becchetti promised to put in as much money as was necessary to achieve the dreams of all Orient fans, and to be fair to him that is what he did.

The deal with Becchetti was done during the 2013/14 season and we were playing really well, eventually finishing third in League One, securing a place in the play-offs. The day we defeated Peterborough United in the play-offs semi-final at Orient was another great day with a huge crowd, great atmosphere and one of the best matches I have seen. It took us into the final at Wembley and I thought this could be the dream exit for me.

It wasn't to be. We lost in the final to Rotherham United via a penalty shoot-out having led 2–0 at half-time. I remember the Rotherham chairman coming up to me at half-time saying, 'You are a far better team, you deserve to win.' I told him to keep his opinions to himself since we were only halfway. How right I was. They equalised with two goals from a former Leyton Orient striker, Alex Revell, and won the shoot-out. When he went up to receive his medal, Alex, a good lad, shook my hand and said sorry. I told him not to be silly. He was just doing his job.

It wasn't our day and I sat there suffering one of the worst disappointments of my sporting life. I would have loved to have gone out on a high, having delivered the fans one season at least of Championship football on the smallest budget ever seen in League One.

Over the next few seasons, Becchetti pumped in around £15m and the club had the biggest wage bill in the division. Unfortunately, he knew next to nothing about football. All he achieved was two relegations in three seasons, out of the Football League and down into the National League. It was heart-breaking for the fans and very disappointing for me after nineteen years building a stable and sustainable club.

Fortunately, Orient subsequently attracted the attention of Kent Teague, a Dallas-based ex-Microsoft businessman, and my friend Nigel Travis, the former president of Dunkin' Donuts and a lifelong Orient fan. They bought out Becchetti, invested substantially, and have turned the club around. They have the passion I had at the beginning and I only hope they last nineteen years like I did. They achieved promotion back into League Two in 2017/18 and I was as happy for them as I was for the fans. Anybody who runs and owns a lower-league club deserves appreciation. I just hope that after the Becchetti debacle the Orient fans appreciate what they had with me and what they now have with the Teague/Travis management. A proper football club for proper people – that in my heart is where Orient should always remain.

When I sold the club to Becchetti, I was offered the position of honorary president for life, an acknowledgment of the nineteen years' work I had put in. I also insisted on having a table for ten in the directors' room for every game for the rest of my life. However, I became so disillusioned with Becchetti's antics, not to mention the two relegations, that I resigned as honorary president. Once he had gone, the new owners offered to reinstate me, and I gratefully accepted. I have no power at all (or aggravation), but it maintains my ties with the club I love.

It was the romantic in me that wanted Leyton Orient to be a club entirely made up of local players. I remember when Tommy Taylor was our manager, he desperately wanted to sign a player from Northern Ireland and, knowing my attitude, he asked me if I thought Northern Ireland was local as it was part of the United Kingdom. I said, 'Tommy, as far as I'm concerned, south London is foreign.'

Of course, we had to move on and inhabit the real world and eventually we had players from all over Europe and beyond, including some great stars, two of whom I shall always remember because we sold them for a lot of money.

First, a central defender called Gabriel Zakuani from the Democratic Republic of the Congo. When Fulham wanted to sign him, they offered £500,000. Steve Dawson wanted to take it as we needed the money, but I felt their interest was keen and told him it was £1m or no deal, and they actually paid. Gaby was a wonderful player and a lovely young man who went on to have a decent professional career, although he only played once for Fulham before they got rid of him. But he went on to play five hundred times for ten different clubs, as well as winning twenty-nine caps for his country. I see him from time to time and I'm happy he has made such a success of his life.

The other great player we had was an outstanding right-winger called Moses Odubajo, who attracted a lot of interest from

Brentford and went for £1m as well. Moses had a decent career, at Sheffield Wednesday and elsewhere, but has been plagued by injuries. However, he is a quality player and still trying. I expect him to come back. Needless to say, when we sold those star players the fans went crazy, but you can never hold sportsmen back in their lives. If they want to move, your job is to get the most money for them. We did in both cases, but unfortunately these were rare instances of financial success in a business that is always condemned to financial failure.

Now that I am out of football, my reflections on the future of the game are not optimistic. There is a disaster waiting to happen and maybe the coronavirus epidemic will begin a rethink of how football is run in this country.

Lower-league clubs will struggle to survive and, to repeat, clubs don't just need benefactors to keep them going, they need multimillionaires. Being chairman of Leyton Orient gave me moments I will never forget, but it was a balancing act between my wallet and my heart all the way and in the end the wallet had to win.

The fundamental problem is that Premier League clubs waste a huge amount of money in their race for success, but don't contribute anywhere near enough money to the grassroots of the game. They make token payments, which is quite clever, and I'm not surprised they're clever because for many years they were effectively run by Richard Scudamore, their chief executive. When I was a director of the Football League, Richard was our chief executive and I recognised his talent straight away. It was no surprise to me that he was head-hunted by the Premier League, which was their gain and the Football League's loss.

Richard knew it was good policy to throw a few million quid at lower-league clubs because it looked as if the Premier League cared about grassroots football, when of course they don't. They just want to buy up the talent that comes through lower leagues.

The Premier League has been an amazing commercial success but somewhere, somehow, someone should have reduced their power to ensure that a good bit of their excess was distributed to lower-league football. It's all very well creating a wonderful flower, but you mustn't forget to maintain the roots, or the flower will die. Until the government takes more control, the Premier League will remain a money-making machine that overpays players and neglects the long-term future. The coronavirus pandemic may well change that attitude when Premier League clubs realise they have not created sufficient reserves within their businesses to guarantee even their own future, let alone help the game. I just hope that message gets across to the government and that they make sure the beautiful game is maintained for the benefit of all of us.

That lesson was dramatically illustrated by the fiasco of the European Super League, when twelve leading clubs from Europe, including six from England, announced unilaterally in April 2021 that they would form their own league, which would involve twenty clubs, all guaranteed to remain in the league, even if they came bottom. It was a closed shop, and it was immediately opposed by fans, administrators and the government.

Clearly, the owners of those clubs had failed to realise that however rich you might be, you do not really own a football club. You are the custodian. The six English clubs swiftly withdrew in the face of such opposition and the proposal collapsed. The spectre of such a league remains and will do until the government grasps the nettle and exerts proper governance of the national game, once and for all.

Back in July 2005, I was sitting in bed in a hotel in Taiwan when I turned on CNN and saw a crowd of kids waving union jacks and celebrating the fact that London had just won the Olympic bid. What's more, these kids were standing in front of Leyton Orient's football stadium, less than half a mile away from the proposed Olympic Park. I was amazed, because like most people, including the Labour government, I thought Paris was bound to win the bid. Nothing like enough work had been put into the planning and logistics of putting on an Olympic Games in London and creating a lasting legacy. And, as many previous host cities had discovered, lack of vision and organisation leads to a complete waste of infrastructure, at huge cost to the taxpayer.

As soon as the celebrations died away, it should have been obvious that with just seven years to prepare, it was a matter of real urgency. In my view, neither Ken Livingstone, the Mayor of London, nor Tessa Jowell, the Minister for the Olympics, approached the challenge in a realistic way. Early budgets suggested that two or three billion pounds would be required. In the end, it cost sixteen billion. But the biggest scandal was not the ineptitude of politicians, or their lack of logistical planning, or the buildings they constructed. The big issue for me was the future of the Olympic Stadium itself.

When the plans started to come together, Livingstone and Jowell favoured the concept of constructing the stadium like a Meccano kit. The lower part of the bowl was to be fully operational and permanent with seats and full facilities, but the upper seating areas would be temporary, easy to dismantle, with no toilets, food outlets or hospitality boxes. The plan from day one was that as soon as the Games were over they would strip out all the additional seats to be left with a 20,000-seater stadium.

It was cost-efficient and made some sense, but they then made an enormous error by listening to Sebastian Coe, the chairman of the Olympic Organising Committee, and accepting his argument that whatever other uses were envisaged, the stadium should remain a large-capacity venue for athletics. Of course, athletics was a major part of the Olympics, but the idea of a football pitch inside an athletics track is anathema to me and all football fans, a real no-go area. There is no atmosphere, any feeling of close contact with your heroes is destroyed, and the layout has never worked anywhere in the world.

Originally, Livingstone and Jowell wanted the local club, Leyton Orient, to have occupancy. That, for them, would constitute the most suitable legacy. I was more than happy for Orient to move into the Olympic Stadium as a 20,000-capacity arena. But once they decided the athletics track had to stay, I lost enthusiasm because it would have killed football at Leyton Orient. I told Livingstone that as much as I wanted the Olympic Stadium for my club, I could not possibly consider it with an athletics track separating the fans and the pitch.

From then on in, it was a series of disasters and a succession of different politicians making equally poor decisions. Finally, it ended on the desk of Livingstone's successor as Mayor of London, Boris Johnson. It was soon clear to me that this was a problem he wanted to get off his desk as quickly as possible.

The Olympic Park Legacy Company, which was charged with sorting it all out, decided that to maximise their financial return they should do a deal with the nearest Premier League football club, West Ham. I had no objection to West Ham being involved, as long as we could share the ground as a community asset. It should have been easy to achieve the right deal: Leyton Orient would play in the Olympic Stadium in front of 10,000 fans, with every chance to progress, and West Ham would be the principal tenant, with much larger crowds and exploiting most of the commercial opportunities.

But West Ham, in particular their chief executive, Karren Brady, had other ideas. They wanted the stadium exclusively for themselves. And although they were only going to be able to rent the stadium, they wanted to give the impression of sole ownership.

For two or three years, we were in and out of the High Court trying to block West Ham's move, initially as the purchaser of the Olympic Stadium (which we succeeded in blocking) and then as the leaseholder.

The contest involving Brady and the bureaucrats and civil servants was a mismatch. She tied them in knots, threatened them, screamed at them and got her own way on just about everything. The final deal was a disgrace and should never have been sanctioned. Put simply, West Ham were allowed to sell their own ground to developers and keep the proceeds. In return for a 99-year lease, they contributed £15m towards the cost of the stadium but by that time the cost of the stadium plus the conversion was probably in excess of £700m. They were charged £2.5m per year as rental but the Olympic Park Legacy Company was responsible for all stewarding, policing and pitch upkeep, so that West Ham were effectively given a free rental.

It was the deal of the century and, as I said at the time, my dog could have struck a better one in the public interest. I told Boris Johnson to his face that it was a terrible deal for the UK taxpayer and that he and his representatives had been out-manoeuvred and out-negotiated at every turn.

I explained that they really had West Ham where they wanted them because West Ham were desperate to leave Upton Park, which was falling to bits. And of course, they were being offered one of the great postal addresses ever for a football club – the Olympic Stadium. I even begged Boris to let me do the job for free, to negotiate a better deal, but nothing doing.

We tried everything we could to block West Ham but eventually we failed. It cost me over a million pounds in legal fees, but I did not feel bad about finally losing out as I had given it my best shot and I was running out of support. Initially, Tottenham Hotspur were on our side. Their chairman, Daniel Levy, had been interested in moving his club to the Olympic Stadium and was incensed that West Ham were effectively getting state sponsorship by being offered an uncommercial deal for a taxpayer asset. But he, too, eventually had had enough and concentrated on building the new Tottenham stadium, which is first class.

Time will tell, but every time I read anything about the London Stadium I know I was right. The operators of the stadium were soon in financial trouble because an arrangement that so favoured the tenant, West Ham, was untenable. The athletics track is still there but is now covered by an inane seating configuration that takes days to install and costs millions to maintain, all for the sake of an athletics track that even British Athletics did not want because there is no demand for more than one or two meetings a year. It is not commercially viable. Sebastian Coe got his athletics track but it is not part of the legacy for which he will want to be remembered. It would have been so much better, and cheaper, for athletics to stay at Crystal Palace, with a refurbished stadium.

The battle against West Ham even extended to the House of Lords, which held a select committee inquiry on Olympic and Paralympic legacy. Karren Brady, for West Ham, stonewalled every time she was asked an awkward question. 'That is confidential, and I cannot answer,' she said repeatedly. Unfortunately, the committee had no power to demand a full and open answer.

My own performance in front of the committee in the House of Lords on 24 July 2013 was, if I say so myself, rather brilliant. From time to time, I have wished my dear mum was still around to see that her efforts to make sure her son made something of himself had not been in vain. I'm sure she would have been proud on this occasion, one of my finest hours.

Baroness Billingham was one of my toughest questioners and we had the following exchange:

Baroness Billingham: I do not understand why you are so determined that you cannot view football across an athletics track. I have viewed football all over Europe and other parts of the world which does just that . . . If you were able to compromise, there would be a saving to the taxpayer and perhaps the release of funds to other sports that are not as wealthy or as popular as yours. May I remind you that we are told that we have the task of the legacy of producing a new sporting nation? Now you are taking a very large portion of that cake.

Me: Before you kill me, I am the largest sports promoter in the world. I promote eleven different sports to a global audience of billions of people every day of my life. I care very passionately about sport. I care very passionately about football. The evidence is that everybody agrees with me that you cannot have football and athletics in one stadium. I am sorry, but you are very much in the minority.

Baroness Billingham: I am asking the question.

Me: The answer is that you cannot play football with atmosphere with fifty metres of athletics track between the front row of the seats and the start of the playing surface. They do it in Europe and it is an abysmal failure. The whole ethos of how football has been built into the national game is that it has been built around accessibility – to all ages, all sexes and all creeds – and the responsibility of people to put on an entertaining show that will provide atmosphere. The fact is that not just I, but obviously West Ham, and now even the LLDC, have finally agreed that this was a colossal mistake, and it was not a question of compromise. I am not good at compromise. I am good at getting things right. That is what I try to do. I do not live in a world of compromise. Compromise, to me, is a completely alien thought . . . We are really excited, because we come from the East End of London, which probably has not had any money spent on it since the Great War. Suddenly, we have these magnificent facilities, and we want to be part of it. I am afraid I disagree with you. When you make mistakes in life, you have to bite the bullet.

It was a long session and I allowed myself a somewhat cheeky farewell to their lordships: 'Thank you for putting up with me. I do appreciate it; thank you. You have been a very good crowd.'

Despite everything, I bear no malice towards West Ham. They should never have been allowed to get away with that deal, but you cannot fault their officials for getting it. For a minimal spend, they elevated the value of their club by several hundred million pounds. There are few people in this world smarter than their chairman David Sullivan, and the late David Gold, the joint-chairman, was no slouch either. It was a major 'touch', and good luck to them. They fought their corner and won. But it was hardly a fair fight.

Successive governments have talked about 'community value' and 'levelling up the country' but this was another case of talking the talk but not walking the walk. The Olympic Stadium could have been a national asset, giving something back to the community. Alas, it was far easier just to hand it over to a large, established commercial entity.

In 2021, West Ham announced the sale of 27 per cent of the club to a Czech billionaire, Daniel Kretinsky, for around £180m, thus valuing West Ham at some £700m. Some way above the less than £100m Gold and Sullivan reportedly paid for West Ham. Job done. A huge part of this valuation is surely attributable to the acquisition of the London Stadium, as I predicted to the House of Lords select committee, and in person to Boris Johnson. Part of me wants to congratulate the shrewd David Sullivan, David Gold and Karren Brady; another part of me thinks that all of us, as taxpayers, have been royally ripped off.

One of the great pleasures of my return as snooker's supremo was admiring the greatest of them all, Ronnie O'Sullivan. Credit: Benjamin Mole

13

The Empty Chair

After the banking crisis in 2008, times were tough commercially. But darts was thriving. Since I had taken over as chairman of the Professional Darts Council, prize money had grown from £500,000 to £5m in seven years. All the top players were making a good living and every player had the opportunity to transform his life, as long as he was good enough.

Snooker, in sharp contrast, was dying. It was moribund, a cosy club, a part-time sport dependent on its contract with the BBC to televise the World Championship. It was really a closed shop in which the leading players, who were guaranteed a certain amount of money and ranking points, held all the advantages. Since the heyday of world snooker, the number of notable tournaments had been reduced to five or six, so few that lower-ranked players had next to no chance of making a living or rising to the top.

In 2009, I had a phone call from Pat Mooney, the manager of John Higgins, the reigning world champion, with a follow-up call from Brandon Parker, who managed several top players. Their message was simple: would I consider coming back into the sport as chairman of World Snooker? Would the poacher turn gamekeeper?

I had enough on my plate and I knew I was not exactly the most popular person among the old guard of the sport's governing body, the World Professional Billiards and Snooker Association. Steve Davis warned me. 'What on earth are you thinking of, getting involved?' he said. 'Do you really need all this aggravation in your life?'

But as Mickey Duff, the old boxing promoter, once said, 'Making money is great, but getting even is better,' and the idea of achieving both was attractive. I knew there was a job to be done and I owed snooker an enormous debt. It had changed my life. I wanted to show everyone how promoting a sport should be done and put an end to the mismanagement that had blighted the sport for many years.

I let it be known that if the players, who had been loud in their criticisms of the board, but very quiet in doing anything about it, voted out the incumbent chairman, Sir Rodney Walker, I would consider stepping in on a short-term basis, and that I would prepare a report to show the way forward and to re-establish snooker as a major global sport. I was determined that there would be many more tournaments, all around the world. To my surprise, the players voted out Walker and three months later I had studied the books, consulted widely and produced a thirteen-page report for the membership. The final line of the report was somewhat brazen: 'Finally, gentlemen, I think I should take over the entire sport.'

With the backing of Pat Mooney, Brandon Parker and several of the top players, I put together a proposal by which I would take control for the princely sum of one pound, guaranteeing to immediately increase annual prize money from £3.5m to £4.5m and to increase it by at least 5 per cent each year. Any surplus would be carried forward into a 'surplus pot' to be used in case of unforeseen circumstances. If I failed to achieve the 5 per cent, the entire company, World Snooker Tour Ltd, would be handed back to the players.

The key meeting at which the players were to accept or reject my plan was set for June 2010. Each of the top sixty-four players in the rankings had a vote and only a simple majority was required. All was set fair until a couple of weeks before the vote, when it became clear that a company called 110Sports, run by a father and son, Ian and Lee Doyle, was lobbying feverishly behind the scenes to scupper my plans.

I had known Ian Doyle, a dour Scotsman, for many years. He was the manager of Stephen Hendry, who had taken over from Steve Davis as the world's best player and inflicted many wounds on my champion. Doyle enjoyed the limelight, but he lacked charm and humour. I once told him that life must be frustrating for him because he was not, and never would be, Barry Hearn.

The Doyles, father and son, were mortified at the thought that I might take over the sport. Eight years earlier, they had tried to do the same themselves when they teamed up with the Altium Group, a venture capitalist company led by a former Olympic shooter, John Davison. Now they tried to revive their earlier bid and Davison offered more money than I did and even said that his bid could be divided between the top sixteen players as a signing-on fee. I regarded that as a blatant bribe.

I decided to assess the enemy camp and invited Davison to have breakfast with me at Simpson's in the Strand. He turned out to be a thoroughly decent fellow and I suggested he should withdraw his offer and in return I would give him 16 per cent of the company and a seat on the board. He turned it down on the Doyles' advice and we were back to lobbying the players, trying to secure proxy votes from those who would not be attending in person. Brandon Parker lobbied stalwartly on my behalf, but the Doyles had a dozen or so players under management contracts, so they had a clear advantage.

I thought it would be a good idea, a last chance maybe, to have a presidential-style debate in which Davison and I would address the players at the critical meeting. On the eve of the Extraordinary General Meeting in Sheffield, I was astonished to hear that Davison would not be appearing. My understanding is that he was warned by the Doyles that I would slaughter him in debate. They also believed they had secured enough votes to win anyway. And here, yet again, one of my lessons in life kicked in: complacency is a killer.

My speech to the assembled players was short. 'Gentlemen, you see before you on the podium two chairs. One of these chairs is occupied by me, a passionate snooker fan and someone who has been involved in the sport for the past thirty years. You know me. I am a hard-headed businessman and I have a plan to take this game to new heights. The other seat is empty, which I personally find disrespectful to you. You have spent money on airline tickets, train tickets or petrol to get here to listen to my opponent give his version of the snooker plan going forward. If that's the type of person you want running this game, then I leave it to you and your judgement.'

Four or five players changed their minds, and I won the vote by thirty-five votes to twenty-nine. Commercially, this was one of the great days of my life. I had acquired control of World Snooker and its commercial assets in perpetuity, for one pound. Steve Dawson and I enjoyed a few bottles of champagne on the train back to London.

When we finished all the negotiations, there was an ownership split of 51 per cent for Matchroom Sport, 5 per cent for Steve Dawson (who would be chief executive of World Snooker), 5 per cent for my son Eddie, 13 per cent for Brandon Parker and 26 per cent for the WPBSA to make sure the players' interests were always represented and considered. Over time, those shareholdings changed. Today, Matchroom owns 74 per cent and the WPBSA, the players' association, retains 26 per cent.

Jason Ferguson, the chairman of the WPBSA, has been a huge asset to snooker. As a former player, he brings a deep passion to the game and has worked tirelessly from 2010 to promote snooker globally, establishing academies and organising training sessions for players and referees all over the world. An amazing job and an amazing guy.

I believe I have delivered. After ten years of my stewardship, the snooker tour pre-Covid comprised twenty-six tournaments played in eleven countries, with prize money of £15m a year. As with darts, the number of players able to make a substantial living has increased enormously. The Covid-19 pandemic had damaging effects, just as it had for every sport, but this was where our idea of a surplus pot proved invaluable. By then it stood in excess of £45m. As they say in *The A Team*: 'Don't you love it when a plan comes together!'

My first major problem when I bought snooker was an inquiry involving John Higgins, who had been filmed in a clandestine meeting with some Eastern European potential sponsors who suggested he might like to throw the odd match. The videotape was very damaging and once it had been made public I phoned up Higgins. He assured me it had been taken out of context, but I had to tell him: 'This video does not look good, John.'

That was probably the understatement of all time, for it did look as if he was agreeing to take a dive. But the truth was that these potential sponsors were asking John to give local players a few frames so that they wouldn't be humiliated in front of their own fans. John served a sentence of suspension for failure to report an approach, not for any match-fixing. I take the view that he was trying to encourage local sponsorships rather than being crooked. In fact, the matches never took place, so no serious offence was committed.

After that affair, and mindful that sports such as snooker, which are so reliant on bookmakers' sponsorship, need to be whiter than white, I decided to set up an integrity unit. I was introduced to Lord John Stevens, who had been Commissioner of the Metropolitan Police for many years. Lord John is a real down-to-earth man who has wrestled with a whole range of criminal activities. When he left the Met he set up his own integrity-based independent company, Quest International, mostly working for sporting bodies in the Middle East. I explained the situation we had in snooker and Lord John was instrumental in setting up our integrity unit, appointing a chief integrity officer and making sure we did everything in our power to keep snooker a clean sport. In the early days, several players who flouted the rules were caught and banned.

It has been a tough task, but integrity comes above anything else because if you take away integrity from sport then effectively you have no sport. If customers do not believe they are watching real sport, they will turn off. If sponsors feel there is any smell of foul play, they will exit the sport immediately.

Today, we have an excellent integrity officer, Nigel Mawer, whose team monitors every match in our snooker and darts operations. We now have two of the cleanest sports in the world, a view endorsed by the UK Gambling Commission, which described our integrity unit as 'the envy of any sport in this country'.

Unfortunately, Pat Mooney, who had set the ball rolling by suggesting I should take over snooker, became embroiled in the Higgins scandal. The tribunal heard evidence of malpractice and he received a lifetime ban from the sport. I was not party to that legal process so I cannot comment on the details, but I do know that I owe Pat a great deal for his original support.

The demise of 110Sport has been well publicised. They lost their players and their business and no longer have any serious involvement in snooker. That was a shame, because there had been a time when Ian Doyle contributed positively to the growth of the game.

Sadly, Brandon Parker, a tough-talking Mancunian who always said it as it was and who remained a loyal servant to the game and a personal friend, lost his fight against cancer. He died in 2020, fondly remembered.

After a decade of effort from Matchroom, from Jason Ferguson and from the players themselves, who have delivered the highest standard of sporting entertainment, the game has flourished as never before. Support from the BBC and ITV in Britain and from CCTV, the national broadcaster in China, has been critical, but a special mention must be made for Eurosport, who took a chance on snooker with a ten-year deal that has been amazingly successful, spreading the game throughout Europe, East and West. The World Championship has achieved a global audience in excess of half a billion viewers.

The acquisition of World Snooker at that EGM in June 2010 must be placed among the major commercial moments in my life. The others were the acquisition of Lucania Temperance Billiard Halls in November 1974 and of the Professional Darts Corporation in July 2001. Three stepping-stones that helped to transform a one-man band underneath a billiard hall into one of the largest sports promotion companies in the world.

Adrenalin rush: Anthony Joshua regains his world heavyweight
crown by winning his rematch with Andy Ruiz Jnr in
Saudi Arabia. Credit: Mark Robinson

14

I Want 1 Per Cent of Your Adrenalin

Like me, Eddie loved boxing. We sent him to Brentwood, the public school, as a day boy. After school, he liked to take the bus to Romford and go to the Matchroom gym, operated by Freddie King, to watch the professional fighters train. He joined Billericay Amateur Boxing Club, had three fights and won them all. In the first one, he was introduced to the crowd as Eddie Hills. He was devastated and only found out later that the name change was my idea. If they had known who he really was, they might have taken liberties. Eddie won all three fights as Eddie Hills, but when he was sixteen or seventeen, he came home and said he thought he would pack it in. I asked him why. He said he had sparred with some Travellers and realised he would never be as tough as them.

When Eddie was sixteen and I was forty-seven, I decided the time had come to see if he was made of the right stuff. I was always going to test him out when he was eighteen, to see what a rich kid was like as opposed to a poor kid. But he had grown so big – six feet-plus and hefty – that I thought, *Let's do it now*. We put on gloves and headguards and climbed into the ring. My aim was to knock him out.

That would not have gone down too well at home because Susan went potty when she heard about my plan. 'If you hurt my son, don't bother coming back to the house,' she said.

In the first round, Eddie charged at me and I caught him with a heavy shot. I could feel the force going right up my arm as it landed. But he didn't fall over. In the second round, he dropped me twice with body shots and that was the end of it. I was pleased as punch. I knew my boy was a proper man.

Back home, Susan had only one concern: 'Did you hurt him?'

'No,' I said. 'And this won't be discussed again.' I've never put on boxing gloves since and nor will I, ever.

When Eddie was politely asked to leave Brentwood public school, he decided to continue his education at the local technical college. His mother was heartbroken that her little boy had left such a prestigious establishment for what appeared a poor replacement in his further education. She was actually quite wrong. Going to technical college gave Eddie the chance to see life as it really is and not in the protected environment of a public school. A lot of the kids at the college were 'messers' who didn't want to be there in the first place and I think he realised this was his opportunity to either improve or just be consigned to the scrapheap. Eddie always had an eye on how to make a pound note. When we were doing the boxing shows in the early days, he and his friends would sell programmes, and although they did well, I can never remember getting back any of their proceeds. During the evenings, he used to cold-canvass as a double-glazing salesman, which is probably the best experience you could ever get at dealing with rejection and thinking on your feet, desperately trying to get that one interview for which you got a few quid.

Eddie wasn't slow in thinking about making money and once he had finished from the technical college he went to work for a sports management company in the West End, representing golfers on the professional tours. A few years later, in 2004, he came to work for Matchroom and I gave him the golf and poker to look after. He was very successful, but there may have been some passion missing.

One day, Eddie said, 'Dad, I've got to do the boxing.' I told Susan and she said, 'Over my dead body.' She knew what aggravation I had gone through in the world of professional boxing, and she knew I had only been able to handle it because of where I had come from. She was fearful for her darling son.

Susan is the only person in this world who can really strike fear in me, but on this very rare occasion she did not get her way. Eddie took over the boxing and has proved to be a fantastic promoter, much better than me in fact. He soon became the main man at Matchroom Boxing, signing up established fighters, including Carl Froch and Kell Brook, both champions, and most of the country's best prospects. But best of all, Eddie understood the modern world, the demographic of boxing fans, if you like. He knew they are people with money who want entertainment and communicate through social media.

The best example came after Froch's controversial win against George Groves in the Manchester Arena. The build-up, with both fighters making plain their contempt for each other, was reminiscent of the Eubank–Benn rivalry: genuinely nasty and good for business. The fight itself was supercharged, topsy-turvy, with Groves knocking down Froch in the first round and out - boxing him for several rounds. It became a war of attrition until Froch at last wore down Groves and was handing out serious punishment in the ninth round when the referee, Howard Foster, jumped in to stop the contest. At the time, Groves was ahead on the scorecards of all three judges and Foster's intervention was controversial to say the least. Groves claimed he had been robbed, but that robbery helped make him millions. There was such a clamour for a rematch that Froch and Groves were bound to make a fortune if it took place. Here was another example of an unexpected stroke of luck, so long as all concerned could take advantage.

Eddie, who grasped the potential straight away, wanted to stage the rematch outside at Wembley Stadium.

'Don't do it,' I said. 'I've done big shows outdoors and they're horrendous. All kinds of logistical problems and sleepless nights.'

Eddie sent a tweet to his followers saying if you want to know when tickets for the Froch–Groves rematch go on sale, send me your e mail address. He got 37,000 in a day. And when the tickets went on sale, 80,000 seats at Wembley Stadium, they were all sold in under an hour. I thought: *This bloke's on a different level.*

What a show that was. What a right-hand punch Froch unleashed to knock out Groves. Froch revealed later that he and Rob McCracken, his trainer, had noticed that Groves had a tendency to move his head to the left after throwing a certain punch. They claimed that they had planned the knockout with that punch and had practised for it. I can believe it. McCracken, who also trained Anthony Joshua as an amateur and professional, is one of the best in boxing. And just to show how times had changed. Eddie was now taking a management percentage rather than giving the fighter a fixed purse and keeping any profits. He was working for the fighters rather than employing them. It was a quantum change from old-school boxing promotion.

Mind you, Froch was never likely to become impoverished. He was a terrific fighter but just about the tightest I ever encountered. With our new way of working, he essentially owned the show, with a guaranteed percentage, the lion's share of the proceeds. Under our agreement we sent him full accounts of everything, with copies of every bill, every contract and all receipts. We sent it to him thirty days after the fight and it was a substantial folder. Groves received one as well. Groves handed his over to his accountant and when everything was checked and agreed we sent him his money. Froch, though, didn't want to use an accountant, presumably to save money. He went through the folder himself, checking every item.

Froch rang me up with a query. 'Who's so-and-so?' he asked.

'I don't know,' I replied.

'Well, he's charged £14.50 for laundry.'

Then I remembered: so-and-so was one of the boxers on the undercard. A six-rounder, a fellow trying to make a living.

'Well, he's charged £14.50 for laundry in his hotel. That's bang out of order,' Froch said.

'If it's a problem, I'll pay the £14.50,' I said.

'No need for that. I just want you to know it's bang out of order.'

'Look, Carl, you've made eight and a half million pounds.'

'It's still out of order.'

'Carl, you'll always be a rich man,' I said. I recalled that Chris Eubank had been another fighter who checked every figure from every show to make sure he got every last penny to which he was entitled. Then one day, after fighting Ray Close in Belfast, he said, 'Barry, I've checked everything you have done since we started working together and I have never found anything wrong. As from today, I am checking nothing.' Eubank may not have realised it, but he had just paid me one of the biggest compliments I have ever received.

On the undercard of the Froch–Groves rematch at Wembley, making his sixth professional appearance, was Anthony Joshua, the winner of the super-heavyweight Olympic gold medal at the 2012 London Games. After winning the gold medal, Joshua sounded out various promoters before deciding whether he would turn professional or, possibly, carry on as an amateur to the Rio Games in 2016. He came to see us at Mascalls and I could tell straight away he was suspicious. Boxing promoters don't have the best reputation, one rung down from gangsters, people seem to assume. He was wearing a tracksuit, an athlete in his young prime opposite a grey-haired, smart-suited, smart-talking promoter: me and of course the new kid on the block, Fast Car Eddie Hearn.

Joshua knew only too well that, historically, the relationship between promoters and boxers was unequal to say the least. Boxers were not just exploited by promoters but virtually owned by them. Chris Eubank, Lennox Lewis, Naseem Hamed and Ricky Hatton had broken free from that, as did Carl Froch and subsequently many others. They controlled their own destinies and became the guv'nors. They took most of the profits from the big shows and we began to work *for* them, taking either a set fee for staging an event or a small percentage of the show's profit, leaving the lion's share to the fellows who risked their health and lives in the ring. Many promoters of the old school were guilty of not paying their fighters an agreed fee, not paying on time and sometimes not paying at all. I'm proud to say we never did that. We operated with integrity and honesty, and we never had a boxer complain on that score. In over thirty years in the business, we have never had a dispute with a fighter over agreed purses.

Keen to get his signature, I was talking up Matchroom to Joshua and mapping out a golden career for him. But Eddie, who was in on the negotiations, was much more subtle. In fact, he produced a masterstroke by saying to Joshua that he should travel everywhere, talk to everyone, see what offers were available and then come back and see us.

Joshua, a bright, level-headed young man, did exactly that. A year later, he sat down with Eddie, said he had talked to everyone and wanted to sign with us. They have been great friends ever since and we now look on AJ as one of the family.

My relationship with Joshua is different from Eddie's. From the beginning I could sense that, although he'd had no great education, he was very street smart. He gave a lot of thought to every aspect of his career, from training to business, and he had a very clear understanding of where he wanted to go. Of course, he wanted to make a load of money, but he also wanted to make sure he was in control of his own destiny and could secure his name for posterity.

At one of our earliest meetings, we were discussing opponents, career moves, broadcast deals, sponsorships and so forth. Suddenly, he stared straight at me.

'What do you really want out of me?' he said.

'I want 1 per cent of your adrenalin,' I replied. He looked at me quizzically.

'You don't know me well enough yet,' I continued. 'But you will, and when you know me, you'll know you can trust me because I will take a bullet for you, and because you are enriching my life in a way that money can't. When you win the World Championship, when you walk out at Madison Square Garden, when you become a global superstar, for me to get 1 per cent of the adrenalin rushing round your body is payment enough. Eddie will do the deals with you. I will be there for you whenever you need me.'

Looking back, 1 per cent was an underestimate.

After that first appearance at Wembley, Joshua was always top of the bill, Eddie's special project. There were many wonderful nights, mostly at the O2 Arena in Greenwich, which was where Joshua dismantled Dillian Whyte, his old amateur foe, having been rocked himself. It was also where he won the IBF version of the world title in April 2016, knocking out Charles Martin in the second round.

Getting the Charles Martin fight for the world title was another masterstroke pulled off by Eddie. I have always said to athletes, don't worry about what your opponents are getting, worry about what you are getting; and this was a case in point.

Martin was a very fortunate young man to become world champion at all. With moderate fighting pedigree, he won the title in bizarre fashion when his opponent injured his leg. Since he came from a very poor background and hadn't had much financial success in his life, he was certainly open to offers.

We paid Charles Martin a fortune to lure him to the UK to defend his title. It's as simple as that. We effectively bought the title. Joshua never understood why we paid Martin so much money, but it fast-tracked Joshua's career, gave him the heavyweight world title. The fight itself was a formality and Martin didn't seem to be able to protect himself at all when Joshua kept it simple, just punching straight 'down the pipe'. It was all over in the second round and we had a new world champion.

That was the nearest I would come to fulfilling my childhood dream, winning the world heavyweight championship. Joshua had done it and we all felt on top of the world. But the way the championship had been acquired was not wholly satisfactory in sporting terms. Wladimir Klitschko had ruled the division for a decade. He was a truly formidable and dedicated champion, and it was a huge upset when Tyson Fury won a unanimous and deserved points victory against him in Germany. Fury sank into a sea of personal troubles, of course, and forfeited his belts. Charles Martin fortuitously won the IBF belt and Eddie moved fast and made that huge offer to bring him to London.

Two straightforward defences followed, but there was still a perception that Joshua hadn't really earned the right to be looked on as a true champion. That all changed when we arranged Joshua's third defence, against the great Klitschko, who was desperate to win back his titles. That clash of giants, clash of generations, had to be at Wembley.

Saturday, 29 April 2017: what a night it was, for the whole Hearn family. I sat next to Eddie and his wife Chloe in the front row of the ringside seats with Susan. Katie and her husband Dan were close by. For heart-stopping drama, there is nothing like a championship fight that tilts violently one way and then another, especially when the heavyweights are clashing like dinosaurs in some primeval clearing.

Klitschko had looked so poor against Fury that I reckoned he must be 'shot'. In particular, he had been too negative, reluctant to throw his punches, especially his feared right cross and hook. In the opening rounds at Wembley, he looked equally cautious. Very little happened in the first four rounds, but it all kicked off in the fifth. Joshua landed with his right hand and Klitschko was instantly in trouble, trying to grab hold of Joshua, blood seeping from a cut on his left cheek. Joshua kept punching and Klitschko slid to his knees. He got up quickly but looked dazed as Joshua attacked. The shock knocked the caution out of Klitschko. He was desperate and began to fight from instinct. He caught Joshua on the chin with a left hook and now Joshua was swaying, happy to hear the bell so that he could stumble back to his corner.

In the one-minute interval after that fifth round, Susan leaned across and said to Eddie: 'He's gone. Joshua's gone.'

Eddie replied: 'If he gets through the next two or three rounds, he'll win.'

Susan was pessimistic. 'No chance,' she said.

The sixth was one of those rounds that get talked about for years. Klitschko was the aggressor, looking to land that concussive right hand. After little more than a minute, he did it, catching Joshua on the chin and sending him to the canvas. Joshua rose wearily at the count of seven. He had never before been knocked down as a professional and was in serious trouble.

I turned to Eddie and said, 'Have you got the rematch clause?'

'Yes.'

'Thank fuck for that.'

Joshua survived that sixth round, mostly because Klitschko seemed reluctant to go for the kill. Instead of finishing it, he reverted to being careful, staying out of range. Did he get his tactics all wrong? Did he believe he could now coast to a points win? Or was he so tired he could not summon the effort to complete the job? Those would be the questions every pundit and fan tried to answer in the weeks and months ahead. What happened at the time was that Klitschko held off, Joshua was allowed to clear his head, find fresh energy and – being the younger man – grow stronger and stronger. Klitschko was stopped, exhausted, in the eleventh round.

Three wins for Joshua followed, against Carlos Takam, Joseph Parker and Alexander Povetkin. Each of the three opponents posed Joshua some problems but he never looked like losing. Nor did he look remotely likely to lose when Matchroom notched up another notable achievement: our first promotion at the Mecca of boxing, Madison Square Garden, New York City.

I could not have felt prouder as I took my seat in June 2019, front-row ringside, next to Eddie. My company, my son, were staging a world heavyweight title bout at the iconic Garden. This was where Muhammad Ali fought Joe Frazier in 1971, the Fight of the Century attended by countless celebrities, at which Burt Lancaster provided colour commentary and Frank Sinatra contrived to get a photographer's pass and took the cover picture for *Life* magazine. Now it was a Matchroom venue.

Originally, Joshua was going to defend his title against Jarrell Miller, a huge, rotund heavyweight, but Miller failed three drug tests and was refused a licence by the New York State Athletic Commission. Eddie had to find a late replacement and came up with Andy Ruiz Junior, a Mexican-American who was almost as fat as Miller, but with a better record.

Most people, including the odds-makers, who had Joshua at 25–1 on, reckoned it was a mismatch, and when you looked at the two boxers at the weigh-in you could see why. Joshua was all muscle; Ruiz was mostly flab. At the weigh-in, fans chanted, 'Who ate all the pies?'

I warned people not to be deceived. Ruiz hardly had a sculpted figure, but he could fight. He had good feet, a decent amount of power and had been brought up the hard way. Having said that, not for a moment did I imagine that Joshua might lose.

In the third round, Joshua caught Ruiz with three world-class punches and the challenger went down. It looked like an early night. Ruiz had never been off his feet before. When Ruiz got back up, Joshua went for a quick finish. I think he wanted to send a message to the boxing world. That year, all the talk and endless negotiations had been about a fight between Joshua and Deontay Wilder, the holder of the WBC version of the title. Wembley Stadium had even been booked for it, but the talks broke down and Wilder went on to fight Dominic Breazeale instead. Wilder, the biggest puncher in boxing, knocked Breazeale spark out in the first round at the

Barclays Center, New York, just two weeks before Joshua fought Ruiz.

Joshua waded into Ruiz looking for his own spectacular knockout, hit him with a solid right hand but got caught by a punch to the forehead. He was hurt and was soon on the canvas. Before the end of that third round, he was down again. In the seventh round, Ruiz knocked Joshua down yet again and the referee stopped the fight. It was the biggest upset in heavyweight boxing since Mike Tyson was knocked out by Buster Douglas back in 1990. In fifty years of watching boxing, I had never been so shocked.

In the dressing-room, Joshua said he knew he had been hit on the forehead in the third round but remembered nothing after that. It was concussion. And, once again, complacency had done its deadly business.

Sometimes, an apparent disaster turns out to be one of the best things that can happen. And although most sporting sayings are rubbish, it is true that you tend to learn more in defeat than from victory. That was the case with Joshua's shock defeat by Andy Ruiz.

Joshua had earned a huge amount of money for fighting in Madison Square Garden, but the best was just around the corner. We exercised our option on Andy Ruiz's first defence and, despite having some legal arguments with his team, we agreed a sensible compromise whereby he got a few million more than he was promised. He also agreed to fight Joshua in any venue we could find. Well, that venue happened to be more than a little controversial – Saudi Arabia.

Eddie had started conversations with the Saudis, in particular through Prince Fahad, an avid boxing fan who wanted to stage major fights in his country. Frankly, the Prince would not take no for an answer and paid a huge site fee to bring both Joshua and Ruiz to Riyadh. We took a lot of stick from the newspapers and various groups, including Amnesty International, who claimed that the sponsorship and site fee for this fight was no more than 'sports-washing' to deflect attention from the human rights problems within Saudi Arabia.

From our point of view, it was just about sport, and it was up to governments to define what we could and couldn't do. As pretty well everybody was trading with Saudi Arabia commercially, and as many other sports, including golf and motor racing, were operating in Saudi Arabia, I did not think we were doing anything untoward. Our fiduciary duty was to maximise the financial return for our clients.

The fight itself showed how much Joshua had matured and learned from his previous defeat, as he boxed Ruiz's head off. His was a punch-perfect, precision performance. Once again, we had the unified world heavyweight champion, and his next contest, a knockout win over Kubrat Pulev, cemented his position as the number-one heavyweight on the planet, although this claim was contested by the Gypsy King, Tyson Fury.

Every boxing fan wondered or had an opinion about who was the better heavyweight, Joshua or Fury? As a committed Joshua fan, I was biased, but I could understand some of the fans' insistence that the Gypsy King was the main man. In terms of the quality of his opponents, Joshua was in a league of his own, but the Gypsy King was the man who had beaten Wladimir Klitschko in Germany and stopped Deontay Wilder in a classic exhibition of boxing, having previously drawn with him. He then went on to conclusively defeat Wilder in their third contest. Let us hope that the question will one day be answered. But it is surely exciting that a heavyweight merry-go-round to rival the great welterweight and middleweight contests of the 1980s has developed. Back in the day, we had Marvin Hagler, Sugar Ray Leonard, Thomas Hearns and Roberto Duran fighting for supremacy. Today, we have Anthony Joshua, Tyson Fury, Deontay Wilder and Oleksandr Usyk, with Dillian Whyte and Joe Joyce in the wings.

Following the win against Kubrat Pulev, Joshua's next contest was against a mandatary challenger, Usyk. Actually, this was not a fight anyone really wanted, except Usyk himself. The fight every fan wanted to see was Joshua versus Fury for the undisputed heavyweight title. Negotiations for that showdown had been going on for ages. The culmination of countless discussions came when Eddie negotiated a massive site fee from Saudi Arabia to host the fight.

That was when the complications really set in. Fury was co-promoted by Bob Arum and Frank Warren but effectively controlled by his management company in Dubai. All management decisions emanated from Dubai and basically Arum and Warren were told what to do by Tyson Fury's management. I don't believe Arum or Warren ever thought that Eddie could really deliver the fight the whole boxing world wanted to see but when he did they had to make a big decision: take the fight and risk everything while earning a life-changing amount of money, or look elsewhere.

That decision became irrelevant when Deontay Wilder applied for an injunction to compel Fury to honour a rematch clause in the contract for their second fight. Wilder won his case and Fury was forced to box him for a third time.

I was intrigued that, despite the huge amounts of money available for the Joshua–Fury fight, no effort was made by the Fury camp to negotiate a step-aside payment for Wilder to allow that fight to happen. Perhaps Fury didn't fancy the fight or Wilder wouldn't take any amount of money to step aside, but I believe the real reason lay in the egos of Arum and Warren, who wanted to keep control rather than allow that young upstart, Eddie Hearn, to prove once again that he is the best operator in the business.

I know that if Fury's management had asked us for a contribution towards a payoff for Wilder and asked the Saudis for a similar contribution, we would definitely have paid up, because the sums of money from the site fee were so enormous. The fact that they didn't ask and didn't try to postpone the Wilder–Fury fight suggests that they didn't fancy the Joshua fight in the first place.

Once that blockbuster fight was off the agenda, Joshua, the consummate professional, agreed to face his mandatary challenger, Oleksandr Usyk, who was the undisputed world cruiserweight champion and, like Joshua, a gold-medal winner in the 2012 Olympics. In my mind, he was one of the finest boxers of the modern era, although clearly lacking the punching power possessed by Joshua.

The fight, at the Tottenham Hotspur Stadium on 25 September 2021, was interesting but essentially technical, like a chess match. Joshua seemed to be trying to out - box a boxer and that fell right into the hands of Usyk, a great technician. Once again, there was an upset, with Usyk clearly winning on points, and once again the question had to be asked: did complacency do its deadly work?

I think not. Joshua was just beaten by a better boxer. AJ and his team got their tactics wrong. Joshua was left with a chance of salvation, having exercised the rematch clause. Meanwhile, Fury cemented his claim to be the number-one heavyweight with a sensational eleventh-round knockout of Wilder. The soap opera of heavyweight boxing rolls on!

I have grown tired trying to count the number of sports governing bodies who should not be allowed to run a newsagent's, let alone a major or minor sport. They may be passionate about their sport, but they have no idea how to develop it commercially. They forget the principle that sport must be able to change lives and that, inevitably, involves money.

How true that was with gymnastics, a sport that I really care for, one that requires tremendous discipline and expertise from its athletes. The trouble is that for the athletes themselves, unless they are at the top of the tree, like Simone Biles or Max Whitlock, there isn't enough in the pot to change their lives or even to reward them for the sacrifices they make every day.

I started looking at gymnastics around 2014, and decided I liked it. I had met Whitlock and his trainer and a few of the other kids down at their local club in Basildon. I was amazed how many people were there from all ages, and seeing the mums and dads watching their kids go through their routines was inspirational. I was thinking of enrolling my grandchildren until I found out that they had 3,000 members and a huge waiting list, a very good sign when you are looking for a progressive sport to get involved in.

I did some research and found this was being replicated almost everywhere – not enough facilities to meet the demand, an ideal recipe for success. Gymnastics was underdeveloped, and I knew I could revolutionise the finances and make sure the athletes were better rewarded. I started working on ideas for formats and I knew that with my expertise I could bring in television and sponsorship at levels never seen before in the sport.

After I had been looking at this for some time, I had a surprise phone call from the head of the British Gymnastics Association, Jane Allen, who told me she had heard I was looking at gymnastics. Yes, I replied, and I think there is some potential in it.

She had a suggestion: 'Rather than start up from scratch yourself and get into confrontation with the existing bodies, why don't we do something together?'

Her proposal was that we would jointly promote the World Cup of Gymnastics in London and give it the special Matchroom treatment, but it would be officially sanctioned to give it credibility. This seemed to be a short cut to where I wanted to go, so we had a meeting at the Waldorf Hotel and agreed on a fifty-fifty joint venture to stage the World Cup in 2017. It was a three-year deal with a one-year break clause in case we didn't get on.

It wasn't too difficult to work out why British Gymnastics needed Matchroom and me – they were losing a fortune on the event. Their losses were around £300,000, which was not a very encouraging sign, but as usual I looked beyond what was being achieved today and concentrated on what could be accomplished in the long run. I went ahead with the deal and we promoted one of the best ever World Cups. We just about sold out the O2 Arena and the athletes had a ball. They were allowed to express themselves, to improvise creatively, and they came up with original routines throughout. What's more, they promoted the event on social media and through their own contacts and worked endlessly with the press and broadcast media. Sky TV were delighted with it all. So was I, because it was an excellent event and the £300,000 loss had been transformed into a substantial profit. Mission accomplished.

We had a follow-up meeting at the Waldorf a few weeks afterwards, which I assumed was to discuss our future plans. But Jane Allen said that as there was a break clause in the agreement after one year, they would exercise it. They wanted to go it alone, without us.

I suppose they didn't like the freedom the athletes had been given to improvise, to be creative and have fun, but they did like the fact that it made a profit. We had given the event our best shot, had completely turned it around, and now they were walking away from us. I was annoyed that an opportunity had been lost and made my feelings clear. I was sorry for the sport, sorry for the athletes who had embraced the concept with such enthusiasm. But there was nothing to do but walk away, and walk away I did, leaving them with their own version of the World Cup which has since struggled financially.

I did get some form of revenge because when the gymnastics blazers went back to their offices to organise the World Cup without my help, they suddenly realised that the contract with the O2 was with Matchroom, not British Gymnastics. Jane Allen phoned me to ask a favour. Would I please write to the O2 and tell them that the contract would now be taken over by British Gymnastics? I told her she had more chance of playing centre-forward for Leyton Orient.

I decided to stage a rival event, the Superstars of Gymnastics. I am not going to claim it was as good as the World Cup, but it was different, and it featured some of the best gymnasts from around the world, including the best of all, Simone Biles. We pretty well sold out the O2 and made money. But it still was not the event I really wanted to do. They say that revenge is a dish best

Wielding the willow: like most bowlers, I fancied myself as a batsman, but it took me thirty years to score the first of my two centuries (so far).

Sure touch: a leg glance, against an Essex XI, that was
reminiscent, perhaps, of the great Ranjitsinhji.

True hero and
inspiration: Michael
Watson, almost
fatally injured in
the ring in 1991,
completes the
London Marathon,
2003. Credit: Paul
Gilham/Getty.

Million-pound equaliser: Jonathan Téhoué's late goal gave Leyton Orient a draw against mighty Arsenal and secured an FA Cup replay at the Emirates.
Credit: Simon O'Connor.

Sweet promotion: Lee Steele celebrates his winner against Oxford United, congratulated by Matt Lockwood, the world's best left back.
Credit: Simon O'Connor.

My first Champion Mark Reefer.

...ptain courageous: John Mackie, Orient's captain when we won promotion, was ...e kind of man you want next you to in the trenches. Credit: Simon O'Connor.

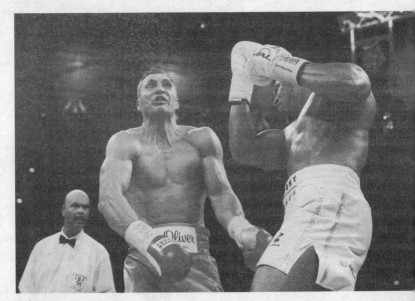

King of kings: when the reigning heavyweight champion, Anthony Joshua, defeated the former champion, Wladimir Klitschko, at Wembley, AJ and Matchroom Boxing were on top of the world. Credit: Reuters.

World Champion Scouser: Tony Bellew, pictured with Hearn father and son, fulfil every ambition when he triumphed at Goodison Park. Credit: Lawrence Lustig.

My daughter Katie's wedding: when I gave her away, I was the proudest man in the world.

Eddie and Chloe's wedding, another great day.

Love between equals: my marriage with Susan,
the only person I fear, has been tender and tumultuous.

served cold, and I made life as difficult for British Gymnastics as I possibly could. They lacked the vision to understand that we were trying to take gymnastics to a wider audience in big arenas with international television exposure. Looking back, I believe I was wasting my time trying to educate them. It was their loss, not mine.

Time to pass over control, but I am still keeping an eye on things.
Credit: Paul Stuart

15

The Clock Is Ticking

Christmas was joyful in December 2019. Matchroom had had its best ever year, with a consolidated group profit of just over £28m. We looked set to really push on and establish ourselves as a major player on the global scene. Complacency is the enemy of course, but we were not complacent. Like the rest of the world, we were ambushed by the unforeseen: Covid-19.

I started hearing rumours of something not being right in China in January 2020. Matchroom has offices in Shanghai and Beijing and word came through that a virus was spreading. It was the beginning of the pandemic. In my forty years of involvement in the sports business, I have had many challenges: three recessions, a banking crisis and goodness knows how many other problems with companies crashing, debtors defaulting, opportunities missed. I had survived them all, learned from every setback and should have been armour-plated. But no previous crisis could be compared with the effects that Covid-19 had on our business and the sporting world. When we went into the first lockdown, life seemed unreal. With 650 event days planned for the year, we were faced with the prospect of having no events whatsoever.

Quite soon, our resilience kicked in. We gathered together as a group and tried to work out what we could do that might be relevant, that could give employment to the legion of sports stars we work with, and that might even yield a profit. Our biggest decision was that we would not reduce prize money by a penny. We stood our corner and knew it was our responsibility to look after our sports men and women as best we can. We let no-one down. One of our first moves was to open discussions with the Department of Culture, Media and Sport. Crucially, we were able to get elite-athlete status for our performers. That meant they were exempt from the travel restrictions. Mind you, it was hardly simple to get people to travel from all round the world. One of the early, creative ideas came from the PDC, who decided it might be fun to organise a darts tournament filmed on iPhones. The quality was not great, but there was a nine-dart finish from someone's kitchen. Most TV stations had no sport to screen at all and our home-spun event was shown around the world and won innovation awards from the sports industry.

Matchroom was determined not to follow the crowd, not to follow all those sports administrators who seemed to have their heads in the sand, asking to be woken up when it was all over or holding out their begging bowls to the government. Our darts, snooker and multisport divisions all prepared Covid-19 policy documents, creating safe environments for the sportsmen and -women as well as those producing shows. Somehow, we managed to come up with thousands of hours of sports coverage to entertain the nation – and how we needed to be entertained – and to sell overseas. We actually created more indoor events behind closed doors than we do in a normal year.

Early in the pandemic, the government allowed certain pilot events to go ahead, including the World Snooker Championship. We were limited to 25 per cent of a capacity crowd, with social distancing and every kind of health and safety measure in place. World Snooker, led by Nigel Oldfield, the operations director, did an outstanding job. Naturally, I was up in Sheffield for the first session, which began at 10am. Twenty-five minutes later, we had a message from Downing Street to say they had changed their minds. No more crowds would be allowed after Day One. After all the work and expense, we had had the rug pulled from beneath our feet. I was gutted. The extra cost of organising such a safety-first championship came to a little over £100,000. (I'm still waiting for my cheque for compensation from the government.) Then, believe it or not, they changed their minds once more and we were allowed crowds again for the last two days of the championship.

There were all sorts of frustrations, but we bashed on, determined not to be beaten. One of the craziest and best ideas came from Eddie, who came into my office one day.

'Boxing,' he said. 'Dad, we've got to do some boxing.'

'Yes, but there's no crowd, and that's a huge chunk of your revenue.'

'I've had this idea: why don't we do it here, at Mascalls, in our back garden?'

'Have you any idea what it is going to cost to construct the kind of structures we need to stage, film and promote big-time boxing in our garden?'

'Yes, actually. I've calculated it'll cost a little over a million pounds to set it up and even without a crowd I reckon we can make money. It's certainly worth a gamble.'

Looking back at his call to stage the Froch–Groves rematch at Wembley, which I was against, I'd learned my lesson.

'OK. Just go and do it, son.'

The joke was that we had gone from MSG to MSG: Madison Square Garden to Matchroom Sports Garden. Eddie called it Fight Camp and he staged events for four consecutive weeks in high summer. The highlight was the world-class heavyweight fight between Dillian Whyte and Alexander Povetkin. That was on pay-per-view. Imagine that: a pay-per-view event from your back garden.

Eddie's idea and implementation were brilliant, and it further convinced me that the time had just about come when I would have to hand over the reins. In many ways the pandemic has made our company stronger. We have emerged as a more cutting-edge organisation. We have proved we can get past any obstacle, that we refuse to accept defeat and that a can-do, creative approach can work near-miracles. Yes, profits were down by 20 per cent over the year, but they improved to dramatically the following year. The future looks bright for the Matchroom group and the lessons learned through Covid has changed the way we run our business to our casting benefit. The teams led by Emily Frazer (Matchroom Multi Sport), Matt Porter (Darts), Frank Smith (Boxing) and Steve Dawson (Snooker) really delivered, not just for Matchroom but for the whole country because people needed to be entertained. I was very proud on the final two days of the snooker World Championship in 2021 when we provided a sporting full house for the first time in Britain since the Covid-19 lockdowns were imposed.

The skills we acquired will surely take our company to new levels, helping all those self-employed sportsmen and women to survive in difficult times. We have put ourselves in the best possible position to take advantage when the world opens up.

My Principle Number Two is to tell the truth, and it is even more important to tell yourself, as well as other people, the truth. And one truth you must tell yourself, however unwelcome it might be, is your sell-by date.

In June 2018, when I turned seventy, I was already thinking of taking a backward step. The Matchroom business was going great guns and I was gratified to see how well our young management team, led by Eddie, Katie and Steve Dawson, had developed. They were surely ready to take over, and Eddie in particular, wanted to be the group chairman. He was itching to be the man in control.

But two events in the spring of 2020 – my second heart attack and the beginning of the Covid-19 pandemic – brought a temporary delay to the implementation of my exit plans. I was determined to stay on and lead from the front, to make the most of my experience in overcoming past crises. As I have outlined, we did not let Covid beat us and we created more events and produced more hours of TV sport than we did in a normal, pre-Covid year.

Covid was a test and we passed it, proving our resilience, creativity and character. So I adjusted my plans, waiting for the time when the lockdowns were less drastic to hand over the reins.

The perfect moment to leave the stage came during the World Snooker Championship in 2021. The Crucible had been chosen as the first indoor event at which spectators would be allowed back in and sport could begin to return to normal. That was a great success and a great honour. It was also forty years on from the breakthrough moment when Steve Davis won his first world title and I disgraced myself with that wild celebration (which I still do not regret).

As well as handing over to Eddie, I took advice on the tax implications of formal retirement and as a result my shareholding in Matchroom was reduced While Eddie's and Katie's were increased, so they effectively have control. Furthermore, under my tax arrangements, I can no longer be a serving director and have become non-executive president, with a brief to oversee strategy and global development, both very close to my heart.

I believe William Gladstone, one of our greatest prime ministers, said when he was in his eighties: 'I have been a learner all my life.' That certainly applies to me. Another inspiration has been Warren Buffett, the American investor of genius, who has always insisted that the most important quality of any business is its management. Assets come and go but it is management that builds a business and changes people's lives.

With those truths in mind, I know I was right to step aside and that my timing was spot-on. I don't lie to myself. There are very few operators who are as good as me at what I do, but the marketplace post-Covid has changed and what I do best is no longer what counts the most. It takes a young brain to appreciate how to exploit the social and digital opportunities that now make up the marketplace. Times change: management must change, companies must change.

Eddie has become a major social media figure, and one with a superb business brain, especially in his chosen business, boxing promotion. His business relationships with Len Blavatnik and his video-streaming service, DAZN, are transformative. Eddie signed a $1bn deal with DAZN in 2018 to stage shows in the US and in June 2021 he announced that after many years providing Sky Sports with boxing, Matchroom would be leaving to join DAZN exclusively, both in the UK and globally.

This was a huge decision, a major gamble, perhaps. After all, Sky had been the main source of our success. When they came to the UK market in 1990, they were like the cavalry coming over the hill to our rescue, and for thirty years working with them was a joyful and rewarding experience.

But attitudes change, people change, and money certainly changes. Companies such as DAZN are able to muscle in on a market, pay more money to begin with to be disruptive while they create their own market, taking advantage of the fact that youngsters no longer want to sit on the settee at home and watch TV with Mum and Dad. They want to watch wherever they want to be and on whatever device they choose. It all points to a whole new operation in terms of pay TV. Time will tell whether DAZN will be the ones to get it right, but my guess is they will and in so doing will become the Netflix of sport.

For me, it was sad to remove our boxing from Sky, although we still have long-term commitments for darts and some other sports. Unfortunately, Sky failed with one of my ten principles, the avoidance of complacency. Our long-term contract with Sky ended on 30 June 2021 and there should have been discussions about a renewal from at least a year before that. The reasons that Sky did not initiate such discussions were twofold: they believed we had nowhere else to go, and they were arrogant, believing that Sky is best and no one would leave them. A change of leadership did not help. Barney Francis, the head of sport, left and instead of giving his job to his second-in-command, Jonathan Licht, they brought in someone new, a round peg in a square hole. Straight away, our relationship with Sky was not as strong and communications were not what they were. By the time Licht was given the job, it was too late. If Sky had approached us to renew the five-year deal a year before it ran out, we would have done so in a heartbeat. But they did not and that left it open for DAZN to make an offer that exceeded our Sky deal by many times and gave us the chance to build the business the way we wanted to, by taking over programme production as well as programme content.

That brings in Katie and our in-house production team, Matchroom Media, which started operations on 1 July 2021. With Matchroom's involvement in world darts and snooker, and having developed such talented people as Matt Porter, Emily Frazer, Frank Smith and all the others, the carefully thought-out plan of backing the right people at the right time and giving them the chance to change their lives and our company is clearly working.

Now, at the age of seventy-three, I can ride off into the sunset with a clear conscience and the knowledge that the company I built from nothing is in the best possible hands. I shall carry on with my cricket, golf, fishing and competitive table-tennis against my grandchildren. I will give my all every time but bear in mind that the body does start to wear out. The clock keeps ticking, but I am trying to slow it down as much as possible.

I have always been very health-conscious, despite being a smoker in my early life. I have paid my dues in the gym and on the road, which may be why I have survived two heart attacks and can still lead a very energetic life with no signs of slowing down. I do listen to doctors and my medical advisers because I know the adventure will stop one day, and I want to postpone that day for as long as possible.

Naturally, I am a member of East Hanningfield Cricket Club. Our beautiful ground and handsome pavilion are on my land. With semi-retirement in April 2021, I have decided to concentrate a bit more on cricket, my first love. I have enjoyed playing for East Hanningfield and really enjoyed the challenge of playing for Essex over-seventies Second XI and First XI; but, being the character I am, I am never going to settle for just that. I have made it clear that, all being well, I am going to have a real crack at making the England over-seventies team in 2022. It might be an impossible task, but that has never stopped me in the past. I like the impossible; self-belief can fulfil dreams and isn't that what sport is all about, isn't that what this book has been about – maximising your potential, living the life and changing your life in the process? Most of the players I am playing with in the Essex side were better than me thirty or forty years ago, but as time goes on and my fitness and mental strength kick in, the ability gap is narrowing. I can't explain how much I enjoy still being active in sport at this stage of my life. It's a real bonus. If I keep myself fully fit, 2022 is going to be the year of dreams; and if not, I'll do my best to make it happen the following year.

I reckon there are three main stages in life, at least for me. The first is when you are selfish, doing everything and anything to be a success. The second is when you have achieved a certain amount and you can look after your family properly and be a better person. The third is when you look at the community from which you came and can give something back. In my case, the Matchroom Charitable Foundation is beginning its vital work in children's hospices and charitable endeavours in our areas of geographical and business interest. This will be our way of creating a different kind of legacy for our company. I will be donating my advance and all royalties I receive from sales of this book to our charitable foundation. So well done if you've bought this book — you've made a contribution to a very good cause.

Financial matters still form the backbone of my belief in running successful businesses. It is vital, not just necessary, to make a profit if you are to run an efficient business, reward both staff and professional players properly and create a sustainable business plan with adequate reserves for emergencies.

The level-headed approach I have always applied to business and my reliance on young management promoted from within rather than recruited from outside have been fundamental to our success. It is vital to me that Matchroom staff understand the basics and ethos of our business, our passion for sport and the people that play it. It is important that they understand the debt that we owe great sportsmen and -women who have dedicated their lives to entertain us, and with that debt there comes a responsibility for us to do everything in our power to reward them properly and change their lives financially. It is always a pleasure to watch past Matchroom stars develop their own life, learning, I hope, from a little Matchroom advice along the way.

Starting out in 1982 as a small business underneath a snooker hall with just me, a PA and a part-time bookkeeper, and turning it into one of the world's major sports promotion businesses, is something of which I could barely dream. Remember, the reason I started Matchroom in the first place was to have some fun – making money is easy but really enjoying your life requires work. The figures tell just a part of the story. The first year of Matchroom's trading in 1982 produced a turnover of £338,000 and pre-tax profits of £74,000. Not a bad start, I thought back then. The figures for 2022 at the time of writing are likely to be huge, and certainly enough to confirm our position as one of the largest sports promotion companies in the world, which is almost unbelievable. It comes down to good management, having bright ideas, a relentless work ethic and a refusal to accept defeat.

It has been an amazing life and I am hesitant to say that there is still more to come; but I have a feeling that the legacy is in the capable hands of some wonderful people, and I am very much looking forward to them taking Matchroom as a company to its next level.

I began this book with my ten guiding principles. It seems appropriate to conclude with what I call my Matchroom Rules of Life. I wrote them down when I realised that in many ways motivating yourself to make the most of your life is actually more difficult when you are born into money than when you're skint. That's one of the reasons I am so impressed with my children,

Katie and Eddie. They had every excuse, with that silver spoon, to take it easy, to be idle and fail to put in the work that they do. But in fact, they think poor and work hard.

I framed these rules for Eddie's daughters, Isabella and Sophia, and Katie's sons, Sam and George, and gave them each one for Christmas. My rules are not just a collection of pretty sentences but a discipline, a code of conduct. They are hanging in their bedrooms, and I hope they at least glance at them now and again. When they come of age, I hope they will not rest on the laurels of inherited wealth but will go out and make their own mark. I have a feeling that that is exactly what they will do.

- *Our job is to create opportunities for sportsmen and -women with as few barriers to entry as possible, to have fun and make a profit. We judge ourselves on prize money levels, tournament numbers, TV ratings and profit.*
- *We value our staff, and if they deliver either in extra effort or extra profitability, we reward them properly.*
- *We have a plan for each event, a short- and long-term strategy, and we do not waver from that plan unless we experience changing circumstances.*
- *We do not listen to uninformed criticism.*
- *We always over-deliver, and our handshake is better than any contract.*
- *We are honest and legal, with integrity in all we do.*
- *We are on a mission from God. We are relentless.*
- *We accept we will make dozens of mistakes, but we will make thousands of decisions.*
- *We never say we are the best sports promoter in the world, but we know we are in a group of one.*
- *We love our jobs. It is not a quick fix. It is a long-term marriage.*
- *We pay our way: no charity, no handouts, just graft.*
- *We tell the truth. We can afford to and that's a luxury.*
- *We think poor in everything we do. We want value for money and so do our clients.*

- We go the extra mile and no one can ever live with our work ethic.
- We understand that everything ends one day, and so we'll enjoy every second of it.
- There is never any complacency in our lives.
- We acknowledge how lucky we are.
- We are a special family.

My Top Ten Sporting Moments

When I look back over my career and the moments that gave me the greatest pleasure and satisfaction, the key word is adrenalin, the occasions when I was literally out of control with joy and excitement.

I have selected ten of my greatest, the ones that have been fundamental not just to the success I've enjoyed in business but the exhilaration of living my life, a life in sport. At this point, some might say the adrenalin rush is like a drug. Well, I have never experimented or tried any form of drug other than cigarettes, and they have now been consigned to history. I have always felt that people who take drugs are doing it as an excuse for a fast fix and, as you probably know by now, I don't like fast fixes. I like sustainable approaches that shape not just your business life but your character. Non-medical drugs are for cowards. If you need something artificial to stimulate your senses, then perhaps you should have a closer look at yourself and ask why you can't create such feelings internally.

My ten great moments are not all about the big money or events in a sold-out arena with 90,000 in attendance. They are the ones that get the heart racing, the head thumping and the adrenalin racing round your body like a train on a track in your attic.

1. Steve Davis, World Snooker Championship, 1981
I have already made clear the impact Steve Davis has had on my life and how fortunate I am to have known him and to have had

him as my best friend for so many years. But to appreciate the momentousness of the occasion, the first really big win, let's wind it back to the Crucible Theatre, Sheffield, 1981.

Steve and I were uncomplicated but driven people. I was incredibly ambitious and did not care what I had to do to succeed; Steve was totally committed to snooker and did not care what sacrifices he had to make to achieve his goal. So we were very similar: both council-house boys, no money in the family, no great education but a desire to be winners.

Over the years, we had often sat beside a fire, with a glass in hand, talking about what we were going to do with our lives. Steve wanted to be the best player on the planet. I wanted to be one of the richest men on the planet. We were miles apart but joined at the hip in our desire to get there.

We might discuss everything from acceptance speeches to changing endorsement values, advertising, personality development and so on, but it all came down to that day when you stand in the theatre of dreams – the Crucible – and you hold up the Joe Davis trophy, the one Joe largely paid for himself in 1927 when he won £6.10s for winning the inaugural world title. The name of every snooker player of significance is on that trophy apart from Jimmy White and Steve desperately wanted his to be added to it. I wanted to be managing the world champion, the number-one player in the world, to see the dawn of a new era for the sport.

There we were in the final against Doug Mountjoy and frankly Steve was just too good for him. But anticipating a win is not the same as experiencing one and as we got closer to the climax of the tournament, the final session, the final frames, the pressure mounted. Negative thoughts intrude. What happens if the tip comes off Steve's cue? Will the other guy suddenly find a level at which he is unbeatable (as most top pros can)? Will the roof fall in? Will there be a riot or a streaker who destroys the TV moment? Such are the irrational horrors that go through your mind. It's like a stomach ulcer. You are scared, scared you might get close and lose what means more to you than anything. That was me, watching on. Fortunately, Steve had the ability to play like an iceberg.

For me, this was a much bigger emotional roller-coaster ride. It was not just the chance to manage the world snooker champion, but the chance for me to change my life, to have real power, to have clout, leverage. I could see the opportunities opening up in front of my eyes, but it was just out of my reach. We needed to get our hands on that bloody trophy!

I was sitting next to Susan, mumbling, 'Don't do anything stupid, don't do anything stupid,' and then Steve was on the pink ball for the match – and as he potted it, simplicity itself, with the crowd applauding, I did something very stupid. I don't know how, but somehow I ran out through the seats on to the stage and I gave Steve a body-check hug that would have knocked over most men. I was on another planet. You only have to look at my face on the infamous BBC archive clip of the incident to see what it meant to me, my teeth clenched, fist-pump raised to the balcony where the Romford supporters sat throughout the championship. There were no words coming out of my mouth but if it had been a cartoon there would have been a bubble: 'We've done it, we've done it, we've fucking done it.'

It was and remains the pinnacle, the number-one moment of my sporting life, my business life, the day my life changed forever.

2. Chris Eubank vs Nigel Benn, 1990

The second-biggest adrenalin rush in my professional career came when Nigel Benn defended his WBO world middleweight title against Chris Eubank.

Benn was everyone's hero, an out-and-out warrior, ex-Army, so he had discipline, but I imagine he was a handful for anyone on the cobbles when he was younger. He took that belligerent approach into his professional career with a series of stunning knockouts. Unlike Eubank, he traded punches, happy to take shots so that he could land bigger bombs. He was a more concussive puncher than Eubank, but not half the stylist.

Eubank had a great chin and was also very good at avoiding being hit. He had studied the art of pugilism, whether it was in the first gyms he went to, in New York, or just watching old fights and adopting his own version of the moves he liked. A counterpuncher rather than a devastating come-forward fighter, he had enough power to inflict serious damage.

Come the day of the fight, relations between the camps were intense to put it mildly. Ambrose Mendy, Benn's principal adviser, was playing games, tricks. He gave Eubank a very poor dressing-room, with dirty towels because he knew Eubank hated filthy towels. They did everything they could to get inside our heads, probably because, as I found out afterwards, they had their own problems because Benn was struggling to make the weight.

I was getting more and more annoyed with every stroke they pulled. On our walk into the arena, to our usual Tina Turner number, 'Simply the Best', the music suddenly stopped and it was clear they had sabotaged it in an effort to further upset us. I steamed up a ladder into the PA room to see a young man with a broken tape in his hand and a look on his face that said 'It just broke, it just broke.' I did not accept that and things got very physical; I had to be dragged down the stairs by a couple of security people because I wanted to kill him, such was the enormous pressure we were under. Once again, the adrenalin was really pumping.

I got down the stairs and Eubank looked at me and said quietly, 'Bazza, they gave me a shitty dressing-room, they gave me dirty towels and now they have ruined my entry music. Can you please calm down and let me go and spank this geezer.' I felt about an inch tall and just lamely let him get into the ring, meekly following in his footsteps.

From round one, it was a war, with Benn the aggressor, Eubank the counter puncher, but nearly always having the last punch in every exchange. Eubank gave a master class of boxing, but he had to weather storm after storm as Benn just refused to forsake his aggressive, come-forward style. One uppercut from Benn split Eubank's tongue down the middle as if someone had cut it with a knife, but still the pace was frenetic. It went on round after round, with Eubank gradually becoming stronger and stronger in what was probably the best fight and best fighting performance I have seen.

As the tide turned more and more into Eubank's favour, the referee, Richard Steele, was constantly looking at Benn to see whether he was in danger of being seriously hurt, although you would never know because Benn was the ultimate warrior. Eventually, the barrage of punches became too much; Steele jumped in to save Nigel Benn from further punishment and Eubank became the WBO world middleweight champion.

All the risk and aggravation had proved worthwhile and Matchroom had a second world champion in a second sport. We were truly on our way.

3. Mark Reefer vs John Sichula, 1989

When I started out in the boxing business, I made a huge amount of money on the Bruno–Bugner fight and thought boxing was an easy touch. How wrong can you be? It was and remains a business fraught with problems, betrayal and dishonesty.

I persevered but after nearly two years I still did not have a champion of my own. It was frustrating. As a fight fan I wanted to see great fights but I also wanted to be involved with great fighters, and that made me believe that if I kept promoting great fighters I would become a great promoter. It's said that great fighters make trainers great, and I think that applies to promoters and managers as well. Managers and promoters come and go, but the one who gets in the ring is the one whose actions determine his own success and the success of those around him. It's no use thinking we are something we are not: talent is the king.

And so it was that in Bethnal Green in September 1989 we matched Mark Reefer, the local super-featherweight, against one of the top fighters to come out of Africa, John Sichula from Zambia, for the Commonwealth super-featherweight title. Reefer was a decent fighter and a nice guy. He was the local hero and the wonderful York Hall, the best small-hall venue on the planet, was banged out with a very partisan crowd. But we all knew that for Reefer it was going to be a tough night in the office.

I was desperate for a champion but halfway through the fight it did not look very likely. Sichula was a very competent boxer and was more than holding his own with Mark, who had suffered a terrible cut early on. Still, the cornermen did their job and Reefer's heart kept him in the fight and in the later rounds he began to overwhelm Sichula. When the bell went for the end of round twelve, no one knew for sure who had won it. Eventually the referee, Adrian Morgan, held up Reefer's hand as a points winner, 118 points to 117.

I had my champion and went nutty in the ring, jumping up and down, getting my suit covered with blood, grease, Vaseline, all from Reefer's body. I didn't care.

Sichula could have argued he deserved at least a draw, but he did not expect any favours and didn't moan. He went back to Africa and never boxed again. I don't know whether he just fell out of love with the game or realised he was not going to get many more opportunities from boxing. He died five years later at just thirty-nine years old.

Reefer, an intelligent man, enjoyed a fine career and retired at the right time. I hope and believe he has since had a successful life, but for me he will always have a special place as my first champion in the ring. Oh, the joy of winning!

4. Catch of the Century

I am going to allow myself one indulgence by including my finest single moment as a sports participant rather than promoter or fan.

This is my book, after all. I was down in Sussex at Arundel Castle, playing cricket for the Lord's Taverners against Lavinia, Duchess of Norfolk's XI. The usual mix of greats and celebrities was playing, plus me, and a crowd of several thousand had assembled on a perfect summer's day in unmistakeably English surroundings.

Barry Norman, the late, great film critic, was bowling. He was a purveyor of rather unorthodox leg breaks, which really meant that the ball went up in the air and nothing happened when it pitched except that it got hit very hard by the batsman. On this occasion, the batsman was a South African who played for Somerset. He hit a ball from Norman that went up to the moon. I have never seen a ball hit so high – not so far as to go for six, but about a mile high.

I was fielding at long off, on the boundary, and I thought this ball way up in the sky was going to end up around the deep cover boundary, so I started trotting round the outfield at a fair pace towards it. After a second or two, I realised that I might just have a chance of getting to the ball before it hit the ground, so I accelerated to top speed – my top speed – and the crowd began to cheer me. I was nearly there, agonisingly close and, being somewhat flash and wanting to be the hero, I launched myself into a full-length dive and in mid - air the ball hit my outstretched hand and stuck. The catch had been taken. I hit the ground, bouncing forward with my own momentum, like a Dambusters' bomb. When I stood up, still clutching the precious ball, the crowd, in their thousands, went mental. I did a lap of honour right round the boundary – which, I admit, was a touch excessive. Even the batsman, an international cricketer, said it was one of the best catches he had ever seen. The result of the match? I have no idea.

Many years later, I was flying to Hong Kong, first class on Cathay Pacific. The pilot came in from the cockpit, spotted me and said, 'You're Barry Hearn, aren't you?'

I agreed and he said: 'You took the finest catch I've ever seen. It was at Arundel, wasn't it?'

'It was.'

5. Tony Bellew's world title, 2016

Tony Bellew is a Scouser; without doubt, a proper Scouser!

That means he is full of chat, has an opinion on everything and is a proper handful. He is also one of the nicest people you could meet. Tony came off the streets of Liverpool and I'm sure in his younger life he was in plenty of trouble and heading for worse. However, he decided to go down the right path and became a great example of how boxing can change people's lives for the better.

The reason Tony makes my top ten adrenalin moments comes down to a spectacular night at Goodison Park stadium, Liverpool, on 29 May 2016 when he fought Ilunga Makabu for the vacant WBC world cruiserweight title.

But you have to look behind that night to fully appreciate the significance. Tony is a lifelong Everton football fan and the club he supports was just as important to him as his boxing career. An Everton nutter, he dreamed of one day fighting for a world title at his stadium of dreams.

Through a very decent career at the highest level, the dream lived on, and suddenly the opportunity came up where he could challenge for the world title in front of his own people. Tony had been a great fighter for us to promote and had become a loyal, honest friend, so Eddie and I just could not say no to him when the chance came up. Strangely enough, Tony had been a supporting actor in *Creed*, a successful boxing film in which he actually boxed at Goodison Park, so we were turning fantasy into reality.

We knew we were bound to lose money: the promotion had to be thrown together quite quickly and there were a huge number of problems in getting Goodison Park as the venue. It came down to two people – the Mayor of Liverpool, Joe Anderson, who just about moved heaven and earth to make sure we had all the necessary permissions, and Bill Kenwright, the theatre impresario and chairman of Everton, who understood how important it was to Tony to challenge for the title at his beloved club.

I spoke to Bill some weeks beforehand, wondering if it might really be possible to stage the contest within such a short timeframe and with such a tangle of red tape. Bill settled me down with a single, wonderful sentence: 'Tell Tony his chairman won't let him down.'

That was it. With the support of the mayor and Bill Kenwright, nothing could stop us. We just had to accept that this fight was never going to make money and Tony had to accept that he was in for a really tough fight against a dangerous opponent. Makabu, from the Democratic Republic of the Congo, lost his first fight in 2008 and then won nineteen in a row, with only one going the distance. He was a spectacular puncher, and most people didn't give Tony much of a chance.

Still, everyone agreed that Tony deserved his day in the sun, and you could see on his face how proud he was when he walked out at Goodison Park with the *Z Cars* theme blaring.

It all went tits-up in the first round when Makabu landed a right hand that put Tony on the canvas. I turned to Eddie. We both knew this had got disaster written all over it. The crowd was decent but hardly full and now we were not only losing a lot of money, but our guy looked as if he was going to get knocked out, and it would all end in tears.

The gods of boxing had ordained a different script. Tony survived the initial onslaught and in the third round launched a blistering attack that finished with Makabu on the ropes, standing up but completely unconscious thanks to a ferocious left hook from Tony.

The adrenalin kicked in, the crowd went crazy and the tears flowed. Bill Kenwright stood on the ring apron with Eddie and me, all of us hugging like long-lost brothers. The Scousers all celebrated in proper Liverpool style. Tony went on to have two big-money fights with David Haye, both of which he won, and a tough assignment against Oleksandr Usyk, the best cruiserweight in the world at the time, but it was that night at Goodison Park in his home town that meant more to him than anything.

It was a very special moment in my life and career, so well done, Tony. Thanks for being who you are, for the support you have given us and the excitement you generated. Top Scouser!

6. Leyton Orient vs Arsenal, FA Cup, 2011

I bloody love the FA Cup! You can forget the Champions League and Premiership as far as I'm concerned. For atmosphere and passion, there is nothing like the FA Cup, football's oldest competition, the one that throws the minnows in with the sharks, the one that provides upsets that live in the memories of millions of fans.

Leyton Orient fans still talk about the 1978 semi-final against Arsenal at Stamford Bridge, with victories along the way over Chelsea, Norwich, Blackburn Rovers and Middlesbrough, but for me nothing comes close to the drama on 20 February 2011 at Brisbane Road, once more against the mighty Arsenal.

Orient went into the fifth-round match after an amazing run of only one defeat in their previous twenty games, but we were given no chance against an Arsenal team that had beaten Barcelona just a few days earlier. Once again, complacency kicked in as Arsenal's manager, Arsène Wenger, made ten changes to his midweek team, no doubt believing he had very little to beat in Leyton Orient. Arsenal had lots of possession but were limited to a one-goal lead as we approached the final moments.

I was sitting with Susan and Eddie and the rest of our gang of hardened Orient supporters led by Matt Porter. Our dream was still alive, but only just.

The seconds ticked away as we contemplated an inevitable defeat, softened by the knowledge that we'd had a great run to the fifth round with some brilliant wins along the way. Then in the eighty-eighth minute Jonathan Téhoué danced through the Arsenal defence and smashed the ball past their goalkeeper,

Manuel Almunia. Everyone, apart from the Arsenal followers in the sold-out Brisbane Road crowd, went nuts and suddenly the notion of actually drawing against Arsenal and getting a very profitable return leg at their new stadium became a tantalising, graspable reality.

But it wasn't over. As the clock ticked down, the adrenalin rush rose. The computations swirling around my brain were endless: £1.5m gate money, which meant that Leyton Orient might actually make a clear profit for the season for once; the credit due to the players; the bonuses and sponsorship benefits; the TV rights; and of course the bragging rights that little Leyton Orient could hold the mighty Arsenal to a draw.

Like a kettle coming to the boil, the atmosphere built and built. Ninety minutes were up, and the board came out to announce three minutes of added time. They were the longest three minutes of my life and I was not at all shocked when Eddie jumped up with a foul-mouthed instruction to the referee: 'Blow the fucking whistle!' Edward was put in his place by his mother, who told him to sit down and mind his language, but we all felt the same – all we wanted to hear was the final whistle. When it came, the relief, the joy, the sheer love of the FA Cup was overwhelming. Little Leyton Orient had created another memory for our children and their children to be reminded of as they developed into Leyton Orient supporters.

Once again, the FA Cup had created something that money cannot buy: history.

7. Mosconi Cup, Steve Davis v Earl Strickland, 2002

Golf's Ryder Cup has been one of my favourite sporting competitions for many years. I love the format and the transatlantic nature of the clash, USA vs Europe, so felt no shame at all in borrowing it to showcase the game of pool.

Hence the Mosconi Cup, named after the late, great Willie Mosconi, and an event that excites such pride and passion that the money becomes secondary at best. It's all about playing and winning for your team. The event began in 1994 and after the first two matches both teams had won once. Then the Americans had a run of six consecutive and increasingly embarrassing wins, culminating in 2001 when Europe were slaughtered at York Hall, Bethnal Green – home turf – by twelve games to one.

This prompted a rethink by the European team, and they became a lot more professional, bringing in two top Germans, Oliver Ortmann and Ralf Souquet, along with the experienced Mika Immonen and Marcus Chamat and the exciting Nick van den Berg. It was a little like Seve Ballesteros riding to the rescue of the Ryder Cup.

It worked. In the 2002 event, Europe built a good lead, 11–9 in the race to twelve wins, and looked the likely winners when Steve Davis entered the arena to play the legendary Earl 'The Pearl' Strickland. This was a tough assignment. I had always asked Steve to play the Mosconi for me as a favour because he was a famous face, and we were building the event. He was quite good but would admit himself he was not a really good pool player, just a very good cueist.

The event was back at York Hall, Bethnal Green, which is like a bear-pit, with four or five hundred seats on the ground floor and a balcony overlooking the pool table, almost close enough to touch it. The fans gave the Americans so much stick that at one point their captain, Johnny Archer, wanted to take some of them outside for a fight. Strickland was another fiery character. He was also one of the greatest pool players in the world and would usually be strongly fancied to beat Steve Davis, especially in an extended game. But this was just the best-of-nine racks: anything could happen.

Strickland was in control of the final rack and it seemed a formality that he would clear the last few balls. Inexplicably, he overcut the five ball into the bottom pocket and suddenly Steve was five balls away from snatching victory. Icy as ever, he never looked like missing and as each ball was potted the crowd noise grew louder. The hairs on the back of my neck were standing up straight.

As the final ball went in and Steve turned to shake Strickland's hand, the rest of Team Europe ran out to celebrate, jumping up and down like madmen. Steve rates it the greatest atmosphere he ever experienced.

Six years of frustration flooded out and every member of that team was in tears when they finally presented the Mosconi Cup. And to think that an event that started in a bowling alley in Romford had become a global sports event, one that people really cared about and players were desperate to win. Willie Mosconi would have understood, and I trust he would have been proud to have his name so honoured.

8. Oxford United vs Leyton Orient, 2006

Let me set the scene. Under Martin Ling's excellent management, we'd had a terrific season. Martin had assembled a team of real character. They may not have been world-beaters in terms of skill, but they would do anything, put in any effort, for the cause. For much of the season, it looked as though their efforts would be rewarded by automatic promotion to League One. But, of course, with Leyton Orient it is never that easy. It all came down to the final day of the season. If we won at Oxford, we were up. But if we drew or lost and Grimsby won their final game, at home against Northampton, they would be up, and we would have to endure the play-offs.

Our task was not made easier by the fact that Oxford had plenty to play for as well. After a dire campaign, they needed to win to avoid relegation. However, they made a mistake that played into our hands. They gave us a whole stand for our away support.

I was sitting in the main stand, opposite our fans, in the Oxford directors' box, along with Eddie, Susan and the rest of the Leyton Orient board. After fourteen minutes, Oxford took the lead and that familiar sense of dread intruded. But not for long. Three minutes later, Craig Easton equalised for the O's. The Oxford keeper seemed to have saved his header, but the ball clearly crossed the line and the referee, for once, was in exactly the right position. The score was one each at half - time, but the bad news was that Grimsby were in front. It looked like we would have to win to go up.

Uncertainty turned to optimism in the sixty-fourth minute when Gary Alexander, one of the Orient's great centre-forwards, received the ball just outside the Oxford penalty area and curled a delightful shot into the top right-hand corner of the Oxford goal: 2–1 ahead and all our dreams were coming true, so long as we could hold on for twenty-six minutes – not a long time, but a lifetime for the Orient fans.

Of course, there were other twists in the tale. Two minutes after Alexander's wonder goal, Chris Willmott equalised for Oxford. The game was heading for a draw, and if Grimsby remained ahead, that would not be enough.

Then the most amazing minute of my football life unfolded. Well into injury time, the crowd suddenly went crazy when the news came through that Northampton had equalised against Grimsby. That meant a draw was now good enough for Orient to seal promotion.

Unfortunately, no one had told the Orient players, who still believed they had to win and were attacking like Genghis Khan's hordes, with nine players up front and the defence non-existent. Martin Ling, our manager, had heard there had been an equaliser at Grimsby and he was screaming at the Orient team to go back, go back, defend, defend, keep the ball, don't take chances.

The Orient players took no notice but went on a kamikaze attack with less than thirty seconds of injury time to go. Matt Lockwood passed up to Alexander, who passed to Jabo Ibehre inside the penalty area. Jabo decided he didn't want the responsibility of scoring the winner and let the ball through to Lee Steele, who poked it past Billy Turley in the Oxford goal. It doesn't get better than that.

Oxford kicked off again, but it was just a few seconds before the referee blew his whistle. What a scene, with the Oxford fans distraught that they were relegated and the Orient faithful beyond joyful, going nuts in their stand. Eddie and I began to walk across the pitch to go to them but the police advised us that since the Oxford fans were so disappointed it might be safer to go back inside. After a few seconds' thought, and still walking on air, we agreed.

9. Phil Taylor vs Raymond van Barneveld, World Darts final, 2007

I have witnessed dozens of darts matches of great quality and pulsating drama over the years, but nothing has quite matched the 2007 showdown between Phil 'The Power' Taylor and Raymond van Barneveld at the Circus Tavern, Purfleet, the original home of the PDC World Championships.

That night in the Tavern, with the low roof, the smoky atmosphere and 900 darts fans going crazy, supercharged by many, many pints of lager, when the title slipped away from the greatest of them all, will live with me forever. As his manager, I was rooting for Taylor, but as the promoter I knew that for the good of the game a new world champion from Holland would be no bad thing. Taylor was so dominant he was bound to win further World Championships, after all.

The final was the best of thirteen sets, and it looked all over when Taylor went 3–0 up in very quick time. But Barney, four times the winner of the BDO World Championship, kept his composure and battled back to level the match at 6–6, taking it into a deciding set. That set went to five legs all, meaning the world title would come down to one sudden-death leg.

Before a sudden-death leg, the players have to throw for the bull's-eye to determine who throws first, which is a massive advantage. Taylor hit the outer bull's-eye (the 25) but van Barneveld was able to leave Taylor's dart in as a guide (which is no longer allowed) to nestle his dart in the bull itself.

Game on. Barneveld threw first and scored a ton. Taylor took to the oche and threw three perfect darts, 180. Uproar. Van Barneveld stepped up and he too threw 180. Now Sid Waddell, the most erudite and entertaining of all commentators, was screaming in his best Geordie that this was the match of all matches. He was right. Taylor couldn't respond and made a mere 40 on his second visit. Back to van Barneveld, who made 105 to put himself within touching-distance of the title. Taylor responded with 133, but van Barneveld could check out with 116. He scored 76, leaving double-tops for his next visit, unless Taylor could snatch an unlikely win, as he had done so often, by checking out with 148. For once, it was not to be. Van Barneveld took to the oche and threw his thirteenth dart, which went straight into the double-top.

10. Anthony Joshua vs Wladimir Klitschko, Wembley Stadium, 2017

I pride myself on being a good judge when it comes to boxing. But even the best judges get it wrong. I thought the former champion, Wladimir Klitschko, at forty years of age, was well past his best and that young Anthony Joshua, whom we had guided from the Olympic title to the world heavyweight crown, was in for an easy night when they met at Wembley Stadium on 29 April 2017. In fact, I was rather smug and relaxed as I took my ringside seat and waited for my opinion that Klitschko was essentially a 'shot' fighter to be proved correct. Not for long. From the first bell, it was clear that Klitschko was far from 'shot'. He looked deadly serious, and lighter on his feet than any forty-year-old has a right to be. That all gave rise to a little trepidation, but it soon disappeared as Joshua, after four cautious rounds, let go a barrage of punches and decked Klitschko in the fifth round. I was not surprised. I turned to Eddie and grinned, as if to say, that has gone well, let's call it a night – time for Joshua to close it out and start the celebrations.

Klitschko got up and Joshua moved in for the kill, but it was Klitschko who ended the round stronger, landing heavy punches on Joshua's chin. There was fight in the old dog yet. In the sixth round, Klitschko shed all caution and was the aggressor. He knocked down Joshua and the way Anthony went down and rose on unsteady legs convinced me that all our plans were going up in smoke.

I turned to Eddie again: 'Have you got the rematch clause?'

'Yes.'

'Thank fuck for that.'

When he came out for round seven, Klitschko made a mistake. Rather than go for the kill while Joshua was stumbling and befuddled, he seemed to decide he had done enough, that he could cruise to a points victory without taking risks. Joshua was given a couple of rounds to recover and get his brain working. By round eleven, it was clear that Joshua was in the ascendancy. He had got his second wind and sent Klitschko to the canvas again. Klitschko got up but Joshua knocked him down for a second time in the round, then unleashed a barrage of punches while Klitschko was pinned against the ropes, forcing the referee to jump in and stop the fight.

That is the swing of emotions you can get in boxing. Complacency in the beginning, desperation in the middle and pure joy at the end. At the time of the stoppage, Joshua was ahead on two judges' scorecards, 96–93 and 95–93, while the third judge had Klitschko ahead 95–93. It was close, one of the great fights, a career-defining encounter for Joshua.

An OBE for Services to Sport, presented by Prince Charles at
Windsor Castle. It doesn't get better!

Awards, Achievements, Records

Halls of Fame

We all love a pat on the back and people telling us 'well done'. I am no different.

The first time I was inducted into a hall of fame was in 2013 when I was honoured by the Billiard Congress of America. I was inducted alongside Jeanette 'The Black Widow' Lee, one of the greatest women players of all time, and presented with the legendary green jacket and gold ring, worn on every special occasion sanctioned by the Billiard Congress of America.

We shared the stage and made speeches that probably went on far too long, but it was a great honour to be in Las Vegas, with friends from the world of pool and billiards acknowledging my contribution to the sport over the previous twenty-five years. I wear the green jacket with great pride. The Billiard Hall of Fame has been in existence for over fifty years and every great player has been inducted, including the legendary Willie Mosconi in 1968, so I am in good company.

A few months later, I was inducted into the International Boxing Hall of Fame in Canastota, New York. This was very special. All my heroes were there from bygone days. Legends I had seen boxing in black-and-white footage were having a cup of coffee with me and telling me about their career; it was three days I will never forget. I was inducted alongside Oscar De La Hoya, Joe Calzaghe and Felix Trinidad, three of the greatest fighters of all time.

Of course, few people knew me in comparison with those legends, but at least the organisers put my name on the side of the car carrying me in the cavalcade in front of 30,000 people through the streets of Canastota, so that there were shouts of 'We love you, Barry!' I knew they had no idea who I was. But then why should they when Oscar De La Hoya was in the lead car?

After three days signing autographs, having a plaster cast made of my fist and various publicity pictures taken for the International Boxing Hall of Fame Museum, I sat down to dinner with hundreds of the greatest fighters this world has seen. What a spectacular night, and I can't wait to return to Canastota when Eddie is inducted, and we can become the first father and son inductees.

Again, I received a fabulous Hall of Fame ring, which I wear to every world-title fight as a mark of respect to that great organisation. I was waiting for a taxi once in New York on my way to a world-title fight and a stranger asked me: 'Is that a Hall of Fame ring?' Yes, it's very special.

My next great honour came in 2018, when I was inducted into the snooker hall of fame during the annual World Snooker Awards at the Dorchester Hotel in London. I had no idea in advance, but I should have guessed from the moment Steve Davis got up to say a few kind words and to present me with my induction trophy. Snooker has been a massive part of my life and to be part of a hall of fame that has been going for thirty years and has featured every great snooker player and administrator was an honour indeed.

In January 2021, I was inducted into the PDC Darts Hall of Fame. Locked down by Covid-19, there was no awards dinner, so it was an online induction, but it was still a special moment because darts has been such an important part of my life. Helping to take a game from the pubs of Britain to being played in front of 20,000 fans in a German football arena has been a wonderful journey.

Honours

In 2014, I was awarded an honorary doctorate in business from East London University. Now I never went to university, so it was nice to get a degree, especially from East London, 'for services to sport over four decades'. I've always wanted to say, 'Trust me, I'm a doctor.'

In 2020, I received a letter from the Institute of Chartered Accountants, congratulating me on fifty years of membership. Fifty years! Where did the time go, from the day my mum told me at twelve years old that I was going to be an accountant?

I wish she had known that I was a member of the Institute for half a century, that I was awarded a university degree and, above all, that I was honoured by the sovereign. In 2020, I had a letter from the Cabinet Office to inform me that the Prime Minister, on the advice of the independent main honours committee, following an independent assessment process, was to recommend my name to Her Majesty the Queen to receive the OBE for Services to Sport. Now I know I am old-fashioned and a royalist, but I cannot tell you how chuffed I was to read that letter. I saw it as recognition of a life's work. With all the Covid delays, I had to wait until 15 December 2021 to receive my OBE from Prince Charles at Windsor Castle. You can imagine that Bazza at the Castle with long-suffering wife was one of my most surreal and unforgettable experiences.

In September 2021, I was presented with a Lifetime Achievement Award at the Sport Industry Awards. With a massive crowd in attendance at Battersea, London, it was a pleasure to listen to applause for once instead of boos! I suppose you only get recognised with such awards as a way of acknowledging that you might not be here for much longer. That may be a bit cynical, but I was never offered any award in my early life. Now I'm inundated with them, which is very gratifying but somewhat surreal. Receiving the Sport Industry Lifetime Achievement Award was perhaps the greatest compliment, bearing in mind it came from the people who actually support, create, own, stage and televise the wonderful world of sport that has been central to my life.

Records
Fishing
Biggest fish: 2019: carp, 49lb 6oz, Domaine de la Ribière, Limoges, France

Snooker
Best break in competition: 54
Best break in practice: 87

Cricket
For South Loughton Cricket Club 1963–86
Bowling: 1,477.3 overs, 390 maidens, 3,898 runs, 336 wickets: average 11.60
Batting: 157 innings, 18 not-outs, highest score 86 runs, total 1,784 runs: average 12.83
Catches: 76
Double of 500 runs and 100 wickets in a season: 1969 (690 runs, 103 wickets)

Career record
Centuries (2): July 1992 (102); August 1994 (106)
Clubs: Buckhurst Hill CC, South Loughton CC, Old Victorians CC, Brookweald CC, Brentwood CC, East Hanningfield & Great Burstead CC, Lord's Taverners, Essex Over-70s

Golf
Hole-in-one: Rockland Golf and Country Club, New York, September 2012

Marathons

London 1986: 3hr 52min 01sec
New York 1986: 3hr 46min 12sec
São Paulo 1986: 4hr 33min 39sec
London 1987: 3hr 22min 51sec (personal best)
New York 1987: 4hr 15min 47sec
London 1988: 3hr 32min 29sec
Hong Kong 1988: 3hr 59min 55sec
London 1989: 3hr 48min 36sec

Fastest half-marathon: 1hr 31min 59sec
Fastest 15 miles: 1hr 44min 41sec
Fastest 10 miles: 1hr 9min 24sec
Fastest 10km: 41min 40sec

Last Word

Nothing in my life has been remotely as important to me as family. I hope I have made it clear in these pages how much I cared for and owe to my original family, especially my mother. Susan, my wife, has been my partner and most cherished companion in our great adventure, and my children and grandchildren are a constant source of joy and hope for the future.

Matchroom, which grew from humble beginnings and survived substantial setbacks to become one of the world's foremost producers of sport, has remained a family business and every Matchroom employee has become part of my ever-growing family. Important early roles were played by Linda Turner (my first PA), Sharron Tokley (event promotion), Wendy Barker (accounts), Karen Manzi (TV sales) and Karen Mazzone. All have been and remain important members of the Matchroom family.

I believe it fair to say that elevating snooker and darts to star status in the sporting firmament has been my finest achievement. I especially enjoyed bringing snooker back from the precipice of oblivion. But that would not have happened without the very best team pulling together in one direction. Jason Ferguson, chairman of the WPBSA, should be singled out for his amazing work ethic and passion for the amateur game. Plaudits must also go to Nigel Oldfield, World Snooker's director of operations; Miles Pearce, commercial director; Simon Brownell, finance director and now chief executive; as well as my old pal Steve Dawson, who after thirty-odd years living in my shadow is now the main man.

In the world of darts, Matt Porter is leading his PDC team in developing a global sport with a pub background. Of all my commercial successes, I'm sure darts has been number one. To take a game from bar rooms and pubs into the global marketplace, changing the lives of ordinary people who happen to be very good at throwing three little arrows at a sisal board, really takes some believing. We now have a real global sport on our hands, and I love the fact that darts players are suddenly making millions of pounds per year and inspiring kids all over the world to stand tall on the oche.

Emily Frazer continues to excel in running Matchroom Multi Sport, particularly with regard to nine-ball pool, our next major project. My daughter Katie and her Matchroom Media team have created and organised hundreds of thousands of hours of live sport and syndicated it worldwide. What a team! My son Eddie and his boxing team, led by Frank Smith, have changed the whole sport, created and rewarded heroes and gathered a new layer of global interest via social media and digital streaming. Along the way, they have eclipsed anything achieved by the old-timers in boxing, including me. It's a brave new world for the noble art and I'm happy to be on the sidelines with a free ticket to watch the drama unfold. My son-in-law, Dan has done an amazing job developing the PGA EuroPro Tour, much to the benefit of golf; and the unsung heroes, the backroom staff, have been terrific. It has been an honour to work with all of them.

But most of all, my thanks go to the legions of sporting men and women who have dedicated their lives to being the best they can and in doing so have created entertainment for fans throughout the world. They are, and always have been, my heroes and if I have played even a small part in helping them to change their lives and live their dreams, then I'm contented.

Without sport, any community or country is a less attractive place. Sport unifies us all, irrespective of colour, creed or sex, and showcases the backbone and character of our world.

Be grateful for it and enjoy.

Index

loathing of Chris Eubank 142,
151
opponents
Barkley, Iran 142
Chris Eubank (1990) 141–5,
279–81
Chris Eubank (1993) 151,
153–4
Michael Watson 142
success in America 151
Bennett, Roger 1–2, 3
Berbick, Trevor 109
Berg, Nick van den 288
Big Fights Inc. 184
Biles, Simone 260
Billah, Prince 106
Billericay Amateur Boxing Club
247
Billiard Congress of America 295
Billingham, Baroness 235–6
Black Cat Bones 27
Black, George 137–8, 139
Blanchflower, Danny 20
Blavatnik, Len 270
Blind Les 64
Blow, Cindy 26
Blow, David 26
Blow, Deborah 26
Blow, Morris 26, 37
surrogate father to BH 26–7
Blow, Pamela 26, 27
Blyth, Tom 44–5, 69
Bow, Riddick 131
boxing
draws in contracts 155–6
options clauses 143
risks for boxers 161
see also Matchroom Boxing
Brady, Karren 233, 235, 237

Braverman, Al 156
Brazier, Robbo *see* Robbo (BH's
driver)
Breazeale, Dominic 256–7
Brentwood Centre 130
Brentwood Cricket Club 29
Brentwood public school 248
Briggs, Annie 100
Bristow, Burrell & Co. 33, 35, 37,
40, 42
Bristow, Eric 188, 190, 193, 196
British Boxing Board of Control
(BBBofC) 152–3
British Gymnastics Association
261, 262–3
Brook, Kell 249
Brookweald Cricket Club 29
Brown Bear pub 79
Brownell, Simon 301
Bruno, Frank 169
fight preparation 113
opponents
James 'Bonecrusher' Smith
132
Joe Bugner 109–14
Mike Tyson 132
Tim Witherspoon 132
punch fodder for 110–11
BSkyB *see* Sky TV
Buckhurst Hill Cricket Club
28–9
Buckhurst Hill Grammar School
18, 29, 30
Buckner, Marlene 113
Buffer, Michael 223
Buffett, Warren 269
Bugner, Joe
opponents
Frank Bruno 109–14

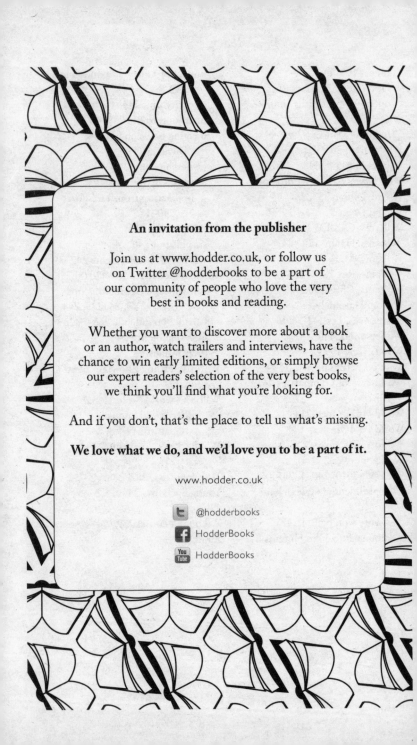

An invitation from the publisher

Join us at www.hodder.co.uk, or follow us
on Twitter @hodderbooks to be a part of
our community of people who love the very
best in books and reading.

Whether you want to discover more about a book
or an author, watch trailers and interviews, have the
chance to win early limited editions, or simply browse
our expert readers' selection of the very best books,
we think you'll find what you're looking for.

And if you don't, that's the place to tell us what's missing.

We love what we do, and we'd love you to be a part of it.

www.hodder.co.uk

@hodderbooks

HodderBooks

HodderBooks